Supplement to "The Laws of Innkeepers

—for Hotels, Motels, Restaurants, and Clubs"

Supplement to "The Laws of Innkeepers—*for Hotels, Motels, Restaurants, and Clubs*"

JOHN E. H. SHERRY

Cornell University Press

ITHACA AND LONDON

International Standard Book Number 0-8014-9327-7
Library of Congress Catalog Card Number 81-67174
Printed in the United States of America
Librarians: Library of Congress cataloging information
appears on the last page of the book.

The paper in this book is acid-free and meets the guidelines for
permanence and durability of the Committee on Production Guidelines
for Book Longevity of the Council on Library Resources.

Preface

This softcover supplement reflects the growing number of lawsuits that have engulfed the hospitality industry since publication of *The Laws of Innkeepers, Revised Edition*. This phenomenon has created a demand for an authoritative yet practical update to enable educators, lawyers, and managers to cope with existing and new problems. Its purpose is twofold: first, to update existing chapter sections, appendixes, and bibliographies of law review articles to reflect current cases and materials; second, to add new chapter sections to incorporate developments since publication of the revised edition. Underlying the choice of format is the wish to provide freshness in subject matter at economical cost without sacrificing accuracy and completeness of coverage.

To accomplish these goals, chapter section titles and page numbers of the revised edition have been included for easy reference, new illustrative cases have been shortened, as indicated by ellipsis points or bracketed notations, and unnecessary footnotes and legal citations have been omitted. Short paragraphs highlighting similar or contrary decisions in cases in other states have been inserted. Numbered footnotes are reported from the cases; lettered notes are my own.

The author gratefully acknowledges the research efforts of Helen M. Alvare and Gregory A. Smith. Ms. Alvare is a graduate of the Cornell Law School and a member of the Pennsylvania Bar. Mr. Smith is a third-year Cornell law student. Each of them has made many practical suggestions that have enhanced the usefulness and readability of the text.

A special word of thanks to Dean John J. Clark, Jr., is in order. His encouragement and support of faculty research and publication have been evident throughout the project and have greatly facilitated the preparation of the supplement.

JOHN E. H. SHERRY

Ithaca, New York

Contents

*New section.

Chapter 2. The Nature of an Inn and Other Places of Public Accommodation

2:8 *Inn and Hotel Defined*

Insert at end of section, p. 23:

In 1983, statutory hotel tenants sought rent abatement for defendant landlord's alleged breach of warranty of habitability. Finding in tenants' favor, the court then dealt with the further issue of whether tenants were entitled to rent reductions for landlord's alleged failure to provide customary hotel services:

WHITEHALL HOTEL v. GAYNOR,
121 Misc. 2d 736, 470 N.Y.S.2d 286 (N.Y. City Civ. Ct. 1983)

McKAY, J.: "The second issue common to all respondents concerns hotel services under the New METHISA [Metropolitan Hotel Industry Stabilization] Code which became effective on July 23, 1982. Only one other reported decision has been found on this subject since the new Code has been in effect, *Brewster v. Gavins*, 117 Misc. 2d 952, 459 N.Y.S.2d 561 (Civ. Ct. N.Y. Co. 1983) which is not regarded as dispositive of the issue of which hotel services, if any, are mandated by the new code. [Footnote omitted.] The Conciliation and Appeals Board (CAB), the principal administrative agency authorized to hear cases under the Code, has not yet decided what hotel services are required under the new Code.

"This case, therefore, presents an issue important to both sides and is regarded by them as one of first impression. In view of the fact that all respondents have been withholding all of their rent for several months to date, and considering the sense of urgency conveyed to this court by both sides for a speedy trial and decision in all of these non-payment summary proceedings, this court would be hard-pressed to defer a decision pending action by the CAB. (Compare *Saljen Realty v. HRA*, 115 Misc. 2d 553, 455 N.Y.S.2d 39 (App. Term 1st Dep't 1982)). Nevertheless, the court is deciding these cases without prejudice to what the CAB may rule hereafter upon the proper application of any appropriate party for reclassification of the building and to set proper rents. See RSL, § 43(b), N.Y.C. Admin. Code, § YY51–3.1(b) as amended June 26, 1983.

"Factually, the trial established that petitioner is currently providing to respondents the following services: desk service, including some mail service, some rough equivalent of bellboy services performed by one or two lobby attendants and minimal telephone service. New carpeting has also been provided to all respondents, but not upkeep of the carpeting. The parties stipulated that these services constitute 20% of all the hotel services set forth in the METHISA Code, (although the list in the Code does not purport to be exhaustive). The remaining 80% which are services not provided by petitioner to respondents, are 'maid service, furnishings and laundering of linen, and use and upkeep of furniture and fixtures.' METHISA Code, § 13(h).

"The stipulation just referred to above also included an estimate of the relative value of the hotel services in relation to the respondents' rent. The stipulation reads in full as follows:

"1. That if all hotel services set forth in the Metropolitan Hotel Industry Stabilization Code were given to the respondent-tenants herein said services would constitute 25% of the rent charged for each of the respondents' apartments.

"2. It is conceded and stipulated that the petitioner-landlord is providing only 5% of the services and that the services that are not being provided to the respondents would comprise 20% of the rent being charged.

"3. This stipulation is in lieu of expert testimony and without prejudice to landlord's claim that it does not have to provide hotel services to the respondent-tenants herein.

"It should be emphasized here that consistent with all the petitions and as recognized and conceded by petitioner at trial, with no opposition from respondents' counsel, petitioner is a member of METHISA, and all of the units in question are currently governed by the METHISA Code. However, it is also apparent to this court that petitioner has been undergoing a serious "identity crisis" as to whether in its newly renovated condition it should be, or even wants to continue to be, part of METHISA. [Footnote omitted.] For example, it advertised these newly renovated units as apartments, not as hotel rooms or suites, and it used the rent stabilized lease form and tenants' rights riders without reference to hotel stabilization or METHISA for each of respondents' leases. [Footnote omitted.] Furthermore, petitioner offered one and two year leases, instead of six months ones. Thus, with the exception of the name of the owner, 'Whitehall Hotel Corp.' and article 42 of the leases concerning the purported waiver of 'hotel services'—to be discussed below—there is not a single reference in these multi-page leases to the fact that this building is a hotel or that the lessees are supposed to be hotel tenants. [Footnote omitted.]

"Although these facts and circumstances demonstrate the ambivalent attitude of petitioner toward METHISA, these units are still currently under the METHISA Code and this court will not attempt to affect or alter this classification in the context of these non-payment summary proceedings. See Rent Stabilization Law ('RSL') § 43, N.Y.C. Admin. Code § YY51–3.1 as amended June 26, 1983.

"With respect to the waiver clause, article 42 of the leases [footnote omitted] referred to above, if the court were to find a valid, enforceable waiver here by each of the tenants, such a finding would seem to dispose of the 'hotel services' issue in favor of petitioner. This would require a careful analysis of the Code because Section 7 of the New Code declares certain waivers to be void. It reads as follows:

> "WAIVER OF BENEFIT VOID—Any agreement by a tenant to waive the benefit of any provision of the RSL, the EPTA, or this Code shall be void unless permitted by this Code."

"Accordingly, the waiver clause in each of the leases is void if the hotel services purportedly waived comprise (1) benefits provided for in the METHISA Code or the enabling statute, RSL and (2) the waiver of such benefit is not otherwise permitted by the METHISA Code. Of course, the same careful analysis of the Code would be required to determine whether petitioner has violated the statute or the Code in the first place, apart from the validity of any waiver. We turn therefore to the analysis of the new Code.

"The first reference in the Code to 'hotel services' is found in 'DEFINI-TIONS', Section 3(h). That subsection reads in full as follows:

> "Section 3. DEFINITIONS . . .
>
> (h) 'Hotel'—Any Class A or Class B Multiple Dwelling containing six or more dwelling units which on June 1, 1968 was and still is commonly regarded as a hotel, transient hotel or residential hotel, which customarily provides hotel services such as maid service, furnishings and laundering of linen, telephone and bellboy service, secretarial or desk service and use and upkeep of furniture and fixtures.

"It should be noted here that one of the differences in this amended Code from its predecessor is found right in the definition of hotel. The prior Code included the words, 'provides or makes available hotel services such as . . .', while the new Code eliminates the words 'or makes available.' This change made the Code definition identical with a definition of 'hotel' in the statute itself, the RSL, N.Y.C. Admin. Code §YY51–3.0(a)(1)(e), except that this particular statutory definition in RSL refers only to Class A multiple dwellings. The Commissioner of the Department of Housing Preservation and Development ('DHPD') in his Explanatory Statement to this new Code labels this difference as one of the 'more significant changes,' which 'requires the owner to actually provide customary hotel services instead of merely claiming that they are available in order to take advantage of the benefits under the Code . . .' Since the Commissioner's comment relates only to the definition section, it must be understood to refer to a threshhold classification issue, that is, whether the building is properly a hotel in the first place, an issue concerning which this court defers to the CAB as more fully explained below, and not necessarily, as urged by respondents to mean that the definition section by itself automatically confers any additional benefits on these tenants-respondents. In any event, to the extent that this explanatory statement does intend to express the latter interpretation, this court declines to follow it. See generally 56 N.Y. Jur. Statutes § 179.

"Without exception, every other reference in the Code to 'services' [footnote

omitted] speaks exclusively in terms of services which were furnished or required to be furnished as of a certain date. In all cases, the controlling date is the
date of the initial commencement of a given tenancy where such commencement
is later than the base dates of May 31, 1968, May 29, 1974 or July 1, 1974. See
subsection 3(p) of the Code. Any decrease in such required services is strictly
regulated by the Code and the CAB. See § 42 of the Code. However, nowhere in
this new Code is it specified which particular hotel services, if any, are required.
Moreover, the official Rider for hotel tenants subsequently approved by DHPD
[Department of Housing Preservation and Development] for attachment to hotel
stabilized leases repeats the admonition of the Code that services provided or required on the date occupancy commences (or, if later, on the date the unit first
became subject to Rent Stabilization) may not be decreased. This official Rider
then goes on to state:

> . . . "Required services include building-wide services such as heat, hot
> water, janitorial service, maintenance of locks and security devices, repair
> and maintenance and may include elevators, air conditioning, doorman and
> other amenities [footnote omitted] . . . *Required services may also include*
> services within the dwelling unit, such as maintenance and repair of appli-
> ances, cleaning, linens and painting every three years." [Emphasis
> supplied].

"It is understood that the Rider quoted above was published for informational
purposes only and does not become part of any lease, nor does it replace or mod-
ify the RSL or the Code. Nevertheless, the Rider underscores the ambiguity
which permeates the Code itself with respect to required hotel services, or put
more positively, it demonstrates the studied decision of the drafters of the Code
to refrain from specifying which particular hotel services would be required.

"It is therefore apparent to this court that the free market bargaining approach
for the setting of agreed rents and services at the commencement of new tenancies, which has been traditionally employed in hotel stabilization, remains essentially intact under the new Code. The Code continues to provide for strict regulation of the increase or decrease in services from the base date, which for new
tenants is the commencement of their tenancy.

"The threshold issue of what minimal hotel services, if any, or what minimum
percentage of hotel services are mandated for this and other buildings to fit the
definition of 'hotel' under the new Code, will have to be left to the CAB. Deference to the CAB on this issue is appropriate for a number of sound administrative
and judicial reasons, including the circumstance that the 'hotel status' of the
building within METHISA was not seriously disputed or litigated before this
court. See *Saljen Realty Corp. v. HRA,* supra. The CAB has more flexibility to
inquire into the issue both from a historical and current perspective and to fashion appropriate remedies, if necessary. Now, however, it is all the more necessary to defer to the CAB on this issue in view of a very recent amendment to the
housing laws, Section 43 of chapter 403 of the Laws of 1983, amending the

RSL (N.Y.C. Admin. Code § YY51–3.1) (June 26, 1983) cited previously. By that amendment the legislature has directed it shall henceforth be the business of the CAB to determine upon application of a tenant or owner, 'if such building is a hotel covered by this law, based upon the services provided and other relevant factors.' *Ibid.*

"Based on the foregoing analysis, this court holds that the current METHISA Code does not require this petitioner to furnish any one or more specific hotel services to these respondents other than those few services already being provided.

"In view of this conclusion it follows that Section 7 of the Code ('Waiver of Benefit Void') does not apply to or render void the waiver of hotel services signed by these respondents. These tenants can and did agree to forego receiving the traditional hotel services, signified in part by the waiver clause (Article 42) in each of the leases, and by their overall agreement to pay the specified rents without these services. This may be contrary to the spirit of the new METHISA Code, but not to its letter, as read by this court. Hence, no reductions in rent are warranted at this time on account of the lack of those services. To reiterate, however, this ruling is without prejudice to what the CAB may hereafter order if application is made for reclassification and the fixing of rents.

"This is not an unjust or inequitable result. Not one of these tenant-respondents ever even remotely suggested at trial that he or she wanted or expected these additional hotel services at the outset of their tenancy, nor is there any evidence that any of these tenants made inquiries or requests of the landlord about these services. [Footnote omitted.] What they sought at trial, instead, were rent reductions. Clearly, they all had agreed to the rent fixed in their leases knowing full well that the rent did not include these services. Moreover, I credit the proof offered by petitioner that the rents would have been set significantly higher if these traditional hotel services were to have been provided and included, especially considering the fact that all utilities were already included in these rents."

2:9a   *(New Section) Municipal Hotel-Room Use and Occupancy Taxes*

Insert immediately after 2:9, p. 28:

Many states have authorized city governments to impose hotel-room use and occupancy taxes under newly enacted constitutional home-rule powers available to cities that otherwise qualify. Since these taxes may be levied in addition to statewide sales taxes, affected local hotel and motel associations have resisted these burdens by challenging the legality of the cities' exercise of this new source of potential revenue-raising authority.

The two cases that follow illustrate differing interpretations of whether and under what circumstances such taxes are proper exercises of municipal home-rule powers or unconstitutional usurpations of fiscal powers reserved to the states.

MONTANA INNKEEPERS ASS'N V. CITY OF BILLINGS
671 P.2d 21 (Mont. 1983)

McCARVEL, D.J. [footnote omitted]: ". . . The . . . Montana Innkeepers Association, hereinafter referred to as 'Innkeepers,' instituted a declaratory judgment proceeding . . . against the City of Billings, Montana, . . . hereinafter referred to as 'City,' to declare Ordinance No. 83–4461 enacted by the City Council of Billings, Montana, to be illegal and void. . . .

"Prior to the 1972 Constitution of the State of Montana, local governments could exercise only such powers as were expressly granted to them by the State together with such implied powers as were necessary for the execution of the powers expressly granted.

"The 1972 Montana Constitution . . . opened to local governmental units new vistas of shared sovereignty with the state through the adoption of the self-government charters. Whereas the 1972 Montana Constitution continues to provide that existing local governmental forms have such powers as are expressly provided or implied by law (to be liberally construed), Art. XI, Sec. 4, 1972 Mont. Const., a local government unit may now also act under a self-government charter with its powers uninhibited except by express prohibitions of the constitution, law or charter, Art. XI, Sec. 6, 1972 Mont. Const.:

"*Self-government powers.* A local government unit adopting a self-government charter may exercise any power not prohibited by this constitution, law or charter . . .

". . . The City of Billings is a municipality in the State of Montana, which has adopted a charter form of government with self-governing powers. On August 23, 1982, the City of Billings adopted Ordinance No. 82–4461, which provides for a 'fee' of $1.00 per adult transient occupant for each day of occupancy of a room in a hotel, motel, or other place of lodging within the City when the occupancy is for a period of one day or more, but not exceeding fourteen consecutive days. The ordinance was referred to the electors of the City of Billings at the election held in November 1982, the voters approved it, and the ordinance became effective January 1, 1983.

"The owner or operator of a lodging establishment is obligated to collect the fee and remit the same to the City monthly, less 2 percent administrative costs, and is subject to penalty for noncollection, audit and inspection.

"Section 5.10.010 of the ordinance states specifically its purpose:

"Purpose of the occupancy fee imposed by this ordinance is to provide a portion of the revenue necessary to construct and reconstruct the arterial and collector streets of the City in a good substantial condition and a portion of the necessary expense of police and fire and allocable incidental administration costs. The fees imposed hereby will enable those persons non-resident of the City to pay a portion of the services of the city that extant within the City for their benefit and protection during their sojourn within the City.

"In addition the city council could allocate up to 20 percent of revenue to promote tourism, conventions and other similar activities within the City.

"Innkeepers is a nonprofit corporation organized under the laws of the State of Montana. It is a voluntary trade association organized and existing for the benefit of the lodging industry of the State of Montana. Members thereof are the owners and operators of lodging establishments within the City of Billings wherein they provide, among other things, overnight lodging services for the general public.
. . .

"The sole issue on appeal is whether the tax imposed by the ordinance is a tax prohibited by statute, and specifically section 7–1–112(1), MCA, which provides as follows:

> "A local government with self-government powers is prohibited the exercise of the following powers unless the power is specifically delegated by law:
> "(1) the power to authorize a tax on income or the sale of goods or services, except that this section shall not be construed to limit the authority of a local government to levy any other tax or establish the rate of any other tax.

"The power to tax the sale of goods or services has not been delegated to local governments.

"The District Court held that the renting of a hotel or motel room is the sale of a service, but since the ordinance imposed the tax on the person occupying the room and not on the transfer of that room, it is not a tax on the sale of goods or services. Counsel for the City argued that the renting of the room has nothing to do with the tax imposed. Therefore, every nonresident of the City upon entering the City is subject to the tax. However, hotel and motel operators are the only businesses permitted to levy the tax. Restaurants, bars and other businesses may not collect the tax from a transient nonresident. This reasoning of course is fallacious. The renting of the room cannot be divorced from the collection of the tax. Therefore, the tax is a tax on the sale of a service and prohibited by section 7–1–112(1), MCA. *J.A. Tobin Const. Co. v. Weed* (1965), 158 Colo. 430, 407 P.2d 350. 68 Am. Jur. 2d *Sales and Use Taxes,* § 5.

"Hotels and motels sell a product or service which is temporary lodging. The occupant is the consumer since he purchases the service. No title changes hands, but the consumer comes into temporary possession of the room. A tax placed on that transaction is a sales tax. . . .

"Ordinance No. 82–4461 enacted by the City is illegal and void. The judgment of the District Court is reversed."

SPRINGFIELD HOTEL-MOTEL ASS'N V. CITY OF SPRINGFIELD
119 Ill. App. 3d 753, 457 N.E.2d 1017 (1983)

WEBBER, J.: "This case concerns the home rule taxing powers of the City of Springfield; specifically, whether the proceeds collected from a tax imposed upon the rental of hotel and motel rooms may be used by the city for general corporate purposes, or whether such proceeds are restricted to the promotion and development of tourism and conventions.

"In 1972 the city adopted an ordinance which in substance provided for a tax upon the use and privilege of renting a hotel or motel room. The tax was to be collected from the renter, and after payment of some of the indebtedness of the Springfield Metropolitan Exposition and Auditorium Authority, the balance of the proceeds from the tax was to be paid into a special fund to promote tourism and conventions in the city.

"In 1976 the ordinance was amended to remove the requirement that the tax proceeds be used for the development of tourism and instead diverted the tax proceeds into the city's treasury. Provision was made for payment to the exposition authority and the balance was to be retained until lawfully appropriated and expended by ordinance.

"In 1982 the city adopted its annual appropriation ordinance which provided for the anticipated use of $200,000 of hotel-motel tax receipts in order to balance the city's budget. Within a few days after the adoption of this ordinance, the plaintiffs, a hotel-motel association and certain operators of hostelries in the city, filed the instant suit against the defendants, the city, its mayor, and its commissioners. . . . [T]he complaint was . . . dismissed by the trial court on motion of the defendants. This appeal followed.

"The . . . complaint alleges the history of the ordinances as set forth above and sought as relief: (1) a declaratory judgment that the 1976 ordinance violated the provisions of article VII, sections 6(e) and 6(g), (h) and (i) of the Illinois Constitution of 1970, and section 8–3–14 of the Illinois Municipal Code (Ill. Rev. Stat. 1981, ch. 24, par. 8–3–14); and (2) a permanent injunction prohibiting the defendants from transferring the hotel-motel tax funds to any fund other than that for the promotion of tourism, conventions and other special events in the city.

"It is undisputed that Springfield is a home rule city and thus possesses the power to tax under section 6(a) of article VII of the Illinois Constitution of 1970. Any limitation on that power must be found in section 6(e) which provides:

"A home rule unit shall have only the power that the General Assembly may provide by law . . . to license for revenue or impose taxes upon or measured by income or earnings or upon occupations. Ill. Const. 1970, art. VII, § 6(e).

"The root question here is whether the Springfield tax is one upon an occupation; if it is not, the city has ample power under section 6(a) to impose the tax without limitation; if it is, then the city must follow the General Assembly guidelines.

"Plaintiffs' principal argument is that the latter alternative is the correct one; that the tax is one upon an occupation, and therefore the city must follow what has been mandated by the General Assembly. This mandate is found, according to plaintiffs, in section 8–3–14 of the Illinois Municipal Code, which provides:

"The corporate authorities of any municipality containing at least 25,000 and less than 500,000 inhabitants may impose a tax upon all persons engaged in such municipality in the business of renting, leasing or letting rooms in a hotel, as defined in 'The Hotel Operators' Occupation Tax Act,' at a rate not to exceed 5% of the gross rental receipts from such renting, leasing or letting, excluding, however, from gross rental receipts, the proceeds of such renting, leasing or letting to permanent residents of that hotel, and may provide for the administration and enforcement of the tax, and for the collection thereof, from the persons subject to the tax, as the corporate authorities determine to be necessary or practicable for the effective administration of the tax.

"Persons subject to any tax imposed pursuant to authority granted by this Section may reimburse themselves for their tax liability for such tax by separately stating such tax as an additional charge, which charge may be stated in combination, in a single amount, with State tax imposed under 'The Hotel Operators' Occupation Tax Act.'

"Nothing in this Section shall be construed to authorize a municipality to impose a tax upon the privilege of engaging in any business which under the constitution of the United States may not be made the subject of taxation by this State.

"The amounts collected by any municipality pursuant to this Section shall be expended by the municipality solely to promote tourism, conventions and other special events within that municipality or otherwise to attract nonresidents to visit the municipality.

"No funds received pursuant to this Section shall be used to advertise for or otherwise promote new competition in the hotel business. Ill. Rev. Stat. 1981, ch. 24, par. 8–3–14.

". . . This forms the basis for plaintiffs' argument: prior to the adoption of the Illinois Constitution of 1970 with its home rule powers, all municipalities were subject to the 'Dillon rule,' which in essence held that they had only such powers as might be delegated to them by the General Assembly. . . . The 1970 constitution intervened, but the Dillon rule was preserved in article VII, sec. 6(e). The enactment of section 8–3–14 subsequent to the adoption of the 1970 constitution indicates an intent on the part of the General Assembly that a hotel-motel tax is a tax upon an occupation and hence is regulated by delegated powers.

"We do not agree. In our opinion section 8–3–14 was enacted to allow non-home-rule units of government, within limitations, to impose hotel-motel taxes under the Dillon rule which still applies to them. Home rule units derive their power from section 6(a) of article VII of the 1970 constitution, unfettered by the Dillon rule.

"The leading case on this subject is the recent supreme court decision of *Commercial National Bank v. City of Chicago* (1982), 89 Ill. 2d 45, 59 Ill. Dec. 643, 432 N.E.2d 227. There the court struck down a tax by the city of Chicago on the purchasers of professional and commercial services. The court found that taxes upon these services were of the type that the delegates to the Illinois Constitutional Convention wished to limit by adopting section 6(e) of article VII. The court found that this was an occupation tax despite the fact that the city of Chicago expressly stated that it was a tax on the purchasers of the services. In coming to this conclusion the supreme court discussed the interplay of sections 6(a) and 6(e) in depth.

"After reviewing the constitutional provisions and statements of the delegates to the constitutional convention, the court in *Commercial National Bank* found that sales and excise taxes were clearly within the grant of the power 'to tax' conferred upon home rule units by section 6(a) of article VII of the constitution and that section 6(e) of that article did not affect or limit the power of a home rule unit to impose such taxes. However, it was just as clear to the court that a tax on services was an occupation tax limited by section 6(e). As the court noted, the distinction between a sales tax and an occupation tax is not always clear. Both are measured by substantially the same standards and both taxes are generally shifted forward to the consumer, with the business firm serving as a tax-collecting agent. As a result, '[t]he difference between the two taxes is primarily one of legislative intent.' 89 Ill. 2d 45, 66, 59 Ill. Dec. 643, 653, 432 N.E.2d 227, 237. . . .

"A tax on the use of a hotel room appears to fall somewhere in between these clearly defined extremes. The question of whether this tax is an occupation tax or not must then be answered by resorting to the intent of the delegates at the constitutional convention.

"In the *Commercial National Bank* decision, the supreme court quoted the report of the Local Government Committee to the constitutional convention. The report contained examples of taxes that would be permissible under the general powers of a home rule unit. The examples included taxes on gasoline, hotel rooms, liquor, food and drugs. The court noted that these were taxes 'which the constitutional convention perceived to be within the power of home rule units to impose, and were considered as not being limited by the restrictions of section 6(e) of article VII.' 89 Ill. 2d 45, 63, 59 Ill. Dec. 643, 651, 432 N.E.2d 227, 235.

"The court also quoted a delegate who stated that either a 'sales or *use* tax' could be properly imposed by a home rule unit. (Emphasis added.) 89 Ill. 2d 45, 56, 59 Ill. Dec. 643, 648, 432 N.E.2d 227, 232.

"The intent of the delegates seems clear. The use of a hotel room is specifically grouped with a list of tangible goods which the convention viewed as freely taxable under section 6(a) of article VII of the Illinois Constitution. While not as tangible as the other examples, the use of a hotel room involves the use of many tangible objects. The rental of a hotel room can certainly be distinguished from the purchase of a lawyer's or doctor's services.

"Moreover, a series of supreme court cases have distinguished allowable section 6(a) taxes from the restricted section 6(e) taxes. These cases were concisely reviewed in *Commercial National Bank:*

". . . In *Town of Cicero v. Fox Valley Trotting Club, Inc.* (1976), 65 Ill. 2d 10 [2 Ill. Dec. 675, 357 N.E.2d 1118], an ordinance was upheld which imposed a flat-rate tax of 10 cents for each person witnessing, participating in, or attending a place of entertainment. It was contended that this constituted an occupation tax. . . . In *Jacobs v. City of Chicago* (1973), 53 Ill. 2d 421 [292 N.E.2d 401], a tax was imposed upon the use and privilege of parking a motor vehicle upon or in a parking lot or garage. The tax was challenged as an attempt to license for revenue, which was beyond the taxing authority of home rule units under section 6(e) of article VII, unless authorized by the General Assembly. This court upheld the tax. *Here, as in the other cases, the tax was clearly within the scope of the examples set out in the majority committee report. There is no distinction between the tax on a hotel room noted in the examples given and a tax on the use of a parking place for a vehicle.* (Emphasis added.) 89 Ill. 2d 45, 59, 59 Ill. Dec. 643, 649, 432 N.E.2d 227, 233.

"We are thus led to the conclusion that *Commercial National Bank* controls this decision and that the Springfield tax is a tax upon the use of tangible personal property and not upon an occupation. The city is then free to dispose of the tax proceeds as it sees fit under section 6(a) of article VII; it is not constrained by section 6(e) of article VII. . . .

"To paraphrase, if a product is only incidental to a service, it is a service tax and subject to the restrictions of section 6(e) of article VII. The corollary is that if the service is only incidental to the product, it is a sales or use tax which may be freely applied under section 6(a) of article VII.

"In the case of the rental of a hotel or motel room, it is our opinion that any service, *e.g.*, maid service, television, telephone, *et al.*, is only incidental to the use of the tangible property, *i.e.*, the structure and the appointments and accouterments in the room. . . .

"Plaintiffs' final contention is that if this case were remanded for a trial on the merits, they could show that when the 1972 ordinance was enacted, the declared intent of the Springfield council was to promote tourism. Such evidence would be immaterial. Obviously by 1976 the council had changed its mind as it had a right to do under section 6(a) of article VII.

"Plaintiffs have also argued that if the hotel-motel ordinance withstands constitutional attack, there will be no end to the proliferation of local taxes. Such a possibility exists without doubt, but its resolution is properly assigned to the political rather than the judicial arena.

"The order of the circuit court of Sangamon County dismissing the plaintiffs' complaint is affirmed.

"Affirmed."

Chapter 4. Discrimination in Places of Public Accommodation: Civil Rights

4:1   Innkeeper's Common-Law Duty to Admit All Who Apply

Insert immediately after Jacobson v. New York Racing Association, Inc., p. 41:

Subsequent to *Jacobson,* a New York appellate court upheld the common-law right to exclude without cause except where such exclusion is based on race, creed, color, or national origin, with regard to a private-for-profit harness-racing track. *Arone v. Sullivan County Harness Racing Association, Inc.,* 90 A.D.2d 137, 457 N.Y.S.2d 958 (1982). The court maintained that since the trainers, drivers, and owners who brought the action could still race at six other tracks, there was not the requisite showing of "economic necessity" or "monopoly power" needed to invoke a *Jacobson*-type action. Moreover, regulation by the state, though heavy, was not sufficient ground for a finding of state action. The dissent argued, however, that denying plaintiffs use of the local track, with the subsequent damage to their reputations, had as great an impact from the plaintiffs' point of view as if there were no other facilities available.

4:5   Injunctive Relief against Discrimination in Places of Public Accommodation — Title II

Insert at end of section, p. 51:

In holding that a Virginia golf club had not met its burden of establishing as a matter of law that it was a private club, legally entitled to bar nonwhite applicants from membership, the federal district court for the District of Virginia elaborated on the factors affecting private-club status in *Brown v. Loudon Golf & Country Club, Inc.,* 573 F. Supp. 399 (E.D. Va. 1983), at 402–403:

> In determining whether an establishment is a truly private club, . . . [t]he key factor is whether the club's membership is truly selective. *See, e.g., Wright v. Salisbury Club, Ltd.,* 632 F.2d 309 (4th Cir. 1980); *U.S. v. Eagles,* 472 F. Supp. 1174 (E.D. Wis. 1979); *Cornelius v. Elks,* 382 F. Supp. 1182, 1203 (D. Conn. 1974). Relevant here are the size of the club's membership fee, whether and how many white applicants have been denied membership relative to the total number of white applicants, *see Tillman v. Wheaton-Haven Recreation Association, Inc.,* 410 U.S. 431, 438 n.9, 93 S.Ct. 1090, 1094 n.9, 35 L.Ed.2d 403 (1973); *Wright,* 632 F.2d at 312; *Eagles,* 472 F. Supp. at 1176, whether the club advertises its memberships, *Wright,* 632 F.2d at 312–13, and whether the club has well-defined membership policies, *Nesmith [v. Young Men's Christian Association,* 397 F.2d 96 (4th Cir. 1968)], 397 F.2d at 107. That the Club here has a substantial admission fee, a membership ceiling, a requirement that two members sign applications, and a requirement that the Board approve membership application does not, without more, establish that the Club's membership is sufficiently selective. The cases have held clubs to be actually

open to the public despite the existence of one or more of these formal admission requirements. *See Tillman, supra* (membership ceiling); *Wright, supra* (2 member sponsorship & board approval requirements); *Nesmith, supra* (substantial annual dues & membership committee); *Eagles, supra* (2 member sponsorship & board approval requirements, membership committee). The crucial inquiry is whether formal admission procedures operate in practice to make the Club's membership selective. *Nesmith, supra* at 101.

4:6a *(New Section) Discrimination on Account of Age in Public Accommodations*

Insert immediately after 4:6, p. 53:

Title II of the Federal Civil Rights Act does not prohibit age discrimination in places of public accommodation. No federal statutes address this issue, but several states do include age as a prohibited basis for treatment by owners or operators of public accommodations. Louisiana includes such a prohibition in its state constitution. La. Const., article I, Section 12 (1977).

The range of what is included as a public accommodation will vary from state to state, as will the age groups protected. The Illinois statute covers only persons aged forty to seventy. Ill. Rev. Stat., chapter 68, 1–104 to 9–102 (Smith-Hurd Supp. 1982–83). In Connecticut, minors are not included. Conn. Gen. Stat. Ann., Sections 46a–64(b)(4) (West Supp. 1983–84). Certain exceptions may exist to the statutes; in Connecticut, for example, federal- and state-aided housing and municipal housing are beyond reach of the statute. See generally Howard C. Eglit, 1 *Age Discrimination,* chapter 11 (1983).

In *O'Connor v. Village Green Owners Ass'n,* 33 Cal. 3d 790, 662 P.2d 427 (1983), the Supreme Court of California held that a nonprofit condominium development association is a "business establishment" within the Unruh Civil Rights Act and thus barred an age restriction in the association's covenants that limited residency to persons over the age of eighteen. Because innkeepers market condominiums, this decision is important, since it reflects the stated public policy of a leading tourist real estate development jurisdiction.

4:7a *(New Section) Discrimination in Employment under Title VII*

Insert immediately after 4:7, p. 56:

Title VII prohibits discrimination in employment on the basis of race, color, religion, sex, and national origin, but it excepts bona fide private membership clubs from its ambit. In *Equal Employment Opportunity Commission v. Wooster Brush Company Employees Relief Ass'n,* 727 F. 2d 566 (6th Cir. 1984) the federal Circuit Court of Appeals ruled that the Association was not an employer but a bonafide private club. As such, it did not discriminate against female employees by refusing to pay pregnancy related disability benefits although it did pay benefits for other disabilities that rendered pregnant employees unable to work. Only the Company had violated Title VII.

In the following North Carolina case, a former employee brought an action against defendant, a private club, alleging discrimination in employment on the basis of race. The court held that the uncontested status of the defendant as a private membership club within the meaning of the Civil Rights Act of 1964 was a sufficient ground for dismissal of the claim and that this exemption as an "employer" also protects such clubs from employment suits brought under the Civil Rights Act of 1866. The court reasoned as follows.

HUDSON v. CHARLOTTE COUNTRY CLUB, INC.
535 F. Supp. 313 (W.D. N.C. 1982)

POTTER, D.J.: "The Plaintiff, Alfred A. Hudson, was hired by the Defendant, Charlotte Country Club, Inc., in April of 1977 to perform various maintenance duties in and around the club's main clubhouse. However, in December of 1977, the Plaintiff was fired by the Defendant due to his behavior on several occasions toward female employees and guests of the club. The Plaintiff, a black, thereupon filed a complaint with the EEOC alleging that his termination was racially motivated, and that the payment and treatment accorded to him by his former employer had been less than that provided to white employees.

"Finding the Defendant to be a private club, exempt from the provisions of Title VII, the EEOC dismissed the Plaintiff's charge for lack of jurisdiction and granted him a 'right to sue' letter. The Plaintiff thereupon filed this suit pursuant to 42 U.S.C. § 2000e, *et seq.* (Title VII) and 42 U.S.C. § 1981, alleging discrimination in employment on the basis of his race. . . .

III. *The § 1981 Claim*

"The only remaining issue for this Court to decide is whether the private club exemption of Title VII, by implication, exempts such clubs from discrimination in employment suits brought under § 1981.

"The Civil Rights Act of 1866, 42 U.S.C. § 1981 provides in pertinent part that

"All persons within the jurisdiction of the United States shall have the same right in every State and Territory to make and enforce contracts, . . . and to the full equal benefit of all laws and proceedings for the security of persons and property as is enjoyed by white citizens. . . .

"Case law has established that this statute 'affords a federal remedy against discrimination in private employment on the basis of race.' *Johnson v. Railway Express Agency,* 421 U.S. 454, 459–60, 95 S.Ct. 1716, 1719–20, 44 L.Ed.2d 295 (1975). *See also, Jones v. Mayer,* 392 U.S. 409, 88 S.Ct. 2186, 20 L.Ed.2d 1189 (1968).

"In *Johnson,* the Supreme Court considered the question of whether the statute of limitations with regard to both a Title VII claim and a § 1981 claim was tolled by the EEOC filing in the Title VII claim. The Court held that Title VII and § 1981 offered distinct remedies and that by filing the Title VII claim, a plaintiff did not preserve his § 1981 claim. Consequently, the § 1981 claim filed over three years after the Title VII claim was barred by the statute of limitations.

"The private club exemption of Title VII was not before the Court in *Johnson,* yet the opinion includes *dicta* that touches on the subject. As a premise to finding that Title VII and § 1981 claims were governed by separate statutes of limitations, the Supreme Court necessarily found that

"the remedies available under Title VII and under § 1981, although related, and although directed to most of the same ends, are separate, distinct, and independent. 421 U.S. at 461, 95 S.Ct. at 1726.

"It is apparent from the *Johnson* opinion that, for the purpose of deciding the narrow statute of limitations question, the Supreme Court considered Title VII and § 1981, from a general standpoint, as creating separate and distinct causes of action. However, the Court did not address the possibility that the later Act, Title VII, might, in very specific situations, have preempted or limited certain causes of action under § 1981. Thus, the Supreme Court in *Johnson* cannot be fairly said to have directly decided the issue of whether the bar on suing private clubs in Title VII is also applicable, by statutory implication, to suits brought under § 1981. . . .

"The term 'employer' under Title VII 'does not include . . . a bona fide private membership club (other than a labor organization) which is exempt from taxation under section 501(c) of Title 26.' 42 U.S.C. § 2000e(b). To be exempt from Title VII coverage under the 'bona fide private membership club' exception, the club must be tax exempt and must be a private membership club. Tax exempt status alone under the Internal Revenue Code is insufficient to bring an organization within the Title VII exception. *See Quijano v. University Federal Credit Union,* 617 F.2d 129, 131 n.12 (5th Cir. 1980). *See also Tillman v. Wheaton-Haven Recreation Ass'n.,* 410 U.S. 431, 93 S.Ct. 1090, 35 L.Ed.2d 403 (1973) (Title II); *Wright v. Cork Club,* 315 F. Supp. 1143 (S.D. Tex. 1970) (Title II).

"The Association's tax exempt status under 26 U.S.C. § 501(c)(9) is undisputed. The Court must therefore determine whether the Association is a private membership club under Title VII.

"The First Circuit Court of Appeals has articulated four criteria that must be met in order for an organization to achieve private membership club status. First, the organization must be a club, i.e., an association of persons for social or recreational purposes or for promotion of a common literary, scientific, or political objective. Second, the organization's objective must be legitimate and not a sham. Third, the organization must be private, not public. Fourth, the organization must require meaningful conditions of limited membership. *Quijano v. University Federal Credit Union, supra* at 131.

"The Association was not created for social or recreational purposes or for

promoting common literary, scientific, or political objectives. The sole reason
for the Association's existence is to provide disability benefits for individuals
who are members, i.e., for individuals who contribute to the Association and
work for the Company. There is no evidence in the record that the members com-
mingle in their capacity as Association members and with a common purpose.

"No one faults the origins of the Association as an organization originally established to aid fellow employees. Moreover, the Court finds that providing disability benefits is a legitimate reason for the Association's existence. The Court
therefore declines to find that the Association is a sham for analysis of the Association's status as a bona fide private membership club under Title VII.

"The Court views the third and fourth criteria set out in *Quijano* as being
closely related. While members of the general public are not admitted to the Association, neither does the Association impose meaningful conditions of limited
membership. Access is premised, first of all, on being employed by the Company. Then, if a member meets the physical requirement and pays monthly dues,
he or she can become and remain a member. As stated earlier, there is no common social, recreational, literary, scientific, or political requisite for Association
membership. The binding objective of Association membership is personal benefit in case of disability while employed at the Company.

"The Court accordingly concludes that the Association is not a bona fide private membership club as intended under Title VII. *See Chattanooga Automobile
Club v. Commissioner of Internal Revenue*, 182 F.2d 551, 554 (6th Cir. 1950)
(denying tax exempt status to automobile clubs). The Association's contention,
then, that it is excluded from Title VII coverage because of status as a private
membership club, is rejected.

"The most recent significant statement by the Supreme Court in this area was
made in *New York City Transit Authority v. Beazer*, 440 U.S. 568, 583–4 n.24,
99 S.Ct. 1355, 1364 n.24, 59 L.Ed.2d 587 (1974). Although the private club exemption was not at issue, with regard to the relationship between claims brought
under Title VII and § 1981 the Supreme Court held that

"Our treatment of the Title VII claim also disposes of the § 1981 claim without the need of a remand. Although the exact applicability of that provision
has not been decided by this Court, it seems clear that it affords no greater
substantive protection than Title VII.

"If § 1981 provides 'no greater substantive protection than Title VII,' then it
would appear that a suit against a private club could not be brought under § 1981
when it is specifically barred by Title VII.

"This is the position that has been taken by the Fourth Circuit as stated in its
opinion in *Tillman v. Wheaton-Haven Recreation Association, Inc.*, 451 F.2d
1211, 1214–15 (1971), *rev'd on other grounds*, 410 U.S. 431, 93 S.Ct. 1090,
35 L.Ed.2d 403 (1973) with the Supreme Court specifically reserving a ruling on
the present issue. In speaking of Title VII's exemption of private clubs with regard to membership practices, the Fourth Circuit in *Tillman* stated that

"[t]his exception to the ban on racial discrimination of necessity operates as an exception to the Act of 1866, in any case where that Act prohibits the same conduct which is saved as lawful by the terms of the 1964 Act. . . . If Wheaton-Haven is a private club as defined in the 1964 Act, the exemption contained in that Act is equally applicable to the earlier statutes. (Footnote omitted.)

"Several other courts in dealing with the specific issue have arrived at the same conclusion as that reached by the Fourth Circuit in *Tillman,* most notably, *Kemerer v. Davis,* 520 F. Supp. 256 (E.D. Mich. 1981); *Wright v. Salisbury Club, Ltd.,* 479 F. Supp. 378 (E.D. Va. 1979), *rev'd on other grounds,* 632 F.2d 309 (4th Cir. 1980); and *Cornelius v. Benevolent Protective Order of Elks,* 382 F. Supp. 1182 (D. Conn. 1974). The principal justification for finding that the private club exemption of Title VII supersedes and impliedly limits § 1981 actions insofar as they conflict, was best expressed by the District Court opinion in *Wright, supra,* in its analysis of Title VII's legislative history. Relying in part upon the *Tillman* decision, *supra,* the District Court found that

"When Congress enacted the 1964 legislation, it did not and could not have known about the conflict with the 1866 Act. Indeed, not until 1968, four years after the 1964 Act became law, did the Supreme Court first determine that the Civil Rights Act of 1866 prohibited 'private' as well as officially sanctioned discrimination. *Jones v. Mayer Co.,* 392 U.S. 409, 88 S.Ct. 2186, 20 L.Ed.2d 1189 (1968). Thus the conflict between the two statutes was latent when Congress drafted the 1964 legislation, and the absence of express language in the 1964 Act limiting the 1866 Act is inconsequential.

"479 F. Supp. at 386.

"The Fourth Circuit reversed the district court's ruling in *Wright* on the grounds that the defendant was not truly a private club and thus did not rule upon the district court's holding that § 1981 was limited by the private club exemption in Title VII. 632 F.2d at 311, n. 5.

"In light of the fact that the Fourth Circuit has not modified its holding in *Tillman,* in view of the analysis of Title VII's legislative history as expressed so well by the district courts in *Cornelius* and *Wright,* and with deference to the Supreme Court's recent statement in *New York City Transit Authority v. Beazer,* this Court finds that 42 U.S.C. § 1981 does not afford any greater degree of protection than Title VII, and that suits against private clubs that are barred by Title VII, are also barred under § 1981.

"Indeed, this ruling makes sense, from both the legislative and judicial viewpoints. As the Fourth Circuit noted in *Tulman,* 'it is unquestionable that in 1964 Congress acted in the belief that in outlawing discrimination . . . it was writing on a clean slate.' 451 F.2d at 1214 n.5. Thus, if private clubs, exempt from employment discrimination suits under Title VII, are nonetheless liable to suit under § 1981 for exactly the same alleged offense, then the exemption in Title VII has no meaning and no practical effect.

"Consequently, having previously found the Defendant in this case, Charlotte Country Club, Inc., to be a bona fide private club exempt from the provision of Title VII, this Court finds that such exemption in Title VII supersedes and limits § 1981 so as to bar the employment discrimination suit under § 1981 as well.

"THEREFORE IT IS HEREBY ORDERED . . .

"(2) that the Defendant's motion for summary judgment with regard to both the Title VII and § 1981 claims is granted, and the entire case is dismissed."

4:13 Protecting Civil and Public Rights according to the New York Civil Rights Law

Insert at end of section, p. 58:

Other states that have enacted statutes prohibiting sex discrimination in places of public accommodation include District of Columbia, Illinois, Kentucky (naming only restaurants, hotels, and motels), Maryland, Michigan, Minnesota, Missouri, Montana, Nebraska, North Dakota, Ohio, Rhode Island, South Dakota, Tennessee, and Wyoming.

4:14 Cases Interpreting Sections 40 and 41 of the New York Civil Rights Law

Insert immediately before Noble v. Higgins, *p. 59:*

In 1982, however, section 40–c of the New York Civil Rights Law was amended to include sex, marital status, and disability as prohibited grounds for discrimination in a person's civil rights. Harassment, as defined in section 240.25 of the penal law, in the exercise of civil rights was also prohibited. Section 40–c applies to all persons, firms, corporations, and institutions and to the state and any agency or subdivision of the state.

4:17 Other Forms of Discrimination

Correction, p. 66: Hales v. Ojai Valley Inn was decided in 1977.

Insert immediately after Hales v. Ojai Valley Inn, *p. 68:*

In rejecting the claim of exemption by reason of a Boy Scout council's private nonprofit associational status, thereby nullifying the council's expulsion of a male member on the ground of his homosexual preference, a California appellate court resolved the competing interests of free association and the commands of the Unruh Civil Rights Act as follows.

CURRAN V. MOUNT DIABLO COUNCIL OF BOY SCOUTS,
147 Cal. 3d 712, 195 Cal. Rptr. 325 (1983), *appeal dismissed* —— U.S. ——,
104 S.Ct. 3574, 82 L.Ed.2d 873 (1984)

THOMPSON, A.J.: ". . . [D]efendant argues that any construction of the Unruh Act to bring the Boy Scouts within the meaning of 'business establishment' would constitute an infringement of its rights of privacy and free association as a membership organization. The 'governing principle,' defendant asserts, is found in the following dissenting opinion of Mr. Justice Douglas in *Moose Lodge No. 107 v. Irvis* (1972) 407 U.S. 163, 179–180, 92 S.Ct. 1965, 1974–1975, 32 L.Ed.2d 627: 'The associational rights which our system honors permit all white, all brown, and all yellow clubs to be formed. They also permit all Catholic, all Jewish, or all agnostic clubs to be established. Government may not tell a man or woman who his or her associates must be. The individual can be as selective as he desires. So the fact that the Moose Lodge allows only Caucasians to join or come as guests is constitutionally irrelevant, as is the decision of the Black Muslims to admit to their services only members of their race.'

"Taking this principle literally as 'governing' would afford protection to the most flagrant form of discrimination under the canopy of the right of free association. The answer is, of course, that those with a common interest may associate exclusively with whom they please *only* if it is the kind of association which was intended to be embraced within the protection afforded by the rights of privacy and free association. (See Note, *Association, Privacy and Private Club: The Constitutional Conflict* (1970) 5 Harv. C.R.—C.L.L. Rev. 460, 466–467.) 'The character and extent of any interference with the freedom of association must be weighed against the countervailing interests.' (Note, *Sex Discrimination in Private Clubs* (1977) 29 Hastings L.J. 417, 422.)

"Accordingly, these constitutional provisions only restrain the Legislature from enacting anti-discrimination laws where *strictly* private clubs or institutions are affected. (See, e.g., *Burks v. Poppy Construction Co., supra,* 57 Cal. 2d 463, 471, 20 Cal. Rptr. 609, 370 P.2d 313; *Stout v. Y.M.C.A.,* (5th Cir. 1968) 404 F.2d 687. *Nesmith v. Y.M.C.A.* (4th Cir. 1968) 397 F.2d 96; *National Organization for Women, Essex Chapter v. Little League Baseball, Inc.,* (1974) 127 N.J. Super. 552 [318 A.2d 33].) . . .

"Since the essence of a private club or organization is exclusivity in the choice of one's associates, we find this approach ensures that private organizations remain protected. However, those entities which are not in fact private must comply with the mandate of the Unruh Act.

"Moreover, we find that to allow an organization to offer its facilities and membership to the general public, but exclude a class of persons on a basis prohibited by law would be contrary to the public policy expressed in the Unruh Act. Although our research discloses no California cases directly on point, cases decided under the federal and sister states' public accommodations statutes are persuasive here. For example, in *Tillman v. Wheaton-Haven Recreation Assn. Inc.* (1973) 410 U.S. 431, 438, 93 S.Ct. 1090, 1094, 35 L.Ed.2d 403, a nonprofit recreational association open to all white residents in a certain area was found not to be a private club exempt from the Public Accommodation Law (Title II of the Civil Rights Act of 1964, as amended, 42 U.S.C. § 2000a, et seq.) because it had 'no plan or purpose of exclusiveness.' Similarly, in *Sullivan v. Little Hunting Park, Inc.* (1969) 396 U.S. 229, 236, 90 S.Ct. 400, 404, 24

L.Ed.2d 386, a community park open to all area residents who were not black was held not to be a private club since '[i]t is not to be open to every white person within the geographic area, there being no selective element other than race.' In *National Organization for Women v. Little League Baseball, Inc., supra,* 127 N.J. Super. 522, 318 A.2d 33, a membership organization for boys was held to be a public accommodation under New Jersey's public accommodation law. There, the court said: 'Little League is a *public* accommodation because the invitation is open to children in the community at large, with no restriction (other than sex) whatever.' (318 A.2d at pp. 37–38.)

"We therefore conclude that the concept of organizational membership per se cannot place an entity outside the scope of the Unruh Act unless it is shown that the organization is truly private. . . ."

The United States Supreme Court dismissed the Boy Scouts' appeal (no. 83–1513, July 5, 1984).

4:21 *The Male-Only Civic Club*

Insert at end of section, p. 73:

In *Whitten v. Petroleum Club of Lafayette,* 508 F. Supp 765 (W.D. La. 1981), women in the petroleum industry brought a class-action suit challenging the men-only policy of a petroleum-industry private membership club. The Petroleum Club of Lafayette, a tax-exempt and nonprofit membership club, had always prohibited women from membership, including professional women who had business at the club consistent with the purpose for which the club was formed and presently operating. The court found:

> Substantial dues, membership fees and entertainment expenses are "written off" by members or their companies each year. Approximately ninety [footnote omitted] per cent (90%) of the memberships are corporate memberships. The Petroleum Club, for all practicable purposes, is totally dependent financially on these corporate memberships, and without them, the club would probably have to close its doors.
>
> A great deal of business is carried on at the Petroleum Club. There is no doubt that women employed in the petroleum industries are at a distinct disadvantage in being denied the use of the facility and have suffered in the areas of career advancement, employment advantages, fringe benefits, and access to the market place, because that's where the action is and there is no substitute.

Despite these findings, the court granted the defendants' motion for summary judgment, asserting that the Petroleum Club did not act outside its rights as a private club.

Insert immediately before 4:22, p. 73:

In *United States Jaycees v. McClure,* 305 N.W.2d 764 (1981), the Supreme Court of Minnesota construed the state's Human Rights Law as making the United States Jaycees "a place of public accommodation" and thus unable to bar females from the full membership privileges accorded males in its Minnesota chapters. The decision was made in response to a certified question raising this precise issue made by the United States District Court for the State of Minnesota.

The United States District Court upheld this application of the law to the United States Jaycees (534 F. Supp. 766), and the Jaycees appealed. The United States Court of Appeals for the Eighth Circuit reversed and remanded. In a two-to-one decision, the majority summarized its views at as follows.

UNITED STATES JAYCEES V. MCCLURE
709 F.2d 1560 (8th Cir. 1983), *rev'd sub nom.*, Roberts v. United States Jaycees, —— U.S. ——, 104 S.Ct. 3244, 82 L.Ed.2d 462 (1984)

ARNOLD, C.J.: "The United States Jaycees, a young men's civic and service organization, does not admit women to full membership. A Minnesota statute, as amended in 1972, forbids discrimination on the basis of sex in 'places of public accommodation.' Minn. Stat. Ann. §§ 363.01 subd. 18, 363.03 subd. 3. The Supreme Court of Minnesota has interpreted this phrase to include the Jaycees, and the Minnesota Department of Human Rights has ordered the Jaycees to admit women to its local chapters in Minnesota. In this suit brought by the Jaycees, we are asked to declare the statute, as so applied and interpreted, unconstitutional, as in violation of the rights of speech, petition, assembly, and association guaranteed by the First and Fourteenth Amendments.

"We hold that the Jaycees, a substantial part of whose activities involve the expression of social and political beliefs and the advocacy of legislation and constitutional change, does have a right of association protected by the First Amendment. In our opinion, the interest of the state, in the circumstances of this case, is not strong enough to deserve the label 'compelling,' so as to override this right. In addition, the state law is unconstitutionally vague. The Jaycees is therefore entitled to an injunction restraining the state from efforts to prohibit its membership policy under state law as presently written. This is not to say that no state law could be written to redress this kind of nongovernmental discrimination. Still less do we intend to express our own view of what the Jaycees is doing. But if, in the phrase of Justice Holmes, the First Amendment protects 'the thought that we hate,' it must also, on occasion, protect the association of which we disapprove. The First Amendment guarantees freedom of choice in a certain area. That freedom must, on occasion, include the freedom to choose what the majority believes is wrong. For reasons to be described, we think this is one of those occasions.'"

¹ The Jaycees' refusal to admit women has given rise to several other court or agency opinions. See *Junior Chamber of Commerce of Kansas City, Missouri v. Missouri State Junior Chamber of Commerce*, 508 F.2d 1031 (8th Cir. 1975) (receipt of federal funds (a practice since discontinued) does not make Jaycees a governmental actor for purposes of the Fifth Amendment); *New York City Jaycees, Inc. v. The United States Jaycees, Inc.*, 512 F.2d 856 (2d Cir. 1975) (same); *Junior Chamber of Commerce of Rochester, Inc. v. United States Jaycees*, 495 F.2d 883 (10th Cir.), *cert. denied,*

Footnote 1 to the preceding case lists other relevant cases. Note that the Supreme Court of Alaska has ruled that the United States Jaycees is not a place of public accommodation. *United States Jaycees v. Richardet,* 666 P.2d 1008 (1983). In an analogous situation, however, the New York Court of Appeals has construed the New York State Human Rights Law broadly, following the precedent established by the Minnesota Supreme Court in *United States Jaycees v. McClure.* See *U.S. Power Squadron v. State Human Rights Appeal Board,* 59 N.Y.2d 401, 452 N.E.2d 1199 (1983), in which the Court of Appeals held that the Power Squadron was subject to the Human Rights Law, thus requiring it to admit female members.

On appeal, the United States Supreme Court reversed the federal Circuit Court of Appeals, *sub nom. Roberts v. United States Jaycees,* which follows.

ROBERTS V. UNITED STATES JAYCEES

—— U.S. ——, 104 S.Ct. 3244, 82 L.Ed.2d 462 (1984)

BRENNAN, J.: ". . . This case requires us to address a conflict between a State's efforts to eliminate gender-based discrimination against its citizens and the constitutional freedom of association asserted by members of a private organization. In the decision under review, the Court of Appeals for the Eighth Circuit concluded that, by requiring the United States Jaycees to admit women as full voting members, the Minnesota Human Rights Act violates the First and Fourteenth Amendment rights of the organization's members. We noted probable jurisdiction, —— U.S. ——, 104 S.Ct. 696, 79 L.Ed.2d 162, and now reverse.

I

A

"The United States Jaycees (Jaycees), founded in 1920 as the Junior Chamber of Commerce, is a nonprofit membership corporation, incorporated in Missouri with national headquarters in Tulsa, Oklahoma. The objective of the Jaycees, as set out in its bylaws, is to pursue

"such educational and charitable purposes as will promote and foster the growth and development of young men's civic organizations in the United

---

419 U.S. 1026, 95 S.Ct. 505, 42 L.Ed.2d 301 (1974) (same); *United States Jaycees v. Bloomfield,* 434 A.2d 1379 (D.C. App. 1981) (Jaycees is not a "place of public accommodation" within the meaning of the D.C. Human Rights Act of 1977, D.C. Code § 6–2241(a)(1)(Supp. 1978)); *Richardet v. Alaska Jaycees,* No. 3AN–79–424 CIV (Super Ct. 3d Jud. Dist. of Alaska Sept. 15, 1980) (Jaycees is a place at which amusement or business services or commodities are offered to the public within the meaning of the Alaska public-accommodations law, Alaska Stat. §§ 18.80.230(1), .300(7)); *Fletcher v. U.S. Jaycees,* No. 78–BPA–0058–0071 (Mass. Comm'n Against Discrimination Jan. 27, 1981) (Jaycees is a place of public accommodation within the meaning of Mass. Gen. Laws Ann. ch. 272, §§ 92A, 98).

The question has also been vigorously debated within the organization. On three occasions a resolution favoring the admission of women has been defeated, but each time a larger minority has voted for it.

States, designed to inculcate in the individual membership of such organization a spirit of genuine Americanism and civic interest, and as a supplemen-
tary education institution to provide them with opportunity for personal development and achievement and an avenue for intelligent participation by
young men in the affairs of their community, state and nation, and to develop true friendship and understanding among young men of all nations.
Quoted in Brief for Appellee 2.

"The organization's bylaws establish seven classes of membership, including individual or regular members, associate individual members, and local chapters.
Regular membership is limited to young men between the ages of 18 and 35,
while associate membership is available to individuals or groups ineligible for
regular membership, principally women and older men. An associate member,
whose dues are somewhat lower than those charged regular members, may not
vote, hold local or national office, or participate in certain leadership training
and awards programs. The bylaws define a local chapter as 'any young men's organization of good repute existing in any community within the United States,
organized for purposes similar to and consistent with those' of the national organization. App. to Juris. Statement A98. The ultimate policymaking authority of
the Jaycees rests with an annual national convention, consisting of delegates
from each local chapter, with a national president and board of directors. At the
time of trial in August 1981, the Jaycees had approximately 295,000 members in
7,400 local chapters affiliated with 51 state organizations. There were at that
time about 11,915 associate members. The national organization's Executive
Vice President estimated at trial that women associate members make up about
two percent of the Jaycees' total membership. Tr. 56.

"New members are recruited to the Jaycees through the local chapters, although the state and national organizations are also actively involved in recruitment through a variety of promotional activities. A new regular member pays an
initial fee followed by annual dues; in exchange, he is entitled to participate in all
of the activities of the local, state, and national organizations. The national headquarters employs a staff to develop 'program kits' for use by local chapters that
are designed to enhance individual development, community development, and
members' management skills. These materials include courses in public speaking
and personal finances as well as community programs related to charity, sports,
and public health. The national office also makes available to members a range
of personal products, including travel accessories, casual wear, pins, awards,
and other gifts. The programs, products, and other activities of the organization
are all regularly featured in publications made available to the membership, including a magazine entitled 'Future.'

B

"In 1974 and 1975, respectively, the Minneapolis and St. Paul chapters of the
Jaycees began admitting women as regular members. Currently, the memberships and boards of directors of both chapters include a substantial proportion of

women. As a result, the two chapters have been in violation of the national organization's bylaws for about 10 years. The national organization has imposed a number of sanctions on the Minneapolis and St. Paul chapters for violating the bylaws, including denying their members eligibility for state or national office or awards programs, and refusing to count their membership in computing votes at national conventions.

"In December 1978, the president of the national organization advised both chapters that a motion to revoke their charters would be considered at a forthcoming meeting of the national board of directors in Tulsa. Shortly after receiving this notification, members of both chapters filed charges of discrimination with the Minnesota Department of Human Rights. The complaints alleged that the exclusion of women from full membership required by the national organization's bylaws violated the Minnesota Human Rights Act (Act), which provides in part:

"It is an unfair discriminatory practice:

'To deny any person the full and equal enjoyment of the goods, services, facilities, privileges, advantages, and accommodations of a place of public accommodation because of race, color, creed, religion, disability, national origin or sex.' Minn. Stat. § 363.03, subd. 3 (1982).

"The term 'place of public accommodation' is defined in the Act as 'a business, accommodation, refreshment, entertainment, recreation, or transportation facility of any kind, whether licensed or not, whose goods, services, facilities, privileges, advantages or accommodations are extended, offered, sold, or otherwise made available to the public.' *Id.*, § 363.01, subd. 18.

"After an investigation, the Commissioner of the Minnesota Department of Human Rights found probable cause to believe that the sanctions imposed on the local chapters by the national organization violated the statute and ordered that an evidentiary hearing be held before a state hearing examiner. Before that hearing took place, however, the national organization brought suit against various state officials, appellants here, in the United States District Court for the District of Minnesota, seeking declaratory and injunctive relief to prevent enforcement of the Act. The complaint alleged that, by requiring the organization to accept women as regular members, application of the Act would violate the male members' constitutional rights of free speech and association. With the agreement of the parties, the District Court dismissed the suit without prejudice, stating that it could be renewed in the event the state administrative proceeding resulted in a ruling adverse to the Jaycees.

"The proceeding before the Minnesota Human Rights Department hearing examiner then went forward and, upon its completion, the examiner filed findings of fact and conclusions of law. The examiner concluded that the Jaycees organization is a 'place of public accommodation' within the Act and that it had engaged in an unfair discriminatory practice by excluding women from regular membership. He ordered the national organization to cease and desist from dis-

criminating against any member or applicant for membership on the basis of sex
and from imposing sanctions on any Minnesota affiliate for admitting women.
Minnesota v. United States Jaycees, No. HR–79–014–GB (Minn. Office of
Hearing Examiners for the Dept. of Human Rights, October 9, 1979) (hereinafter 'Report'), App. to Juris. Statement A107–A109. The Jaycees then filed a
renewed complaint in the District Court, which in turn certified to the Minnesota
Supreme Court the question whether the Jaycees organization is a 'place of public accommodation' within the meaning of the State's Human Rights Act. See
App. 32.

"With the record of the administrative hearing before it, the Minnesota Supreme Court answered that question in the affirmative. *United States Jaycees v.
McClure,* 305 N.W.2d 764 (1981). Based on the Act's legislative history, the
court determined that the statute is applicable to any 'public business facility.'
Id., at 768. It then concluded that the Jaycees organization (a) is a 'business' in
that it sells goods and extends privileges in exchange for annual membership
dues; (b) is a 'public' business in that it solicits and recruits dues-paying members based on unselective criteria; and (c) is a public business 'facility' in that it
conducts its activities at fixed and mobile sites within the State of Minnesota.
Id., at 768–774.

"Subsequently, the Jaycees amended their complaint in the District Court to
add a claim that the Minnesota Supreme Court's interpretation of the Act rendered it unconstitutionally vague and overbroad. The federal suit then proceeded
to trial, after which the District Court entered judgment in favor of the state officials. *United States Jaycees v. McClure,* 534 F. Supp. 766 (Minn. 1982). On appeal, a divided Court of Appeals for the Eighth Circuit reversed. 709 F.2d 1560
(1983). The Court of Appeals determined that, because 'the advocacy of political
and public causes, selected by the membership, is not insubstantial part of what
[the Jaycees] does,' the organization's right to select its members is protected by
the freedom of association guaranteed by the First Amendemnt, *Id.,* at 1570. It
further decided that application of the Minnesota statute to the Jaycees' membership policies would produce a 'direct and substantial' interference with that freedom, *id.,* at 1572, because it would necessarily result in 'some change in the
Jaycees' philosophical cast,' *id.,* at 1571, and would attach penal sanctions to
those responsible for maintaining the policy, *id.,* at 1572. The court concluded
that the State's interest in eradicating discrimination is not sufficiently compelling to outweigh this interference with the Jaycees' constitutional rights, because
the organization is not wholly 'public,' *id.,* at 1571–1572, 1573, the state interest had been asserted selectively, *id.,* at 1573, and the anti-discrimination policy
could be served in a number of ways less intrusive of First Amendment freedoms, *id.,* at 1573–1574.

"Finally, the court held, in the alternative, that the Minnesota statute is vague
as construed and applied and therefore unconstitutional under the Due Process
Clause of the Fourteenth Amendment. In support of this conclusion, the court

relied on a statement in the opinion of the Minnesota Supreme Court suggesting that, unlike the Jaycees, the Kiwanis Club is 'private' and therefore not subject to the Act. By failing to provide any criteria that distinguish such 'private' organizations from the 'public accommodations' covered by the statute, the Court of Appeals reasoned, the Minnesota Supreme Court's interpretation rendered the Act unconstitutionally vague. *Id.*, at 1576–1578.

II

"Our decisions have referred to constitutionally protected 'freedom of association' in two distinct senses. In one line of decisions, the Court has concluded that choices to enter into and maintain certain intimate human relationships must be secured against undue intrusion by the State because of the role of such relationships in safeguarding the individual freedom that is central to our constitutional scheme. In this respect, freedom of association receives protection as a fundamental element of personal liberty. In another set of decisions, the Court has recognized a right to associate for the purpose of engaging in those activities protected by the First Amendment—speech, assembly, petition for the redress of grievances, and the exercise of religion. The Constitution guarantees freedom of association of this kind as an indispensable means of preserving other individual liberties.

"The intrinsic and instrumental features of constitutionally protected association may, of course, coincide. In particular, when the State interferes with individuals' selection of those with whom they wish to join in a common endeavor, freedom of association in both of its forms may be implicated. The Jaycees contend that this is such a case. Still, the nature and degree of constitutional protection afforded freedom of association may vary depending on the extent to which one or the other aspect of the constitutionally protected liberty is at stake in a given case. We therefore find it useful to consider separately the effect of applying the Minnesota statute to the Jaycees on what could be called its members' freedom of intimate association and their freedom of expressive association.

A

"The Court has long recognized that, because the Bill of Rights is designed to secure individual liberty, it must afford the formation and preservation of certain kinds of highly personal relationships a substantial measure of sanctuary from unjustified interference by the State. *E.g., Pierce v. Society of Sisters,* 268 U.S. 510, 534–535, 45 S.Ct. 571, 573, 69 L.Ed. 1070 (1925); *Meyer v. Nebraska,* 262 U.S. 390, 399, 43 S.Ct. 625, 626, 67 L.Ed. 1042 (1923). Without precisely identifying every consideration that may underlie this type of constitutional protection, we have noted that certain kinds of personal bonds have played a critical role in the culture and traditions of the Nation by cultivating and transmitting shared ideals and beliefs; they thereby foster diversity and act as critical buffers between the individual and the power of the State. See, *e.g., Zablocki v. Red-*

hail, 434 U.S. 374, 383–386, 98 S.Ct. 673, 679–681, 54 L.Ed.2d 618 (1978); *Moore v. City of East Cleveland,* 431 U.S. 494, 503–504, 97 S.Ct. 1932, 1937–38, 52 L.Ed.2d 531 (1977) (plurality opinion); *Wisconsin v. Yoder,* 406 U.S. 205, 232, 92 S.Ct. 1526, 1541, 32 L.Ed.2d 15 (1973); *Griswold v. Connecticut,* 381 U.S. 479, 482–485, 85 S.Ct. 1678, 1680–1682, 14 L.Ed.2d 510 (1965); *Pierce v. Society of Sisters, supra,* 268 U.S., at 535, 45 S.Ct., at 573. [Citations omitted.] Moreover, the constitutional shelter afforded such relationships reflects the realization that individuals draw much of their emotional enrichment from close ties with others. Protecting these relationships from unwarranted state interference therefore safeguards the ability independently to define one's identity that is central to any concept of liberty. See, *e.g., Quillion v. Walcott,* 434 U.S. 246, 255, 98 S.Ct. 549, 554, 54 L.Ed.2d 511 (1978); *Smith v. Organization of Foster Families,* 431 U.S. 816, 844, 97 S.Ct. 2094, 2109, 53 L.Ed.2d 14 (1977); *Carey v. Population Services Int'l,* 431 U.S. 678, 684–686, 97 S.Ct. 2010, 2015–2016, 52 L.Ed.2d 675 (1977); *Cleveland Board of Education v. LaFleur,* 414 U.S. 632, 639–640, 94 S.Ct. 791, 796, 39 L.Ed.2d 52 (1974); *Stanley v. Illinois,* 405 U.S. 645, 651–652, 92 S.Ct. 1208, 1212–1213, 31 L.Ed.2d 551 (1972); *Stanley v. Georgia,* 394 U.S. 557, 564, 89 S.Ct. 1243, 1247, 22 L.Ed.2d 542 (1969); *Olmstead v. United States,* 277 U.S. 438, 478, 48 S.Ct. 564, 572, 72 L.Ed. 944 (1928) (BRANDEIS, J., dissenting).

"The personal affiliations that exemplify these considerations, and that therefore suggest some relevant limitations on the relationships that might be entitled to this sort of constitutional protection, are those that attend the creation and sustenance of a family—marriage, *e.g., Zablocki v. Redhail, supra;* childbirth, *e.g., Carey v. Population Services Int'l, supra;* the raising and education of children, *e.g., Smith v. Organization of Foster Families, supra;* and cohabitation with one's relatives, *e.g., Moore v. City of East Cleveland, supra.* Family relationships, by their nature, involve deep attachments and commitments to the necessarily few other individuals with whom one shares not only a special community of thoughts, experiences, and beliefs but also distinctively personal aspects of one's life. Among other things, therefore, they are distinguished by such attributes as relative smallness, a high degree of selectivity in decisions to begin and maintain the affiliation, and seclusion from others in critical aspects of the relationship. As a general matter, only relationships with these sorts of qualities are likely to reflect the considerations that have led to an understanding of freedom of association as an intrinsic element of personal liberty. Conversely, an association lacking these qualities—such as a large business enterprise—seems remote from the concerns giving rise to this constitutional protection. Accordingly, the Constitution undoubtedly imposes constraints on the State's power to control the selection of one's spouse that would not apply to regulations affecting the choice of one's fellow employees. Compare *Loving v. Virginia,* 388 U.S. 1, 12, 87 S.Ct. 1817, 1823, 18 L.Ed.2d 1010 (1967) with *Railway Mail Ass'n v. Corsi,* 326 U.S. 88, 93–94, 65 S.Ct. 1483, 1487, 89 L.Ed. 2072 (1945).

"Between these poles, of course, lies a broad range of human relationships that may make greater or lesser claims to constitutional protection from particular incursions by the State. Determining the limits of state authority over an individual's freedom to enter into a particular association therefore unavoidably entails a careful assessment of where that relationship's objective characteristics locate it on a spectrum from the most intimate to the most attenuated of personal attachments. See generally *Runyon v. McCrary,* 427 U.S. 160, 187–189, 96 S.Ct. 2586, 2602–2603, 49 L.Ed.2d 415 (1976) (POWELL, J., concurring). We need not mark the potentially significant points on this terrain with any precision. We note only that factors that may be relevant include size, purpose, policies, selectivity, congeniality, and other characteristics that in a particular case may be pertinent. In this case, however, several features of the Jaycees clearly place the organization outside of the category of relationships worthy of this kind of constitutional protection.

"The undisputed facts reveal that the local chapters of the Jaycees are large and basically unselective groups. At the time of the state administrative hearing, the Minneapolis chapter had approximately 430 members, while the St. Paul chapter had about 400. Report A–99, A–100. Apart from age and sex, neither the national organization nor the local chapters employs any criteria for judging applicants for membership, and new members are routinely recruited and admitted with no inquiry into their backgrounds. See I Tr. of State Administrative Hearing 124–132, 135–136, 174–176. In fact, a local officer testified that he could recall no instance in which an applicant had been denied membership on any basis other than age or sex. *Id.,* at 135. Cf. *Tillman v. Wheaton-Haven Recreational Ass'n,* 410 U.S. 431, 438, 93 S.Ct. 1090, 1094, 35 L.Ed.2d 403 (1973) (organization whose only selection criteria is race has 'no plan or purpose of exclusiveness' that might make it a private club exempt from federal civil rights statute); *Sullivan v. Little Hunting Park, Inc.,* 396 U.S. 229, 236, 90 S.Ct. 400, 404, 24 L.Ed.2d 386 (1969) (same); *Daniel v. Paul,* 395 U.S. 298, 302, 89 S.Ct. 1697, 1699, 23 L.Ed.2d 318 (1969) (same). Furthermore, despite their inability to vote, hold office, or receive certain awards, women affiliated with the Jaycees attend various meetings, participate in selected projects, and engage in many of the organization's social functions. See Tr. 58. Indeed, numerous nonmembers of both genders regularly participate in a substantial portion of activities central to the decision of many members to associate with one another, including many of the organization's various community programs, awards ceremonies, and recruitment meetings. See, *e.g.,* 305 N.W.2d, at 772; Report A102, A103.

"In short, the local chapters of the Jaycees are neither small nor selective. Moreover, much of the activity central to the formation and maintenance of the association involves the participation of strangers to that relationship. Accordingly, we conclude that the Jaycees chapters lack the distinctive characteristics that might afford constitutional protection to the decision of its members to exclude women. We turn therefore to consider the extent to which application of the Minnesota statute to compel the Jaycees to accept women infringes the group's freedom of expressive association.

B

"An individual's freedom to speak, to worship, and to petition the Government for the redress of grievances could not be vigorously protected from interference by the State unless a correlative freedom to engage in group effort toward those ends were not also guaranteed. See, *e.g., Rent Control/Coalition for Fair Housing v. Berkeley,* 454 U.S. 290, 294, 102 S.Ct. 434, 456, 70 L.Ed.2d 492 (1981). According protection to collective effort on behalf of shared goals is especially important in preserving political and cultural diversity and in shielding dissident expression from supression by the majority. [Citations omitted.] Consequently, we have long understood as implicit in the right to engage in activities protected by the First Amendment a corresponding right to associate with others in pursuit of a wide variety of political, social, economic, educational, religious, and cultural ends. See, *e.g., NAACP v. Claiborne Hardware Co.,* 458 U.S. 886, 907–909, 832–933, 102 S.Ct. 3409, 3422–3423, 3436, 73 L.Ed.2d 1215 (1982); *Larson v. Valente,* 456 U.S. 228, 244–246, 102 S.Ct. 1673, 1683, 1684, 72 L.Ed.2d 33 (1982); *In re Primus,* 436 U.S. 412, 426, 98 S.Ct. 1893, 1901, 56 L.Ed.2d 417 (1978); *Abood v. Detroit Board of Education,* 431 U.S. 209, 231, 97 S.Ct. 1782, 1797, 52 L.Ed.2d 261 (1977). In view of the various protected activities in which the Jaycees engage, see *infra,* at 3254–3255, that right is plainly implicated in this case.

"Government actions that may unconstitutionally infringe upon this freedom can take a number of forms. Among other things, government may seek to impose penalties or withhold benefits from individuals because of their membership in a disfavored group, *e.g., Healy v. James,* 408 U.S. 169, 180–184, 92 S.Ct. 2338, 2345–2347, 33 L.Ed.2d 266 (1972); it may attempt to require disclosure of the fact of membership in a group seeking anonymity, *e.g., Brown v. Socialist Workers '74 Campaign Committee,* 459 U.S. 87, 91–92, 103 S.Ct. 416, 419–421, 74 L.Ed.2d 250 (1982); and it may try to interfere with the internal organization or affairs of the group, *e.g., Cousins v. Wigoda,* 419 U.S. 477, 487–488, 95 S.Ct. 541, 547, 42 L.Ed.2d 595 (1975). By requiring the Jaycees to admit women as full voting members, the Minnesota Act works an infringement of the last type. There can be no clearer example of an intrusion into the internal structure or affairs of an association than a regulation that forces the group to accept members it does not desire. Such a regulation may impair the ability of the original members to express only those views that brought them together. Freedom of association therefore plainly presupposes a freedom not to associate. See *Abood v. Detroit Board of Education, supra,* 431 U.S., at 234–235, 97 S.Ct., at 1799.

"The right to associate for expressive purposes is not, however, absolute. Infringements on that right may be justified by regulations adopted to serve compelling state interests, unrelated to the suppression of ideas, that cannot be achieved through means significantly less restrictive of associational freedoms. [Citations omitted.] We are persuaded that Minnesota's compelling interest in eradicating discrimination against its female citizens justifies the impact that application of the statute to the Jaycees may have on the male members' associational freedoms.

"On its face, the Minnesota Act does not aim at the suppression of speech, does not distinguish between prohibited and permitted activity on the basis of viewpoint, and does not license enforcement authorities to administer the statute on the basis of such constitutionally impermissible criteria. See also *infra,* at 3255–3256. Nor do the Jaycees contend that the Act has been applied in this case for the purpose of hampering the organization's ability to express its views. Instead, as the Minnesota Supreme Court explained, the Act reflects the State's strong historical commitment to eliminating discrimination and assuring its citizens equal access to publicly available goods and services. See 305 N.W.2d, at 766–768. That goal, which is unrelated to the suppression of expression, plainly serves compelling state interests of the highest order.

"The Minnesota Human Rights Act at issue here is an example of public accommodations laws that were adopted by some States beginning a decade before enactment of their federal counterpart, the Civil Rights Act of 1875, ch. 114, 18 Stat. 335. See Survey, 7 NYU Rev. L. & Soc. Change 215, 238 (1978) (hereinafter NYU Survey). Indeed, when this Court invalidated that federal statute in the *Civil Rights Cases,* 109 U.S. 3, 3 S.Ct. 18, 27 L.Ed. 835 (1883), it emphasized the fact that state laws imposed a variety of equal access obligations on public accommodations. *Id.,* at 19, 25, 3 S.Ct., at 27, 31. In response to that decision, many more States, including Minnesota, adopted statutes prohibiting racial discrimination in public accommodations. These laws provided the primary means for protecting the civil rights of historically disadvantaged groups until the Federal Government reentered the field in 1957. See NYU Survey 239; Brief for the States of California and New York as *Amicus Curiae* 1. Like many other States, Minnesota has progressively broadened the scope of its public accommodations law in the years since it was first enacted, both with respect to the number and type of covered facilities and with respect to the groups against whom discrimination is forbidden. See 305 N.W.2d, at 766–768. In 1973, the Minnesota legislature added discrimination on the basis of sex to the types of conduct prohibited by the statute. Act of May 24, 1973, ch. 729, § 3, 1973 Minn. Laws 2158, 2164.

"By prohibiting gender discrimination in places of public accommodation, the Minnesota Act protects the State's citizenry from a number of serious social and personal harms. In the context of reviewing state actions under the Equal Protection Clause, this Court has frequently noted that discrimination based on archaic and overbroad assumptions about the relative needs and capacities of the sexes forces individuals to labor under stereotypical notions that often bear no relationship to their actual abilities. It thereby both deprives persons of their individual dignity and denies society the benefits of wide participation in political, economic, and cultural life. See, *e.g., Heckler v. Mathews,* —— U.S. ——, ——, 104 S.Ct. 1387, 1393, 79 L.Ed.2d 646 (1984); *Mississippi University for Women v. Hogan,* 458 U.S. 718, 723–726, 102 S.Ct. 3331, 3335–3337, 73 L.Ed.2d 1090 (1982); *Frontiero v. Richardson,* 411 U.S. 677, 684–687, 93 S.Ct. 1764, 1769–1770, 36 L.Ed.2d 583 (1973) (plurality opinion). These concerns are strongly implicated with respect to gender discrimination in the allocation of publicly available goods and services. Thus, in upholding Title II of the Civil Rights Act of 1964, 78 Stat. 243, 42 U.S.C. § 2000a, which forbids race discrimination in public accommodations, we emphasized that its 'fundamental object . . . was to vindicate "the deprivation of personal dignity that surely accompanies denials of equal access to public establishments."' *Heart of Atlanta Motel v. United States,* 379 U.S. 241, 250, 85 S.Ct. 348, 354, 13 L.Ed.2d 258 (1964). That stigmatizing injury, and the denial of equal opportunities that accompanies it, is surely felt as strongly by persons suffering discrimination on the basis of their sex as by those treated differently because of their race.

"Nor is the state interest in assuring equal access limited to the provision of purely tangible goods and services. See *Alfred L. Snapp & Son, Inc. v. Puerto Rico,* 458 U.S. 592, 609, 102 S.Ct. 3260, 3270, 73 L.Ed.2d 995 (1982). A State enjoys broad authority to create rights of public access on behalf of its citizens. *Pruneyard Shopping Center v. Robins,* 447 U.S. 74, 81–88, 100 S.Ct. 2035, 2040–2044, 64 L.Ed.2d 741 (1980). Like many States and municipalities, Minnesota has adopted a functional definition of public accommodations that reaches various forms of public, quasi-commercial conduct. See 305 N.W.2d at 768; Brief for National League of Cities *et al.* as *Amicus Curiae* 15–16. This expansive definition reflects a recognition of the changing nature of the American economy and of the importance, both to the individual and to society, of removing the barriers to economic advancement and political and social integration that have historically plagued certain disadvantaged groups, including women. See *Califano v. Webster,* 430 U.S. 313, 317, 97 S.Ct. 1192, 1194, 51 L.Ed.2d 360 (1977) *(per curiam); Frontiero v. Richardson, supra,* 411 U.S., at 684–686, 93 S.Ct., at 1769–1770. Thus, in explaining its conclusion that the Jaycees local chapters are 'place[s] of public accommodations' within the meaning of the Act, the Minnesota court noted the various commercial programs and benefits offered to members and stated that, '[l]eadership skills are "goods," [and] business contacts and employment promotions are "privileges" and "advantages". . . .' 305 N.W.2d, at 772. Assuring women equal access to such goods, privileges, and advantages clearly furthers compelling state interests.

"In applying the Act to the Jaycees, the State has advanced those interests through the least restrictive means of achieving its ends. Indeed, the Jaycees have failed to demonstrate that the Act imposes any serious burdens on the male members' freedom of expressive association. See *Hishon v. King & Spalding,*

—— U.S. ——, ——, 104 S.Ct. 2229, 2235, 80 L.Ed.2d —— (1984) (law firm 'has not shown how its ability to fulfill [protected] function[s] would be inhibited by a requirement that it consider [a woman lawyer] for partnership on her merits'); *id.,* at ——, 104 S.Ct., at 2236 (POWELL, J., concurring); [Citations omitted]. To be sure, as the Court of Appeals noted, a 'not insubstantial part' of the Jaycees' activities constitutes protected expression on political, economic, cultural, and social affairs. 709 F.2d, at 1570. Over the years, the national and local levels of the organization have taken public positions on a number of diverse issues, see *id.,* at 1569–1570; Brief for Appellee 4–5, and members of the Jaycees regularly engage in a variety of civic, charitable, lobbying, fundraising and other activities worthy of constitutional protection under the First Amendment, *ibid.,* see, *e.g., Village of Schaumburg v. Citizens for a Better Environment,* 444 U.S. 620, 632, 100 S.Ct. 826, 833, 63 L.Ed.2d 73 (1980). There is, however, no basis in the record for concluding that admission of women as full voting members will impede the organization's ability to engage in these protected activities or to disseminate its preferred views. The Act requires no change in the Jaycees' creed of promoting the interests of young men, and it imposes no restrictions on the organization's ability to exclude individuals with ideologies or philosophies different from those of its existing members. Cf. *Democratic Party v. Wisconsin,* 450 U.S., at 122, 101 S.Ct., at 1019 (recognizing the right of political parties to 'protect themselves "from intrusion by those with adverse political principles"'). Moreover, the Jaycees already invite women to share the group's view and philosophy and to participate in much of its training and community activities. Accordingly, any claim that admission of women as full voting members will impair a symbolic message conveyed by the very fact that women are not permitted to vote is attenuated at best. Cf. *Spence v. Washington,* 418 U.S. 405, 94 S.Ct. 2727, 41 L.Ed.2d 842 (1974); *Griswold v. Connecticut,* 381 U.S., at 483, 85 S.Ct., at 1681.

"While acknowledging that 'the specific content of most of the resolutions adopted over the years by the Jaycees has nothing to do with sex,' 709 F.2d, at 1571, the Court of Appeals nonetheless entertained the hypothesis that women members might have a different view or agenda with respect to these matters so that, if they are allowed to vote, 'some change in the Jaycees' philosophical cast can reasonably be expected,' *ibid.* It is similarly arguable that, insofar as the Jaycees is organized to promote the views of young men whatever those views happen to be, admission of women as voting members will change the message communicated by the group's speech because of the gender-based assumptions of the audience. Neither supposition, however, is supported by the record. In claiming that women might have a different attitude about such issues as the federal budget, school prayer, voting rights, and foreign relations, see 709 F.2d, at 1570, or that the organization's public positions would have a different effect if the group were not 'a purely young men's association,' the Jaycees rely solely on unsupported generalizations about the relative interests and perspectives of men and women. See Brief for Appellees 20–22 and n. 3. Although such generalizations may or may not have a statistical basis in fact with respect to particular positions adopted by the Jaycees, we have repeatedly condemned legal decision-making that relies uncritically on such assumptions. See, *e.g., Palmore v. Sidoti,* —— U.S. ——, —— ——, 104 S.Ct. 1879, 1882, 80 L.Ed.2d 421 (1984); *Heckler v. Matthews,* —— U.S., at —— ——, 104 S.Ct., at 1395. In the absence of a showing far more substantial than that attempted by the Jaycees, we decline to indulge in the sexual stereotyping that underlies appellee's contention that, by allowing women to vote, application of the Minnesota Act will change the content or impact of the organization's speech. [Citations omitted.]

"In any event, even if enforcement of the Act causes some incidental abridgement of the Jaycees' protected speech, that effect is no greater than is necessary to accomplish the State's legitimate purposes. As we have explained, acts of invidious discrimination in the distribution of publicly available goods, services, and other advantages cause unique evils that government has a compelling interest to prevent—wholly apart from the point of view such conduct may transmit. Accordingly, like violence or other types of potentially expressive activities that produce special harms distinct from their communicative impact, such practices are entitled to no constitutional protection. *Runyon v. McCrary,* 427 U.S. 160, 175–176, 96 S.Ct. 2586, 2596–2597, 49 L.Ed.2d 415 (1976). [Citations omitted.] In prohibiting such practices, the Minnesota Act therefore 'responds precisely to the substantive problem which legitimately concerns' the State and abridges no more speech or associational freedom than is necessary to accomplish that purpose. See *City Council v. Taxpayers for Vincent,* —— U.S. ——, ——, 104 S.Ct. 2118, 2132, 80 L.Ed.2d 772 (1984).

III

"We turn finally to appellee's contentions that the Minnesota Act, as interpreted by the State's highest court, is unconstitutionally vague and overbroad. The void-for-vagueness doctrine reflects the principle that 'a statute which either forbids or requires the doing of an act in terms so vague that [persons] of common intelligence must necessarily guess at its meaning and differ as to its application, violates the first essential of due process of law.' *Connally v. General Construction Co.,* 269 U.S. 385, 391, 46 S.Ct. 126, 127, 70 L.Ed. 322 (1925). The requirement that government articulate its aims with a reasonable degree of clarity ensures that state power will be exercised only on behalf of policies reflecting an authoritative choice among competing social values, reduces the danger of caprice and discrimination in the administration of the laws, enables individuals to conform their conduct to the requirements of law, and permits meaningful judicial review. See, *e.g., Kolender v. Lawson,* —— U.S. ——, ——--——, 103 S.Ct. 1855, 1858, 75 L.Ed.2d 903 (1983); *Grayned v. City of Rockford,* 408 U.S. 104, 108–109, 92 S.Ct. 2294, 2298–2299, 33 L.Ed.2d 222

(1972); *Giaccio v. Pennsylvania,* 382 U.S. 399, 402–404, 86 S.Ct. 518, 520–521, 15 L.Ed.2d 447 (1966).

"We have little trouble concluding that these concerns are not seriously implicated by the Minnesota Act, either on its face or as construed in this case. In deciding that the Act reaches the Jaycees, the Minnesota Supreme Court used a number of specific and objective criteria—regarding the organization's size, selectivity, commercial nature, and use of public facilities—typically employed in determining the applicability of state and federal anti-discrimination statutes to the membership policies of assertedly private clubs. See, *e.g., Nesmith v. Young Men's Christian Ass'n,* 397 F.2d 96 (CA4 1968); *National Organization for Women v. Little League Baseball, Inc.,* 127 N.J. Super. 522, 318 A.2d 33, *aff'd mem.,* 67 N.J. 320, 338 A.2d 198 (1974). See generally NYU Survey 223–224, 250–252. The Court of Appeals seemingly acknowledged that the Minnesota court's construction of the Act by use of these familiar standards ensures that the reach of the statute is readily ascertainable. It nevertheless concluded that the Minnesota court introduced a constitutionally fatal element of uncertainty into the statute by suggesting that the Kiwanis Club might be sufficiently 'private' to be outside the scope of the Act. See 709 F.2d, at 1577. Like the dissenting judge in the Court of Appeals, however, we read the illustrative reference to the Kiwanis Club, which the record indicates has a formal procedure for choosing members on the basis of specific and selective criteria, as simply providing a further refinement of the standards used to determine whether an organization is 'public' or 'private.' See *id.,* at 1582 (LAY, C.J., dissenting). By offering this counter-example, the Minnesota Supreme Court's opinion provided the statute with more, rather than less, definite content.

"The contrast between the Jaycees and the Kiwanis Club drawn by the Minnesota court also disposes of appellee's contention that the Act is unconstitutionally overbroad. The Jaycees argue that the statute is 'susceptible of sweeping and improper application,' *NAACP v. Button,* 371 U.S. 415, 433, 83 S.Ct. 328, 338, 9 L.Ed.2d 405 (1963), because it could be used to restrict the membership decisions of wholly private groups organized for a wide variety of political, religious, cultural, or social purposes. Without considering the extent to which such groups may be entitled to constitutional protection from the operation of the Minnesota Act, we need only note that the Minnesota Supreme Court expressly rejected the contention that the Jaycees should 'be viewed analogously to private organizations such as the Kiwanis International Organization.' 305 N.W.2d, at 771. The state court's articulated willingness to adopt limiting constructions that would exclude private groups from the statute's reach, together with the commonly used and sufficiently precise standards it employed to determine that the Jaycees is not such a group, establish that the Act, as currently construed, does not create an unacceptable risk of application to a substantial amount of protected conduct. [Citations omitted.] See *New York v. Ferber,* 458 U.S. 747, 769, n.24, 102 S.Ct. 3348, 3361, n.24, 73 L.Ed.2d 1113 (1982).

IV

"The judgment of the Court of Appeals is *Reversed*.

"Justice REHNQUIST concurs in the judgment.

"The CHIEF JUSTICE and Justice BLACKMUN took no part in the decision of this case.

"Justice O'CONNOR, concurring in part and concurring in the judgment.

"I join Parts I and III of the Court's opinion, which set out the facts and reject the vagueness and overbreadth challenges to the Minnesota statute. With respect to Part II-A of the Court's opinion, I agree with the Court that the Jaycees cannot claim a right of association deriving from this Court's cases concerning 'marriage, procreation, contraception, family relationships, and child rearing and education.' *Paul v. Davis,* 424 U.S. 693, 713, 96 S.Ct. 1155, 1166, 47 L.Ed.2d 405 (1976). Those cases, 'while defying categorical description,' *ibid.,* identify certain zones of privacy in which certain personal relationships or decisions are protected from government interference. Whatever the precise scope of the rights recognized in such cases, they do not encompass associational rights of a 295,000-member organization whose activities are not 'private' in any meaningful sense of that term.

"I part company with the Court over its First Amendment analysis in Part II–B of its opinion. I agree with the Court that application of the Minnesota law to the Jaycees does not contravene the First Amendment, but I reach that conclusion for reasons distinct from those offered by the Court. I believe the Court has adopted a test that unadvisedly casts doubt on the power of States to pursue the profoundly important goal of ensuring nondiscriminatory access to commercial opportunities in our society. At the same time, the Court has adopted an approach to the general problem presented by this case that accords insufficient protection to expressive associations and places inappropriate burdens on groups claiming the protection of the First Amendment.

I

"The Court analyzes Minnesota's attempt to regulate the Jaycees' membership using a test that I find both over-protective of activities undeserving of constitutional shelter and under-protective of important First Amendment concerns. The Court declares that the Jaycees' right of association depends on the organization's making a 'substantial' showing that the admission of unwelcome members 'will change the message communicated by the group's speech.' See *ante,* at 3254–3255. I am not sure what showing the Court thinks would satisfy its requirement of proof of a membership-message connection, but whatever it means, the focus on such a connection is objectionable.

"Imposing such a requirement, especially in the context of the balancing-of-interests test articulated by the Court, raises the possibility that certain commercial associations, by engaging occasionally in certain kinds of expressive activities, might improperly gain protection for discrimination. The Court's focus raises other problems as well. How are we to analyze the First Amendment associational claims of an organization that invokes its right, settled by the Court in *NAACP v. Alabama,* 357 U.S. 449, 460–466, 78 S.Ct. 1163, 1170–1174, 2 L.Ed.2d 1488 (1958), to protect the privacy of its membership? And would the Court's analysis of this case be different if, for example, the Jaycees membership had a steady history of opposing public issues thought (by the Court) to be favored by women? It might seem easy to conclude, in the latter case, that the admission of women to the Jaycees' ranks would affect the content of the organization's message, but I do not believe that should change the outcome of this case. Whether an association is or is not constitutionally protected in the selection of its membership should not depend on what the association says or why its members say it.

"The Court's readiness to inquire into the connection between membership and message reveals a more fundamental flaw in its analysis. The Court pursues this inquiry as part of its mechanical application of a 'compelling interest' test, under which the Court weighs the interests of the State of Minnesota in ending gender discrimination against the Jaycees' First Amendment right of association. The Court entirely neglects to establish at the threshold that the Jaycees is an association whose activities or purposes should engage the strong protections that the First Amendment extends to expressive associations.

"On the one hand, an association engaged exclusively in protected expression enjoys First Amendment protection of both the content of its message and the choice of its members. Protection of the message itself is judged by the same standards as protection of speech by an individual. Protection of the association's right to define its membership derives from the recognition that the formation of an expressive association is the creation of a voice, and the selection of members is the definition of that voice. 'In the realm of protected speech, the legislature is constitutionally disqualified from dictating . . . the speakers who may address a public issue.' *First National Bank of Boston v. Bellotti,* 435 U.S. 765, 784–785, 98 S.Ct. 1407, 1420, 55 L.Ed.2d 707 (1978); *Police Dept. of Chicago v. Mosley,* 408 U.S. 92, 96, 92 S.Ct. 2286, 2290, 33 L.Ed.2d 212 (1972). A ban on specific group voices on public affairs violates the most basic guarantee of the First Amendment—that citizens, not the government, control the content of public discussion.

"On the other hand, there is only minimal constitutional protection of the freedom of *commercial* association. There are, of course, some constitutional protections of commercial speech—speech intended and used to promote a commercial transaction with the speaker. But the State is free to impose any rational regulation on the commercial transaction itself. The Constitution does not guarantee a right to choose employees, customers, suppliers, or those with whom one engages in simple commercial transactions, without restraint from the State. A shopkeeper has no constitutional right to deal only with persons of one sex.

"The dichotomy between rights of commercial association and rights of expressive association is also found in the more limited constitutional protections accorded an association's recruitment and solicitation activities and other dealings with its members and the public. Reasonable, content-neutral state regulation of the time, place, and manner of an organization's relations with its members or with the State can pass constitutional muster, but only if the regulation is 'narrowly drawn' to serve a 'sufficiently strong, subordinating interest' 'without unnecessarily interfering with First Amendment freedoms.' *Village of Schaumburg v. Citizens for a Better Environment,* 444 U.S. 620, 636–637, 100 S.Ct. 826, 835–836, 63 L.Ed.2d 73 (1980); see *Secretary of State of Maryland v. Joseph H. Munson Co.*, 467 U.S. ——, ——, 104 S.Ct. 2839, 2853, 80 L.Ed.2d —— (1984). Thus, after careful scrutiny, we have upheld regulations on matters such as the financial dealings between an association and its members, see *Buckley v. Valeo,* 424 U.S. 1, 25, 96 S.Ct. 612, 637, 46 L.Ed.2d 659 (1976), disclosure of membership lists to the State, see *NAACP v. Alabama, supra,* 356 U.S., at 463, 78 S.Ct., at 1172; *Shelton v. Tucker,* 364 U.S. 479, 486, 81 S.Ct. 247, 251, 5 L.Ed.2d 231 (1960), access to the ballot, time limits on registering before elections, and similar matters. [Citations omitted]. See also *Heffron v. International Society for Krishna Consciousness, Inc.,* 452 U.S. 640, 649, 101 S.Ct. 2559, 2564, 69 L.Ed.2d 298 (1981). By contrast, an organization engaged in commercial activity enjoys only minimal constitutional protection of its recruitment, training, and solicitation activities. While the Court has acknowledged a First Amendment right to engage in non-deceptive commercial advertising, governmental regulation of the commercial recruitment of new members, stockholders, customers, or employees is valid if rationally related to the government's ends.

"Many associations cannot readily be described as purely expressive or purely commercial. No association is likely ever to be exclusively engaged in expressive activities, if only because it will collect dues from its members or purchase printing materials or rent lecture halls or serve coffee and cakes at its meetings. And innumerable commercial associations also engage in some incidental protected speech or advocacy. The standard for deciding just how much of an association's involvement in commercial activity is enough to suspend the association's First Amendment right to control its membership cannot, therefore, be articulated with simple precision. Clearly the standard must accept the reality that even the most expressive of associations is likely to touch, in some way or other, matters of commerce. The standard must nevertheless give substance to the ideal of complete protection for purely expressive association, even while it readily permits state regulation of commercial affairs.

"In my view, an association should be characterized as commercial, and therefore subject to rationally related state regulation of its membership and other associational activities, when, and only when, the association's activities are not predominantly of the type protected by the First Amendment. It is only when the association is predominantly engaged in protected expression that state regulation of its membership will necessarily affect, change, dilute, or silence one collective voice that would otherwise be heard. An association must choose its market. Once it enters the marketplace of commerce in any substantial degree it loses the complete control over its membership that it would otherwise enjoy if it confined its affairs to the marketplace of ideas.

"Determining whether an association's activity is predominantly protected expression will often be difficult, if only because a broad range of activities can be expressive. It is easy enough to identify expressive words or conduct that are strident, contentious, or divisive, but protected expression may also take the form of quiet persuasion, inculcation of traditional values, instruction of the young, and community service. Cf. *Pierce v. Society of Sisters,* 268 U.S. 510, 45 S.Ct. 571, 69 L.Ed. 1070 (1925); *Meyer v. Nebraska,* 262 U.S. 390, 43 S.Ct. 625, 67 L.Ed. 1042 (1923). The purposes of an association, and the purposes of its members in adhering to it, are doubtless relevant in determining whether the association is primarily engaged in protected expression. Lawyering to advance social goals may be speech, *NAACP v. Button,* 371 U.S. 415, 429–430, 83 S.Ct. 328, 335–336, 9 L.Ed.2d 405 (1963), but ordinary commercial law practice is not, see *Hishon v. King and Spalding,* 467 U.S. ——, 104 S.Ct. 2229, 80 L.Ed.2d —— (1984). A group boycott or refusal to deal for political purposes may be speech, *NAACP v. Claiborne Hardware Co.,* 458 U.S. 886, 912–915, 102 S.Ct. 3409, 3425–3427, 73 L.Ed.2d 1215 (1982), though a similar boycott for purposes of maintaining a cartel is not. Even the training of outdoor survival skills or participation in community service might become expressive when the activity is intended to develop good morals, reverence, patriotism, and a desire for self-improvement. [Footnote omitted.]

"The considerations that may enter into the determination of when a particular association of persons is predominantly engaged in expression are therefore fluid and somewhat uncertain. But the Court has recognized the need to draw similar lines in the past. Two examples, both addressed in cases decided this Term, stand out.

"The first concerns claims of First Amendment protection made by lawyers. On the one hand, some lawyering activity is undoubtedly protected by the First Amendment. '[C]ollective activity undertaken to obtain meaningful access to the courts is a fundamental right within the protection of the First Amendment.' *In re Primus,* 436 U.S. 412, 426, 98 S.Ct. 1893, 1901, 56 L.Ed.2d 417 (1978); see *NAACP v. Button, supra,* 371 U.S., at 429–430, 83 S.Ct., at 335–336. On the other hand, ordinary law practice for commercial ends has never been given special First Amendment protection. 'A lawyer's procurement of remunerative employment is a subject only marginally affected with First Amendment concerns.' *Ohralik v. Ohio State Bar Assn.,* 436 U.S. 447, 459, 98 S.Ct. 1912, 1920, 56 L.Ed.2d 444 (1978). We emphasized this point only this Term in *Hishon v. King and Spalding, supra,* where we readily rejected a large commercial law firm's claim to First Amendment protection for alleged gender-based discriminatory partnership decisions for associates of the firm. We found no need to inquire into any connection between gender as a condition of partnership and the speech of the law firm, and we undertook no weighing of 'compelling' state interests against the speech interests of the law firm. As a commercial enterprise, the law firm could claim no First Amendment immunity from employment discrimination laws, and that result would not have been altered by a showing that the firm engaged even in a substantial amount of activity entitled to First Amendment protection.

"We have adopted a similar analysis in our cases concerning association with a labor union. A State is free to impose rational regulation of the membership of a labor union representing 'the general *business* needs of employees.' *Railway Mail Assn. v. Corsi,* 326 U.S. 88, 94, 65 S.Ct. 1483, 1487, 89 L.Ed. 2072 (1945) (emphasis added). The State may not, on the other hand, compel association with a union engaged in ideological activities. *Abood v. Detroit Board of Education,* 431 U.S. 209, 236, 97 S.Ct. 1782, 1800, 52 L.Ed.2d 261 (1977). The Court has thus ruled that a State may compel association for the commercial purposes of engaging in collective bargaining, administering labor contracts, and adjusting employment-related grievances, but it may not infringe on associational rights involving ideological or political associations. *Ibid.* We applied this distinction in *Ellis v. Railway Clerks,* 466 U.S. ——, 104 S.Ct. 1883, 80 L.Ed.2d 428 (1984), decided this Term. Again, the constitutional inquiry is not qualified by any analysis of governmental interests and does not turn on an individual's ability to establish disagreement with the particular views promulgated by the union. It is enough if the individual simply expresses unwillingness to be associated with the union's ideological activities.

"In summary, this Court's case law recognizes radically different constitutional protections for expressive and non-expressive associations. The First Amendment is offended by direct state control of the membership of a private organization engaged exclusively in protected expressive activity, but no First Amendment interest stands in the way of a State's rational regulation of economic transactions by or within a commercial association. The proper approach to analysis of First Amendment claims of associational freedom is, therefore, to distinguish non-expressive from expressive associations and to recognize that the former lack the full constitutional protections possessed by the latter.

II

"Minnesota's attempt to regulate the membership of the Jaycees chapters operating in that State presents a relatively easy case for application of the expressive-commercial dichotomy. Both the Minnesota Supreme Court and the United States District Court, which expressly adopted the state court's findings, made findings of fact concerning the commercial nature of the Jaycees activities. The Court of Appeals, which disagreed with the District Court over the legal conclusions to be drawn from the facts, did not dispute any of those findings. *United States Jaycees v. McClure*, 709 F.2d 1560 (CA8 1983). 'The Jaycees is not a political party, or even primarily a political pressure group, but the advocacy of political and public causes, selected by the membership, is a not insubstantial part of what it does. . . . [A] good deal of what the [Jaycees] does indisputably comes within the right of association . . . in pursuance of the specific ends of speech, writing, belief, and assembly for redress of grievances.' *Id.*, at 1570.

"There is no reason to question the accuracy of this characterization. Notwithstanding its protected expressive activities, the Jaycees—otherwise known as the Junior Chamber of Commerce—is, first and foremost, an organization that, at both the national and local levels, promotes and practices the art of solicitation and management. The organization claims that the training it offers its members gives them an advantage in business, and business firms do indeed sometimes pay the dues of individual memberships for their employees. Jaycees members hone their solicitation and management skills, under the direction and supervision of the organization, primarily through their active recruitment of new members. 'One of the major activities of the Jaycees is the sale of memberships in the organization. It encourages continuous recruitment of members with the expressed goal of increasing membership. . . . The Jaycees itself refers to its members as customers and membership as a product it is selling. More than 80 percent of the national officers' time is dedicated to recruitment, and more than half of the available achievement awards are in part conditioned on achievement in recruitment.' *United States Jaycees v. McClure*, 534 F. Supp. 766, 769 (Minn. 1982). The organization encourages record-breaking performance in selling memberships: the current records are 348 for most memberships sold in a year by one person, 134 for most sold in a month, and 1,586 for most sold in a lifetime.

"Recruitment and selling are commercial activities, even when conducted for training rather than for profit. The 'not insubstantial' volume of protected Jaycees activity found by the Court of Appeals is simply not enough to preclude state regulation of the Jaycees' commercial activities. The State of Minnesota has a legitimate interest in ensuring nondiscriminatory access to the commercial opportunity presented by membership in the Jaycees. The members of the Jaycees may not claim constitutional immunity from Minnesota's antidiscrimination law by seeking to exercise their First Amendment rights through this commercial organization.

"For these reasons, I agree with the Court that the Jaycees' First Amendment challenge to the application of Minnesota's public accommodations law is meritless. I therefore concur in Parts I and III of the Court's opinion and in the judgment."

Chapter 5. Relationship of Innkeeper and Guest: Creation and Termination

5:7 *Guest Need Not Resort to Inn for Both Food and Lodging*

Insert at end of section, p. 79:

It has been held, however, that no innkeeper-guest relationship was established where a couple, visiting Washington, D.C., for the presidential inauguration, on the day of their departure ate at defendant hotel's restaurant, checking their bags with the hotel bellman. *Blakemore v. Coleman,* 701 F.2d 967 (D.C. Cir. 1983); see case at 16:14a.

5:15 *Statutes Requiring the Keeping of Hotel Registers*

Insert at end of Section, p. 89:

Sections 60 and 61 were merged into section 393 in 1970. When the Election Law was recodified in 1976–1977, section 393 was omitted.

The following states also require innkeepers to keep records for the use of election officials: Illinois, Massachusetts, New Jersey, Pennsylvania.

5:17 *True-Name Registration*

Correction, p. 89: First paragraph, second sentence, should read (changes in italics):

". . . every person engaging or occupying a private *room averaging less than four hundred square feet of floor area, excepting a private* dining room not containing a bed . . ."

Insert at end of section, p. 89:

True-name registration laws can be found in the statutes of Arkansas, Massachusetts, New Hampshire, North Carolina, Ohio, and Vermont. Indiana repealed its statute prohibiting false registration in 1978.

5:22 *Lodgers, Boarders, and Tenants Distinguished from Guests*

Insert at end of section, p. 99:

The following Connecticut cases illustrate the care with which innkeepers must distinguish between creating the status of "lodger" and "guest" among room occupants in exercising the right to remove them.

Thomas v. Lenhart

38 Conn. Supp. 1, 444 A.2d 246 (Conn. Super. Ct. 1982)

Melville, J.: "This is an action of forceable detainer brought pursuant to General Statutes § 47a–43. The following are the pertinent facts: On or about

November 2, 1980, the plaintiff and the defendant entered into a written agreement in which the defendant agreed to hire out a furnished room to the plaintiff for his use and the plaintiff agreed to pay the defendant a weekly sum therefor. The agreement further provided that the defendant was reserving unto himself possession and general control of said room subject only to the plaintiff's use thereof. The plaintiff agreed not to use the room as his home or residence. This agreement designated the parties thereto as 'Lodger' and 'Lodging House Keeper.'

"The building in which this room was located contained other rooms which were hired out to other persons under written agreements containing substantially the same terms. Kitchen and sanitary facilities which were located in other areas of the building were shared by all occupants. The plaintiff's room was secured by lock and he was given the key upon payment of the first week's fee. When the plaintiff moved in he brought with him his entire wardrobe and all of his personal effects and possessions. Between November 2, 1980, and January 20, 1981, the plaintiff used his room, slept in it each night and shared the sanitary facilities and kitchen privileges with the other occupants of the building on a daily basis. Sometime before January 20, 1981, the defendant informally notified the plaintiff that he was delinquent in his payments and would have to vacate the room. On January 20, 1981, while the plaintiff was out looking for a job, the defendant entered the room without the plaintiff's knowledge or consent and, without having initiated eviction proceedings under General Statutes § 47a–23, removed the plaintiff's personal effects, changed the lock on the door and rented the room to another person. The defendant further refused to return the plaintiff's clothing and other personal effects until the plaintiff paid all fees due and owing to the defendant which debt the plaintiff concedes was in fact due.

"The plaintiff now brings this action for relief under General Statutes § 47a–43 claiming inter alia that he is entitled to the protection offered tenants under the landlord and tenant statutes, General Statutes §§ 47a–1 through 47a–74. The defendant claims that at all times relevant the plaintiff was a lodger and not a tenant and did not occupy the room as his residence, and, therefore, that the defendant had a right to a lien on the plaintiff's belongings pursuant to the boarding-house lien statute, General Statutes § 49–68. . . .

". . . the only statutory exemption which might apply to the present living arrangement is 'transient occupancy in a hotel or motel or similar lodging. . . .' General Statutes § 47a–2(4). Indeed, the defendant maintains that he is a 'Lodging House Keeper' and that the plaintiff is a lodger. . . .

"Although, in the present case, the plaintiff signed an agreement stating that the room would not be his residence, he indicated at trial that he did not have another residence and, in fact, did consider the room his home. The agreement is dated November 2, 1980, and the dispute arose on or about January 20, 1981. Thus, the plaintiff had occupied the room for approximately two and one-half months at the time the defendant attempted to revoke the plaintiff's use of the room. Furthermore, the agreement itself contained no provision concerning the duration of the occupancy. It is also noteworthy that the plaintiff had with him in the room all his personal belongings, a fact the court finds totally inconsistent with a transient occupancy.

"Although a reading of General Statutes § 49–68 would seem to support the defendant's contention that he may avoid the application of the landlord and tenant statutes by entering into a 'special agreement,' § 47a–2 expressly prohibits such agreements if they are created to avoid the application of designated sections of those statutes.

"That such was the purpose of this agreement is clearly illustrated by the testimony of the defendant at trial that the overriding purpose of effecting such an agreement with the plaintiff and others in the building was to avoid the substantial expenses and time-consuming procedures associated with summary process proceedings. Therefore, the conclusion is inescapable that the plaintiff is a resident and entitled to protection under the landlord and tenant statutes.

"[Judgment for the plaintiff.]"

BOURQUE V. MORRIS
190 Conn. 364, 460 A.2d 1251 (1983)

SHEA, J.: "The plaintiff brought this action for forcible entry and detainer pursuant to General Statutes § 47a–43 after he was locked out of the room he occupied in a hotel owned by the defendant. After a trial to the court judgment was rendered for the defendant and the plaintiff has appealed. . . .

"The subordinate facts found by the trial court have not been challenged. On August 8, 1980, the defendant began his occupancy of a room in the Wauregan Hotel in Norwich, a licensed hotel owned and operated by the defendant. The room was twelve by fifteen feet in area and it contained a bed and sink, but no toilet, bathing or cooking facilities. Toilet facilities used in common with other hotel occupants were available in the hall outside the plaintiff's room. The city of Norwich paid the weekly rental charge for the room of thirty-five dollars per week because the plaintiff was a welfare recipient. These payments continued during August, September and October and then ceased.

"On November 18, 1980, when the plaintiff was two weeks in arrears on his rent, he returned to his room but found that his key would no longer open the door. The plaintiff complained to an employee of the defendant but was told that nothing could be done. Another employee, the maintenance man, found a key to open the door of the room, and the plaintiff was allowed to enter and to remove his possessions. The trial court found that this employee had changed the lock on the door as an agent for the defendant acting within the scope of his employment responsibility. During the period of his occupancy the plaintiff had no place of residence other than his room at the hotel.

"Subsection (4) of General Statutes § 47a–43(a) [footnote omitted] provides that 'when the party put out of possession would be required to cause damage to the premises or commit a breach of the peace in order to regain possession, the party thus ejected, held out of possession, or suffering damage may exhibit his complaint to any judge of the superior court.' The plaintiff relied wholly upon this subsection as the basis for his action. . . .

"The defendant had the burden of proving that his arrangement with the plaintiff was for transient occupancy, as pleaded in his special defense. *Perley v. Glastonbury Bank & Trust Co.*, 170 Conn. 691, 698, 368 A.2d 149 (1976); see *DuBose v. Carabetta*, 161 Conn. 254, 262, 287 A.2d 357 (1971). Since the statute refers to 'transient occupancy' as one of the 'arrangements' excepted from the operation of the landlord-tenant statutes, any unilateral intention on the part of the plaintiff to remain at the hotel indefinitely or to make it his home, of which the defendant had no reasonable notice, would not be determinative in ascertaining what contractual arrangement existed between the parties. The issue must be decided upon the basis of reasonable inferences to be drawn from the circumstances of the transaction between them. *Hess v. Dumouchel Paper Co.*, 154 Conn. 343, 347, 225 A.2d 797 (1966); *Lindsay v. Phillips*, 95 Conn. 96, 100, 111 A. 176 (1920); 43A C.J.S. *supra* pp. 796–98.

"One significant factor in this case is that the defendant was operating a licensed hotel, as the plaintiff must have realized when he moved there. *Buck v. Del City Apartments, Inc.*, 431 P.2d 360, 363 (Okl. 1967). It appears from the evidence that no special arrangement was made in relation to his occupancy as distinguished from that of other hotel guests. The plaintiff was required to sign a hotel registration card like that ordinarily signed by a hotel guest. The defendant could reasonably have assumed that his arrangement with the plaintiff was for transient occupancy, like that with his other guests, in the absence of some reason to believe to the contrary. The fact that the rent was paid weekly does not compel a different conclusion. It appears that the city of Norwich made the arrangements for occupancy of the room by the plaintiff. There was no evidence that the parties could reasonably expect that the city would pay for the room indefinitely. The three month duration of the plaintiff's occupancy of the room was not so extended that the trial court was obliged to view it as 'permanent.' In conjunction with the brief period of occupancy and the operation of the premises as a licensed hotel, the rudimentary nature of the accommodations furnished, without cooking, bathing or toilet facilities in the room, is some indication that only a temporary living arrangement was intended. There was sufficient evidence to support the finding of the trial court under the applicable standard of proof, [footnote omitted] a fair preponderance of the evidence, that the arrangement between the parties was for transient occupancy of the hotel room.

"[Affirmed.]"

5:23 *Dispossession of Tenants by Summary Proceedings*

Insert immediately before Poroznoff v. Alberti, *p. 99:*

Section 711 of the New York Real Property Actions and Proceedings Law was

amended in 1982, deleting the city population requirement. It now reads, in part: "A tenant shall include an occupant of one or more rooms in a rooming house or a resident, not including a transient occupant, of one or more rooms in a hotel who has been in possession for thirty consecutive days or longer; he shall not be removed from possession except in a special proceeding."
Insert at end of section, p. 103:

Section 711 of the New York Real Property Actions and Proceedings Law was also amended in 1982 to make specific reference to hotels. In the following case, a hotelkeeper unwittingly transformed a hotel guest subject to lockout for nonpayment of room charges into a tenant requiring dispossession by court proceedings.

MANN v. 125 E. 50th Street Corp. (Hotel Beverly)
124 Misc.2d 115, 475 N.Y.S.2d 777 (N.Y. City Civ. Ct. 1984)

LEHNER, J.: "The issue raised on this application is whether a person who had resided in a hotel for 4 months may be locked out of her rooms without legal process.

"Here movant, Ms. Marie Mann, rented a room at the Hotel Beverly (a full service hotel) on November 23, 1983, and on February 2, 1984 rented an additional room. On March 22, 1984, when she allegedly owed $11,398.92 (having paid only $250 during her entire stay), she was locked out of her rooms.

"The rule in this state is that a hotel need not invoke court process to remove a transient occupant. (*People v. Lerhinan,* 90 A.D.2d 74, 455 N.Y.S.2d 822; *Jacob v. Jacob,* 125 Misc. 649, 651, 212 N.Y.S. 62; Rasch, New York Landlord and Tenant-Summary Proceedings, 2d Ed., § 1189). However, a landlord-tenant relationship may, aside from statutory provisions, be established between a hotel and an occupant so as to mandate the institution of summary proceedings in order to evict (*Bolotnikov v. Katz,* 95 Misc. 2d 377, 407 N.Y.S.2d 615), and a hotel occupant may, depending on the length of residence and rental, be protected by the Rent Stabilization Law (N.Y.C. Admin. Code §§ YY 51–3.1 and YY 51–5.0–e).

"RPAPL § 711 sets forth grounds upon which a summary proceeding may be commenced. Prior to the enactment of Chapter 739 of the Laws of 1982, the opening paragraph of the section provided that an occupant of a rooming house in possession for thirty days could not be removed except through summary proceedings. The paragraph contained no reference to hotels. The 1982 amendment repealed the foregoing and replaced it with the following.

"A tenant shall include an occupant of one or more rooms in a rooming house or a resident, not including a transient occupant, of one or more rooms in a hotel who has been in possession for thirty consecutive days or longer; he shall not be removed from possession except in a special proceeding.

"In the memorandum submitted with the legislation, the sponsors (Assembly-man Gottfried and Senator Calandra) state that their purpose was to resolve the problem raised in *Bolotnikov v. Katz, supra,* where the court ruled that RPAPL § 711 does not, by reason of the specific language making it only applicable to rooming houses, cover all single room occupancy facilities. The memorandum concludes by indicating that the amendment is intended 'to include all residential hotels (not just rooming houses) where a resident has been in possession for thirty consecutive days or more.'

"The hotel argues that because Ms. Mann registered for a two day stay and was granted extensions only because of certain alleged misrepresentations, she is a transient and not protected by the foregoing amendment.

"Under the wording of the statute a person can be considered a transient and thus be subject to eviction without legal process though having lived in a hotel for over 30 days, as the 30 days residency is not the sole test for determining ap-plicability. If it were, the phrase 'not including a transient occupant' would be surplusage. Hence, the resolution of this motion turns on the definition of the word 'transient.'

"There is no precise test for determining whether one is a transient provided by statute or case law, the meaning depending on the context. See: *State of Connect-icut v. Anonymous,* 34 Conn. Sup. 603, 379 A.2d 1. Webster's New Collegiate Dictionary defines the term as 'passing through or by a place with only a brief stay or sojourn.' 'Transient' has been considered the opposite of 'resident' (see: *The Leontios Teryazos,* 45 F. Supp. 618), and with respect to a hotel, is one who has a home elsewhere and is staying at the hotel for a short period in connection with a trip away from home.

"Under the facts herein, it is clear that movant may not be considered a tran-sient. There is nothing to indicate that she has any other residence, and although hotels normally require a transient guest to provide a home address, the hotel has no other address for her. Here, after being in possession for three months and having paid only $250 on a bill that ran into the thousands of dollars, rather than take action against her, the hotel rented Ms. Mann an additional room. Whether or not she misrepresented her financial status and the source of funds from which she was going to pay the rental bill is irrelevant to the determinationof her status as a tenant.

"Consequently, the hotel acted improperly in locking Ms. Mann out of her rooms. If money was owing to it, the hotel had the obligation of instituting legal proceedings to recover possession. Having instead used self help, it now faces the consequences of its unlawful actions.

"In light of the above, the court grants movant's application and hereby orders the Hotel Beverly to forthwith restore Ms. Mann to possession of the rooms which she was occupying prior to being locked out provided she presents herself to the hotel for restoration within 20 days from the date hereof."

Chapter 6. Legal Excuses for Failure to Receive a Guest and Right to Eject

6:6 *Ejection for Illness*

Insert at end of section, p. 125:

Le Mistral, Inc. v. Columbia Broadcasting System was appealed. The appeal was dismissed at 46 N.Y.2d 940 (1979).

In *Belluomo v. Kake TV & Radio, Inc.*, 596 P.2d 832 (Kan. App. 1979), the Court of Appeals of Kansas cited with favor the *Le Mistral* holding in a case in which a restaurant sued a radio and television station for compensatory and punitive damages arising from publication of information allegedly obtained by a trespass in news gathering. However, the court concluded that the jury verdict in favor of the defendant was supported by the evidence and there was no legal error requiring reversal. The following authorities also approve of the principles set forth in *Le Mistral: Stahl v. State*, 665 P.2d 830 (Okl. Cr. App. 1983), at 841–842; *Prahl v. Brosamle*, 295 N.W.2d 768 (Wis. App. 1980), at 780–782.

Chapter 7. Liability for Failure to Honor Reservations

7:2 *A Reservation as a Contractual Obligation*

Insert at end of section, p. 130:

In *Pennyrile Tours, Inc. v. Country Inns, USA, Inc.*, 559 F. Supp. 15 (E.D. Tenn. 1982), a tour agency orally contracted with the defendant to reserve rooms in a facility being built for the 1982 World's Fair. When the plaintiff became aware that the facility might not be ready in time, it canceled the reservations on 30 days' notice. Defendant refused to return the deposits, asserting that it was company policy not to give refunds. The court found that the cancellation of reservations had not been discussed by the parties when the contract was formed. In holding for the plaintiff, the court looked to the intention of the parties for a fair and reasonable construction and to the surrounding circumstances. One of the surrounding circumstances was trade usage: "The practice of refunding deposits if reservations are cancelled thirty days prior to the scheduled arrival date is a regular method of dealing in the tourist business. Exceptions to the usual practice are made known during initial negotiations between the parties." *Id.* at 16–17. Since the defendant did not raise the exception during negotiations, the plaintiff was entitled to a full refund.

In another case involving the 1982 World's Fair, Greyhound, acting as a tour promoter, advanced $75,000 to reserve rooms at a hotel. *Greyhound Lines, Inc. v. Sharpe*, 565 F. Supp. 419 (E.D. Tenn. 1983). Greyhound was to recover this amount under the following provision in the contract: "That on May 15, 1982, it is understood by the contracting parties that the regular prepayment schedule incorporated herein may be cut back by Greyhound Lines, Inc. to 75% of what would otherwise be allowed under this contract until all advances received by Old Hickory Inn, in the amount of $75,000.00, are repaid to Greyhound Lines, Inc. by the recoupment of this 25% cutback in prepayment." Low interest in the tours caused Greyhound to notify the defendant in June that it was giving 45 days' notice of the cancellation of a large number of rooms, as per the contract. When the fair ended, the defendant still held $52,985.02 of the original $75,000. The contract did not provide for the plaintiff's failure to recover its prepayment. The court found that the intention of the parties was the repayment of "all advances" and that Greyhound was not obligated to pay the "charges" for any reserved rooms for which it had properly given 45 days' notice of cancellation. As the $75,000 was only an advance on these charges, Greyhound was owed the portion of the advance payment not credited toward the use of rooms during the fair. The court also noted, without basing its decision on this ground, that the defendant, if it kept the money, would be unjustly enriched beyond the services actually rendered.

7:7   *Recovery for Mental Suffering and Emotional Distress*

Insert at end of section, p. 151:

In the following case, the plaintiffs had made reservations with the defendant, Holiday Inns, for rooms at a convention of the National Office Machine Dealers Association (NOMDA). The reservations were made through the NOMDA travel coordinator. Confirmation slips were received by the plaintiffs from both the Holiday Inn and the NOMDA housing bureau, the latter indicating that no deposit had been received. Both slips stated that the confirmation would not be held after 6:00 P.M. of the arrival date. Plaintiffs arrived at 3:00 P.M. and were told that no rooms were available. Arrangements were made to put them up in another hotel. Plaintiffs contended that the dishonoring of the reservations by Holiday Inn gave rise to a claim for fraud or misrepresentation and for breach of contract. The federal district court dismissed the first charge absent a showing that the hotel knowingly or willfully misrepresented a material fact to holders of reservations or intended not to reserve a room, and on the second charge it allowed only compensatory damages. The court discussed both *Nader, supra,* and *Dold, supra,* in its opinion.

WELLS v. HOLIDAY INNS, INC.
522 F. Supp. 1023 (W.D. Mo. 1981)

SACHS, D.J.: ". . . Expert testimony indicated that overbooking to some extent is a recognized and accepted practice within the hotel industry. The day that plaintiffs were refused their rooms there was a dishonor rate at that Holiday Inn of almost four percent (4%). However, the hotel's average dishonor rate was much lower, or about half the national average of one-half of one percent. Moreover, the dishonor rate is not completely attributable to the practice of overbooking, but also is affected by such unknowns as unexpected 'stay-overs.' Holiday Inn's practice was reasonable under the circumstances and not generally a significant factor in whether it could fulfill its promises. Compare Judge Richey's statement that an airline's 'nondisclosure of its overbooking practice was misleading and created a false understanding as to the chance of being flown. . . .' *Nader v. Allegheny Airlines, Inc.*, 445 F. Supp. 168, 174 (D.D.C. 1978), rev'd on other grounds, 200 App. D.C. 167, 626 F.2d 1031 (1980). Nothing has been presented to convince the Court that the *Nader* trial court accurately applied the pertinent common law rule, or the rule which would be applied in Missouri or California to hotel overbooking. It seems more likely that the *Nader* ruling might be persuasive in a legislative or administrative context, such as the adoption of regulations by the Federal Trade Commission pursuant to its authority to prevent unfair or deceptive practices. 15 U.S.C. § 45. The evidence before the Court indicates that the FTC has considered but has not been persuaded to adopt such regulations dealing with hotel and motel overbooking, or requiring notice to the public of such a practice. . . .

"Holiday Inns offered space to the Wells party, provided they appeared at the hotel before 6:00 P.M., July 15, 1976. Plaintiffs met the condition, and were legally entitled to performance of the promise. There was a breach of contract which was not waived, compromised or settled. The rulings in *Wasserman v. TWA*, 486 F. Supp. 194 (W.D. Mo. 1980), aff'd 632 F.2d 69 (8th Cir. 1980), and *Christenson v. Northwest Airlines*, 633 F.2d 529 (9th Cir. 1980), are inapposite in that preclusion of recovery in those cases was based on a federal regulation barring recovery if alternative transportation is accepted. There is no comparable regulation applicable to the hotel industry, and the Court finds the existence of the regulation as to airlines insufficient to bar recovery in the instant case. Additionally, there was no 'impossibility' preventing performance for several reasons; among others, there apparently were available rooms when plaintiffs reached the reservation desk, but those rooms were held for guests with guaranteed or prepaid reservations.

"As a general rule, the measure of damages for breach of contract is that 'compensation should be equal to the injuries subject to the condition that the damages be confined to those naturally and proximately resulting from the breach and be not uncertain or speculative.' [Citations omitted.] The principle established in *Hadley v. Baxendale*, 9 Ex. 341, 15 Eng. Rep. 145 (1854) limits recovery for breach of contract to those damages which could reasonably be supposed to have been within the contemplation of the parties at the time they entered into the contract. [Citations omitted.] The rule generally precludes such special, consequential damages as lost profits from transactions not known to the party charged with breach, in addition to barring recovery for disappointment, mental distress, and similar claims, because such items are not normally predictable by the party breaking a contract. [Footnote omitted.]

"The Court is considerably persuaded by the concurring opinion of Judge Marumoto of the Hawaii Supreme Court, in comparable litigation. *Dold v. Outrigger Hotel,* 54 Haw. 18, 501 P.2d 368, 58 A.L.R.3d 360 (1972). In that case the Dold and Manthei families appealed from a denial of punitive damages in an overbooking situation in which the hotel making reservations had a practice of intentionally taking more reservations than it could accommodate, apparently for the purpose of shunting guests to a less desirable hotel, which gave the defendant hotel a 'kickback' on its receipts. The Supreme Court ruled that punitive damages were not allowable, but in dicta endorsed awards of $600 and $400 for emotional distress and disappointment. The majority announced that the awards were justified by facts which present a 'fusion of the doctrines of tort and contract.' Judge Marumoto concurred, concluding however that the recovery was essentially for breach of contract, disregarding possible tort claims. He noted that freedom of contract should be preserved 'unclouded by uncertain legal penalties.' He stated that he would affirm the award to the Dolds and the Matheis, however, by labeling the damages received by them as 'compensatory' in a breach of contract case. He found it 'preferable . . . to strain the traditional concept of compensatory damages (rather) than to rupture the foundations of tort and contract liability.' . . .

"Eliminating mental suffering, unanticipated physical distress, and loss of business opportunities for damage considerations, the only losses within predictable normal categories, and thus recoverable, are cab fares and the garage charge previously noted. The corporate plaintiff had no contract with defendant and, of course, no damages of the type herein found recoverable. It is of interest that recovery, although quite nominal, is in the category recommended by a staff report of the FTC and by an international study to which defendant's hotel practices expert testified."

7:8   *Group Travel Booking*

Insert immediately before last paragraph, p. 155:

In *Marriott Corporation v. American Academy of Psychotherapists, Inc.,* 157 Ga. App. 597, 277 S.E.2d 785 (1981), Marriott booked two conventions for dates that overlapped. Less than two weeks before the opening date, Marriott informed the plaintiff that there was not enough room in the hotel to handle its convention. The plaintiff moved its convention to another hotel and brought a suit alleging, in part, willful misrepresentation of a material fact. The trial court denied the defendant's motion for a directed verdict, and the appellate court affirmed, holding:

"The five elements of fraud and deceit in Georgia are: (1) false representation made by the defendant; (2) scienter; (3) an intention to induce the plaintiff to act or refrain from acting in reliance by the plaintiff; (4) justifiable reliance by the plaintiff; (5) damage to the plaintiff." *City Dodge Inc. v. Gardner,* 232 Ga. 766, 769–770, fn.1, 208 S.E.2d 794. Having reviewed the record and transcript, we find that the jury could reasonably conclude from the evidence presented that defendant was aware of its having overbooked the hotel to such an extent as to create a substantial likelihood that it would be unable to meet plaintiff's needs during its convention, and yet defendant continued to represent to plaintiff that plaintiff's convention could and would be handled by defendant as planned by plaintiff. The jury could also find that defendant continued to make such representations with an intent to induce plaintiff's reliance, and that plaintiff did justifiably rely thereon to its damage. 'Fraud may not be presumed, but, being in itself subtle, slight circumstances may be sufficient to carry conviction of its existence.' Code § 37–706.

Moreover, defendant's reliance upon *Brown v. Hilton Hotels Corp.,* 133 Ga. App. 286, 211 S.E.2d 125, certiorari dismissed as improvidently granted, Id., 234 Ga. 663, 218 S.E.2d 78, as controlling precedent that would bar plaintiff's maintenance of Count One is misplaced. The jury was properly charged in the language of Code § 105–302 regarding wilful misrepresentation of a material fact. As noted, the evidence could support a finding of defendant's liability therefor. Clearly wilful misrepresentation of a material fact as herein alleged constitutes misfeasance sufficiently extrinsic to a mere breach of the instant contract to give rise to an independent cause of action in tort. Accordingly, we find no error in the trial court's denial of defendant's motion for a directed verdict as to Count One of the complaint.

Chapter 8. Innkeeper's Duty to Guest: Courteous and Considerate Treatment

8:4 *Authority of Management and Law Enforcement Agents to Enter Guest's Room and Seize Guest's Property*

Insert at end of footnote 3, p. 158:
The United States Supreme Court denied *certiorari* at 390 U.S. 911 (1968).
Correction, p. 159: Citation in footnote 4 should read 20 Cal. App. 832, 98 Cal. Rptr. 107 (1971).
Insert immediately before last paragraph, p. 160:

A hotel can allow a search by the police once the rental period has expired. *United States v. Akin,* 562 F.2d 459 (7th Cir. 1977), *cert. denied,* 435 U.S. 933 (1978); *People v. Lerhinan,* 90 A.D.2d 74, 455 N.Y.S.2d 822 (2d Dep't 1982). It can allow such a search even once the guest has been justifiably ejected from his or her room. *United States v. Haddad,* 558 F.2d 968 (9th Cir. 1977). If a room is abandoned, the hotel can also authorize its search. *Akin, supra.* In *Com-*

monwealth v. Paszko, 391 Mass. 164 (1984), defendant had paid a week's rent for the week ending June 20. Because of his sudden departure and his subsequent travel out of state, the court found that the room was abandoned on June 18 and that a warrantless search by a police officer on June 19, with the motel's permission, was not legal.

Insert immediately before last paragraph, p. 161:

Where, however, the defendant left his luggage at a motel, assuring the owners that he would return to pay his bill, and, in fact, exhibited an intention of doing so, a police search of the bags at the hotel's request was illegal. *Hackett v. State,* 386 So.2d 35 (Fla. App. 1980). The defendant's consent given at a later time in the "coercive" setting of a police station, without knowledge of the prior search, did not make that search legal.

In *United States v. Prescott,* 480 F. Supp. 554 (W.D. Pa. 1979), defendant had been placed under arrest. From the jail he called the YMCA, where he had been staying prior to his arrest, to indicate that he would send someone to collect his belongings. The dormitory supervisor told defendant that the YMCA would hold his belongings for sixty days. Within a fortnight, an FBI agent contacted the YMCA and asked to see defendant's room. The dormitory supervisor consented and allowed the agent to remove a T-shirt for evidence. In suppressing the evidence from this search, the court held that the defendant had a justifiable expectation of privacy in his belongings and that the YMCA had no authority to consent to a warrantless search of his room.

Insert at end of section, p. 162:

The following New York decision provides a full exposition of New York law on this subject, as well as reviewing relevant out-of-state authorities.

PEOPLE v. LERHINAN
90 A.D.2d 74, 455 N.Y.S.22d 822 (2d Dep't 1982)

LAZER, P.J.: "Because the constitutional validity of hotel and boarding room searches has evoked only limited jurisprudence in this State, this case provides the opportunity to illuminate the relationship between the Fourth Amendment and real property law. The search here challenged turned up the fruits of the crime and resulted in defendant's plea of guilty to burglary in the third degree after his motion to suppress was denied. We conclude that a hotel guest, who has a constitutionally protected right to privacy in his room, loses any reasonable expectation of such privacy when the rental period expires. At that time, the hotel owner may reassert control of the room and validly consent to have the police search it and its contents.

"On February 14, 1979, a number of cases of liquor and a tool and die set were stolen from the bar and storeroom located in the Colony Arms Hotel in Glen Cove. The stolen items were subsequently found by the hotel manager when he entered the room defendant had been occupying at the hotel and looked in the closet. At the time of this entry, the defendant was two weeks in arrears on rent which was payable in advance weekly. The manager testified that while the purpose of the entry was rent collection, if the defendant was not in, he had intended to move the man's belongings to the basement, change the lock and re-rent the room. Hearing no response to his knock on the door, the manager used a passkey to open it and, in the closet, found the cases of liquor and a tool and die set covered with a bed sheet. Recognizing the items as related to the earlier burglary, the manager promptly called the police. When Detective Van Nostrand arrived, he was informed that the rent had been unpaid for two weeks and the missing property had been discovered in the course of eviction of the defendant. Van Nostrand was then led to the room and shown the stolen goods. The defendant was arrested the next day and subsequently moved to suppress the recovered items. The motion was denied on the ground that he lacked standing to challenge the search.

". . . [T]he defendant can obtain a suppression only if he can demonstrate that he possessed a reasonable expectation of privacy in the hotel room at the time it was searched (see *Rawlings v. Kentucky,* 448 U.S. 98, 106, 100 S.Ct. 2556, 2562, 65 L.Ed.2d 633; *Rakas v. Illinois* [439 U.S. 128, 99 S.Ct. 421, 58 L.Ed.2d 387], *supra; People v. Ponder,* 54 N.Y.2d 160, 445 N.Y.S.2d 57, 429 N.E.2d 735). The test is whether he exhibited an actual (subjective) expectation of privacy and whether that expectation is one that society is prepared to recognize as reasonable (see *Katz v. United States,* 389 U.S. 347, 361, 88 S.Ct. 507, 516, 19 L.Ed.2d 576 [HARLAN, J., concurring]; see, also, *Rakas v. Illinois, supra,* p. 143, 99 S.Ct. p. 430). [Footnote omitted.] Although '"[f]reedom from intrusion into the home or dwelling is the archetype of the privacy protection secured by the Fourth Amendment"' *(Payton v. New York,* 445 U.S. 573, 587, 100 S.Ct. 1371, 1380, 63 L.Ed.2d 639, citing *Dorman v. United States,* 435 F.2d 385, 389 (D.C. Cir.)), the individual's privacy interests extend to a variety of settings. Since a guest in a hotel room is entitled to the protection of the Fourth Amendment *(Stoner v. California,* 376 U.S. 483, 84 S.Ct. 889, 11 L.Ed.2d 856; *United States v. Jeffers,* 342 U.S. 48, 72 S.Ct. 93, 96 L.Ed. 59; *Johnson v. United States,* 333 U.S. 10, 68 S.Ct. 367, 92 L.Ed. 436), a hotel employee may not effectively consent to a search of the room during the rental period (see *Stoner v. California, supra; State v. Smith,* 178 N.W.2d 329 [Iowa]).

"Although the Supreme Court has repeatedly repudiated the notion that the subtle distinctions developed in property law control Fourth Amendment determinations (see *Rakas v. Illinois,* 439 U.S. 128, 143, 99 S.Ct. 421, 430, 58 L.Ed.2d 387, *supra;* [citations omitted], 'the Court has not altogether abandoned use of property concepts in determining the presence or absence of the privacy interests protected by that Amendment' *(Rakas v. Illinois, supra,* p. 144, n.12, 99 S.Ct. p. 430, n.12; see, also, *United States v. Salvucci,* 448 U.S. 83, 100 S.Ct. 2547, 65 L.Ed.2d 619). As noted by Justice REHNQUIST:

"Legitimation of expectations of privacy by law must have a source outside of the Fourth Amendment, either by reference to concepts of real or personal property law or to understandings that are recognized and permitted by society. One of the main rights attaching to property is the right to exclude others, see W. Blackstone, Commentaries, Book 2, ch. 1, and one who owns or lawfully possesses or controls property will in all likelihood have a legitimate expectation of privacy by virtue of this right to exclude. (*Rakas v. Illinois, supra,* p. 144, n.12, 99 S.Ct. p. 430, n.12.)

"Analysis of the current issues first requires examination of the nature of defendant's interest in the premises searched to determine whether a legitimate expectation of privacy existed at the time of the search [citations omitted]. Under New York law, there is an express or implied understanding between guest and hotel owner that the former shall be the sole occupant during the time that is set apart for his use (see *People v. Gallmon,* 19 N.Y.2d 389, 280 N.Y.S.2d 356, 227 N.E.2d 284; *De Wolf v. Ford,* 193 N.Y. 397, 86 N.E. 527). The owner retains a right of access only for such reasonable purposes as may be necessary in the conduct of the hotel, not only to take action in the event of a fire or gas leakage (*People v. Gallmon, supra; De Wolf v. Ford, supra*), but obviously to take routine care of necessary housekeeping as well. But since no conventional landlord-tenant relationship is involved in the ordinary rental of hotel rooms (*Ashton v. Margolies,* 72 Misc. 70, 129 N.Y.S. 617; *Wilson v. Martin,* 1 Denio 602; cf. *Smith v. Rector of St. Philip's Church,* 107 N.Y. 610, 619, 14 N.E. 825), [footnote omitted] a hotel owner may dispossess an occupant without resort to the use of summary proceedings (*Morningstar v. Lafayette Hotel Co.,* 211 N.Y. 465, 105 N.E. 656; *Jacob v. Jacob,* 125 Misc. 649, 212 N.Y.S. 62; Rasch, New York Landlord & Tenant Summary Proceedings [2d ed.], § 1189; 27 N.Y. Jur., Hotels, Restaurants & Motels, § 40). Under section 181 of the Lien Law, the owner also has the right to seize the defaulting guest's property and sell it at public auction. [Footnote omitted.] This contrasts with the rental of an apartment, the possession of which may not be disturbed until a warrant of eviction has been executed (RPAPL 749, subd. 3; *People v. Stadtmore,* 52 A.D.2d 853, 382 N.Y.S.2d 807).

"The distinction between the privacy expectation of a hotel guest and a tenant of an apartment building has been recognized in a number of other jurisdictions (see, e.g., *United States v. Croft,* 429 F.2d 884 (10th Cir.) [Kan. law]; *State v. Carrillo,* 26 Ariz. App. 113, 546 P.2d 838; *State v. Taggart,* 14 Or. App. 408, 512 P.2d 1359). The difference between these types of rental arrangements —particularly the relative ease by which a hotel occupancy can be terminated upon nonpayment of rent—cannot be classified as a 'subtle' property law distinction of the unfavored type [citation omitted]; it is instead a highly relevant factor for determining the legitimacy of a defendant's privacy interest (see *United States v. Salvucci,* 448 U.S. 83, 100 S.Ct. 2547, 65 L.Ed.2d 619, *supra; Rakas v. Illinois,* 439 U.S. 128, 99 S.Ct. 421, 58 L.Ed.2d 387, *supra*).

"As a consequence of the hotel keeper's lien and the transitory nature of hotel tenancies, mere nonpayment of the rent terminates any reasonable expectation of privacy in the hotel room and the property contained in it (*Boone v. State,* 39 Md. App. 20, 383 A.2d 412). The cases have uniformly held that the operator of a motel—essentially similar to a hotel—may consent to a warrantless search as soon as the rental period has expired (*United States v. Jackson,* 585 F.2d 653 (4th Cir.); *United States v. Akin,* 562 F.2d 459 (7th Cir.), cert. den. 435 U.S. 933, 98 S.Ct. 1509, 55 L.Ed.2d 531; *United States v. Parizo,* 514 F.2d 52 (2d Cir.); *United States v. Croft,* 429 F.2d 884 (10th Cir.), *supra; Sumdum v. State,* 612 P.2d 1018 [Alaska]; *State v. Carrillo,* 26 Ariz. App. 113, 546 P.2d 838, *supra; People v. VanEyk,* 56 Cal. 2d 471, 15 Cal. Rptr. 150, 364 P.2d 326, cert. den. 369 U.S. 824, 82 S.Ct. 838, 7 L.Ed.2d 788; *People v. Crayton,* 174 Cal. App. 2d 267, 344 P.2d 627; *State v. Mascarenas,* 86 N.M. 692, 526 P.2d 1285; *State v. Taggart,* 14 Or. App. 408, 512 P.2d 1359, *supra; State v. Cox,* 12 Or. App. 215, 505 P.2d 360; *State v. Roff,* 70 Wash. 2d 606, 424 P.2d 643; see, also, Ann., 2 A.L.R. 4th 1173, § 5). The lack of a possessory interest in a hotel room in turn influences the reasonableness of expectations of privacy for:

> "[I]t is commonly known that those who operate such establishments are understandably interested in maximum paying occupancy and thus could be expected to promptly clear the room of a guest who has overstayed so that another guest may be given the room." (2 LaFave, Search & Seizure, § 8.5, p. 743.)

"After the rental period expires, society does not recognize the guest's asserted subjective expectation of privacy to be reasonable (see *State v. Taggart, supra; Sumdum v. State, supra,* p. 1021). Thus under either property law concepts or societal understandings (see *Rakas v. Illinois,* 439 U.S. 128, 143, 99 S.Ct. 421, 430, 58 L.Ed.2d 387, *supra*), a defendant may not be deemed to have legitimate expectations of privacy after the expiration of the rental period.

"Applying these principles, it is our view that the instant defendant had no reasonable expectation of privacy in the hotel room at the time of the search. He had fallen into rent arrears and the hotel management acted to lock him out so that the room could be rented to another guest. Nothing in the record indicates any arrangement between the management and defendant extending credit or permitting him to stay for an indefinite period without a further payment of rent (see *United States v. Akin,* 562 F.2d 459, 464 (7th Cir.), *supra*). On the contrary, the hotel manager testified that he had not seen the defendant for several weeks. Defendant's argument that he never intended to abandon his room is irrelevant, since the matter of abandonment is a necessary inquiry only during the rental period (*United States v. Akin, supra; United States v. Parizio,* 514 F.2d 52, 55 (2d Cir.), *supra*). Thus, when defendant's rental term ended, the owner had the right to enter the room, remove the defendant's belongings, and prepare the room for the next guest (see *People v. Crabtree,* 34 A.D.2d 1024, 310 N.Y.S.2d 899;

People v. Sorise, 58 Misc. 2d 557, 561, 296 N.Y.S.2d 211, aff'd 34 A.D.2d 736, 310 N.Y.S.2d 1016). Since the defendant no longer had a legitimate expectation of privacy in the hotel room, his challenge to the search must be rejected.

"Accordingly, there should be an affirmance.

"Judgment . . . affirmed."

8:5 *Authority to Record Telephone Calls and Transmit to Police*

Insert at end of section, p. 164:

In *State v. Pierson,* 248 N.W.2d 48 (S.D. 1976), the manager of a hotel, whose suspicions were aroused by the defendant's unprosperous appearance, inability to pay in full for the first night, and claim to be visiting his parents in a nearby town when no people by his name were listed in the phone book, listened in on two calls made by the defendant and overheard a discussion related to the sale of drugs. The court found that this constituted illegal eavesdropping but allowed evidence discovered in defendant's room during a routine cleaning to be presented in court because it arose from an independent source.

8:7 *Damages for Unlawful Intrusion into Guest's Room*

Insert at end of section, p. 166:

The following case demonstrates that a mere unintentional intrusion into a guest's room caused by the negligence of a room clerk in reassigning the guest's room to an incoming guest does not give rise to recovery for emotional distress.

POLLOCK v. HOLSA CORP.
114 Misc. 2d 1076, 454 N.Y.S.2d 582 (App. Term, 1st Dep't 1982) *aff'd as modified*, 98 App.Div. 2d 265, 470 N.Y.S. 2d 151 (1st Dep't 1984)

PER CURIAM: "Judgment entered January 20, 1982 unanimously affirmed, with $25 costs.

"We agree with Trial Term that on the first cause of action, plaintiff did not adduce proof of damages compensable at law. An innkeeper is liable for mental distress where his breach of duty is accompanied by insult, indignity, abuse, or humiliation (13 N.Y. Jur., Damages, § 129), but there must be some tortious act 'committed in virtue of a deliberate intent and design . . . not merely negligent' (*Boyce v. Greeley Sq. Hotel Co.,* 228 N.Y. 106, 111). Taking the evidence most favorable to the plaintiff, no willful assault, abuse or maltreatment of a hotel guest was here shown. All that occurred was that through clerical oversight, the defendant checked the plaintiff out a day before his reserved contract of lodging was to terminate and placed another party in possession, with the result that plaintiff was unable to occupy his room when he returned in the early morning hours of the day in question. Undoubtedly, this turn of events was a source of inconvenience and irritation to the plaintiff but absent other circumstances of aggravation, recovery for emotional and mental distress on these facts must be denied (*Kellogg v. Commodore Hotel*, 187 Misc. 319). It is pertinently noted that plaintiff himself testified that defendant's employee was not discourteous or abusive, and it is difficult to find any degree of 'humiliation' in an incident which unfolded in a deserted hotel lobby at 3:00 A.M. witnessed by a solitary and apologetic desk clerk. '[I]t is the publicity of the thing that causes the humiliation' (*Aaron v. Ward*, 203 N.Y. 351, 357). . .

On appeal, the reviewing court held that while there was no claim for mental suffering, the question of physical damages suffered by the plaintiff was within the contemplation of the parties and thus foreseeable once plaintiff became a guest at the inn. Thus the question of physical harm suffered should be submitted to the jury.

Chapter 9. Duty to Provide Safe Premises

9:1a *(New Section) Innkeeper's Duty to Social Invitees of Guests*

Insert immediately after 9:1, p. 175:
Two state reviewing courts have recently extended the reasonable-care rule to include social visitors, invited by guests, on innkeepers' premises. Maryland: *Murrey v. Lane*, 51 Md. App. 597, 444 A.2d 1069 (1982); North Carolina: *Hockaday v. Morse*, 57 N.C. App. 109, 290 S.E.2d 763 (1982), petition for review denied 306 N.C. 384, 294 S.E.2d 209 (N.C. 1982).

9:4 *The Elements of a Cause of Action for Negligence*

Insert at end of first (incomplete) paragraph, p. 179:
In *Pearce v. Motel 6, Inc.*, 28 Wash. App. 474, 624 P.2d 215 (1981), plaintiff slipped in defendant motel's shower stall. The court found reversible error in the trial court's failure to instruct the jury that the inn's reasonable-care duty was triggered only if the inn had actual or constructive knowledge that the condition of the shower created an unreasonable risk of harm.

9:7 *Liability by Reason of Defective Premises: Doctrine of* Res Ipsa Loquitur

Insert at end of section, p. 183:
In *Terrell v. Lincoln Motel, Inc.*, 183 N.J. Super. 55, 443 A.2d 236 (1982), plaintiff guest was injured when he slipped through the door of a shower stall while attempting to escape an unexpected burst of hot water. The New Jersey Superior Court reversed the trial court's decision for defendant and remanded the

case because the trial court failed to instruct the jury that the doctrine of *res ipsa loquitur* should apply if the jury believed the plaintiff's testimony.

9:7a *(New Section) Strict Liability for Defects in Fixtures and Furnishings*

Insert immediately before 9:8, p. 183:

Recently, plaintiffs suing inns for injuries resulting from safety defects have begun to include product liability claims in their complaints. The cases of *Bidar v. Amfac, Inc.*, —— Haw ——, 669 P.2d 154 (1983), and *Livingston v. Begay*, 98 N.M. 712, 652 P.2d 734 (1982), illustrate two methods used by courts to resolve product liability claims in the innkeeper-guest setting.

In *Bidar*, plaintiff guest tried to use the towel rack in her bathroom to support herself as she rose from the toilet. The rack tore loose from the wall, and plaintiff fell. In response to plaintiff's claim that product liability law applied, the court said: "[A] portion of a leased or rented premises . . . [that] prove[s] defective [citation omitted]" does not equal a "product" for purposes of product liability law. *Id.* at 161. The court was careful, however, to distinguish "identified component[s] of a prefabricated building," which can be a "product." *Id.*

In *Livingston*, the court engaged in a more policy-oriented analysis of plaintiff's product liability claim.

LIVINGSTON V. BEGAY
98 N.M. 712, 652 P.2d 734 (N.M. 1982)

PAYNE, J.: "This case presents various questions concerning the liability of a hotel operator for the death of a guest caused by allegedly defective fixtures in the hotel room.

"Peter Begay, plaintiff's decedent, was found dead in his hotel room the morning after he had checked in. The cause of death was asphyxiation by carbon monoxide gas which apparently escaped from a disconnected exhaust vent attached to a gas space heater located in the room. Plaintiff sued the Livingstons, owners and operators of the hotel at the time of death, the prior owner, Nellie Livingston (Nellie); Montgomery Ward and Company, Inc., the alleged supplier of the heater; and Gas Company of New Mexico, supplier of the gas. Plaintiff's complaint included allegations of negligence, *res ipsa loquitur*, and strict liability. The trial court granted summary judgments for the defendants on all counts of the complaint involved here. . . .

"However, the Court of Appeals reversed the grant of summary judgment in favor of the Livingstons on Count IV, thereby applying the doctrine of strict liability to a hotel operator. We hold that this was error and reverse on this point.

"The general rule is that a hotel operator owes its guests a duty to use reasonable care in promoting their safety. Annot., 18 A.L.R.2d 973, 974 (1951). Although a hotel operator must use reasonable care, he is not an insurer of the safety of his guests. The rule has been that the duty of reasonable care applies to cases involving injuries to guests caused by defective furnishings or conditions in their rooms. *Id.* This rule has been followed in cases involving unsafe heating fixtures. *See* cases cited *id.* at § 7. This reasonable care standard of liability has been applied to motel owners in New Mexico. *Withrow v. Woozencraft,* 90 N.M. 48, 559 P.2d 425 (Ct. App. 1976), *cert. denied,* 90 N.M. 255, 561 P.2d 1348 (1977).

"Plaintiff cites no authority for holding a hotel operator strictly liable for injuries to a guest by inherent defects in fixtures or furnishings in a hotel room. Plaintiff proposed to the Court of Appeals that it hold the Livingstons strictly liable on the authority of two California cases, *Golden v. Conway,* 55 Cal. App. 3d 948, 128 Cal. Rptr. 69 (1976), and *Fakhoury v. Magner,* 25 Cal. App. 3d 58, 101 Cal. Rptr. 473 (1972). The Court of Appeals, with one dissent, obliged.

"*Golden* and *Fakhoury* held landlords strictly liable for injuries to tenants caused by inherent defects in fixtures and furnishings provided as part of the lease. Other courts have refused to apply strict liability to lessors of real estate. *Old Town Development Company v. Langford,* 349 N.E.2d 744 (Ind. App. 1976); *Dwyer v. Skyline Apartments, Inc.,* 123 N.J. Super. 48, 301 A.2d 463 (Ct. App.), *aff'd. mem.* 63 N.J. 577, 311 A.2d 1 (1973). The question is one of first impression in New Mexico. Therefore, a brief review of the law of strict liability in New Mexico is necessary.

"In *Stang v. Hertz Corporation,* 83 N.M. 730, 497 P.2d 732 (1972), we approved the rule of strict products liability expressed in Restatement (Second) of Torts § 402A (1964). There we applied strict liability to a lessor of an automobile, reasoning that there is no logical basis for differentiating between a seller of a defective automobile and a lessor of such an automobile. In a lengthy analysis of the development of strict liability, we noted that the theory was adopted '[b]ecause of the shortcomings of the early theories. . . .' *Stang, supra* at 731, 497 P.2d at 733. These theories—negligence and breach of warranty—imposed limitations and difficulties particularly onerous to purchasers of products. The difficulty in proving that a manufacturer was negligent, the common lack of privity between manufacturer and the ultimate purchaser, as well as other contract and sales rules, required development of strict liability as applied to manufacturers. Liability extends to retailers and distributors as well as manufacturers because each is an integral part of the marketing process, *Vandermark v. Ford Motor Company,* 61 Cal. 2d 256, 37 Cal. Rptr. 896, 391 P.2d 168 (1964), and because the shortcomings of the earlier theories are equally applicable to such dealers. In *Rudisaile v. Hawk Aviation, Inc.,* 92 N.M. 575, 592 P.2d 175 (1979), we also noted that an important reason for imposing strict liability was to encourage manufacturers to take care in production activities and to provide adequate warning of dangers. In *Stang* we held that these same rationales apply to lessors of particular products. We reaffirmed this application of *Rudisaile.* However, we decline to extend the § 402A definition of 'seller' to persons in the class represented by the Livingstons.

"The lessors involved in *Stang* and *Rudisaile* were involved in leasing particular products. Leasing automobiles and airplanes is a common means of making these products available to consumers. Henszey, *Application of Strict Liability to the Leasing Industry,* 33 Bus. Law 631 (1978). The relationship between such lessors and the manufacturers is substantially the same as that between retail dealers and manufacturers. Thus, it would be illogical to distinguish between such lessors and retailers or other retail dealers.

"The Court of Appeals apparently considered the Livingstons to be lessors of the hotel room, as well as lessors of the fixtures placed therein. Thus, as in *Golden* and *Fakhoury,* the Livingstons could be strictly liable for injuries caused by defects in the fixtures, much as the lessors in *Stang* and *Rudisaile* were held liable.

"Plaintiff argues that there were three defective products involved: the room itself as a whole, the gas heater, and the vent. Because each of these 'products' has distinctive characteristics, we shall examine the application of strict liability principles to each 'product' separately.

"Plaintiff asserts that Room 7 was a defective product because it had an inherently unsafe design. (The heater was placed near the sink where a guest would be likely to bump it.) Accordingly, plaintiff claims that by offering the room to prospective guests, the Livingstons placed a defective product on the market. We decline to accept this line of reasoning. Although other courts have held that a house is a product for purposes of holding a contractor liable to the initial and subsequent purchasers, we think such an application is neither required nor advisable in the circumstances of this case. The rationales behind application of strict liability do not apply when the injured party necessarily has a direct relationship with the defendant, when proof of negligence is not difficult, and when traditional remedies have proven adequate. The unsafe design of a hotel room is simply not the type of defect for which strict liability was fashioned as a remedy.

"Any inherent defect in the gas heater would, of course, create strict liability in the manufacturer and distributors, including the seller to Nellie Livingston. The question here is whether the Livingstons should be treated as part of the 'chain of distribution,' or, in other words, whether the Livingstons placed the heater in the 'stream of commerce.' A major consideration in holding lessors of commercial products strictly liable was that such lessors possessed expert knowledge of the characteristics of the equipment or machines they leased. *Booth Steamship Co. v. Meier & Oelhaf Co.,* 262 F.2d 310 (2d Cir. 1958). Another consideration is that such lessors, like retailers, deal continually with their suppliers, giving them an enduring relationship which permits them to seek contribution and indemnification. These considerations do not apply when a motel operator makes a one-time purchase of furnishings and fixtures about which he has no special expertise. Therefore, we hold that a motel operator is not strictly liable for defects in the fixtures and furnishings of the rooms he holds out to the public.

"Finally, plaintiff claims the exhaust vent was defective. It appears that this vent was fabricated by the installer. Therefore, there is no chain of distribution to pursue, and liability, if any, can fall only on the Livingstons. The traditional duty imposed upon hotel operators as discussed *supra* is adequate to cover any claim by plaintiff, and strict liability will not be imposed as to this item.

"Accordingly, we hold that a hotel operator may not be held strictly liable for injuries suffered by hotel guests when the injuries are caused by defects inherent in the fixtures or furnishings of the hotel rooms. This holding in no way diminishes the hotel operator's liability under alternative theories. *See Wagner v. Coronet Hotel,* 10 Ariz. App. 296, 458 P.2d 390 (1969).

"We reverse the Court of Appeals as to this issue."

9:10 *Stairways*

Insert immediately before last paragraph, p. 193:

Adequacy of lighting and visibility as factors for the jury to consider on the issue of safe premises was raised in *McNally v. Liebowitz*, 498 Pa. 163, 445 A.2d 716 (1982). In that case, the Supreme Court of Pennsylvania affirmed a jury verdict for a patron in a public restaurant injured because of an inadequately lighted ladies' restroom.

Insert at end of section, p. 196:

In accord with *Buck* is the case of *Kittle v. Liss*, 108 Ill. App. 3d 922, 439 N.E.2d 972 (1982). In *Kittle*, the court held that a property owner is not liable for injuries occurring on the property that result from natural accumulations of ice and snow, unless the owner caused or aggravated the accumulation. The court, however, hastened to add that the presence of ice and snow on property does not abrogate an owner's duty to provide a safe means of ingress and egress for invitees. See, in accord, *Chadwick v. Barba Lou, Inc.*, 69 Ohio St. 2d 222, 431 N.E.2d 660 (1982).

The following two cases illustrate a restaurant keeper's duty to warn a patron of a potential hazard caused by steep stairs and a patron's reciprocal duty to watch one's step when proceeding in a dark area.

ALLGAUER V. LE BASTILLE, INC.
101 Ill. App. 3d 978, 428 N.E.2d 1146 (1981)

ROMITI, P.J.: "Plaintiff filed suit for injuries sustained after she fell down a stairway when leaving defendant's restaurant after dinner. The trial court granted summary judgment for the defendant.

"We reverse and remand for a trial on the merits.

"Le Bastille Restaurant is located on the north side of Chicago in a building owned by the defendant Le Bastille, Inc. The evidence discloses that on May 3, 1974 the plaintiff, Candy Allgauer, went there as a patron to dine along with her husband and two friends. To go up to the restaurant, she entered through an outside door, climbed a stairway and passed through another door into the restaurant itself. After dinner the four prepared to leave the restaurant. Plaintiff's husband opened the door at the top of the stairs. She walked through expecting there to be a landing. Instead there was a step. She fell to the bottom of the stairway and broke her arm. In her deposition, she stated that she knew of nothing on the stairs that would cause her to trip; that she did not recall any stair being in disrepair and she did not remember any debris being on the stairs. There was no contention the lighting was defective. She stated that she had expected to walk out and then walk downstairs and 'I walked and instead of walking onto a level surface, I went down the stairs.' She also stated the stairs seemed narrow. In an affidavit filed in opposition to the defendant's motion for summary judgment, Beth Prince, one of the two friends who had been with plaintiff at the time of the fall stated that the doors opened onto the stairway and blocked one's view of the stairway until they were swung open. At this point there was no vestibule preceding the steps; the steps were immediately in front of one. The steps were very steep and the tread on each stair was narrow. The plaintiff, in opposition to the motion for summary judgment, also presented the evidence of certain ordinances requiring vestibules, and requiring the tread on a stairway to be at least ten inches wide. Defendant refuted these last contentions by pointing out, accurately, that the ordinance requiring vestibules was inapplicable to interior stairs and there was no evidence that the tread on the stairs was less than ten inches wide.

"The defendant had moved for summary judgment contending that:

"1. plaintiff had stated she had no knowledge of what condition or instrumentality caused her to fall and liability could not be based on conjecture;

"2. the crux of plaintiff's claim was that she anticipated a landing which was not there; and although she said the tread seemed narrow, she also said she knew nothing about the stair which would cause her to fall. [This was not accurate; she only said she knew of nothing *on* the stair which would cause her to fall];

"3. the defendant could not be held liable for failing to foresee that plaintiff would anticipate a level landing; rather plaintiff's account raised the inference of contributory negligence in failing to watch where she was stepping. The trial judge granted the motion, apparently finding that plaintiff, having already used the stairs to enter the restaurant, knew of their condition.

"As this court recently ruled in *Kimbrough v. Jewel Companies, Inc.* (1981), 92 Ill. App. 3d 813, 416 N.E.2d 328, 48 Ill. Dec. 297, a plaintiff cannot recover where there is no evidence as to why she fell and that the condition was caused by the defendant. However, we disagree with defendant's contention that plaintiff in this case cannot say what aspect of the stairs or adjacent premises under defendant's control caused her to trip or fall. It is true that plaintiff has not contended that there was debris on the stair, that the lighting was defective, or that the stairs or carpeting were defective. But plaintiff has clearly stated that what caused her to fall was the unexpected dropoff. Her evidence, construed most favorably to her, tends to show that she fell because she stepped down a stair where a landing was expected, that the absence of a landing was concealed by a door which opened out onto the stair, that the stair was steep and narrow and no warning was given of this dangerous condition.

"The owner of business premises has a common-law duty to an invitee to exercise ordinary care and maintenance of his property (*Duffy v. Midlothian Country Club* (1980), 92 Ill. App. 3d 193, 415 N.E.2d 1099, 47 Ill. Dec. 786), and to prevent injury to those entering the premises. (*Kylavos v. Polichrones* (1942), 316 Ill. App. 444, 45 N.E.2d 99 (Abst.).) The defendant owed plaintiff the duty to exercise ordinary care to have the premises in a reasonably safe condition to use in a manner consistent with the invitation, or at least not to lead her into a dangerous trap, or expose her to an unreasonable risk. (*Geraghty v. Burr Oak Lanes, Inc.* (1955), 5 Ill. 2d 153, 125 N.E.2d 47; *Mock v. Sears, Roebuck and Co.* (1981), 101 Ill. App. 3d 103, 427 N.E.2d 872, 56 Ill. Dec. 540.) It owed a duty to discover dangerous conditions existing on the premises and to give sufficient warning to plaintiff to enable her to avoid injury. (*Perminas v. Montgomery Ward & Co.*, 60 Ill. 2d 469, 328 N.E.2d 290 (1975); *Duffy v. Midlothian Country Club*, 92 Ill. App. 3d 193, 415 N.E.2d 1099, 47 Ill. Dec. 786 (1980); *Chapman v. Foggy*, 59 Ill. App. 3d 552, 375 N.E.2d 865, 16 Ill. Dec. 758 (1978); *Hutter v. Badalamenti*, 47 Ill. App. 3d 561, 362 N.E.2d 114, 5 Ill. Dec. 801 (1977). A concealed stairway may be a trap or pitfall where no warning is given. (*May v. Hexter* (Mo. App. 1950), 226 S.W.2d 383.) A steep staircase without any landing or with one beginning before the end of the edge of the door when it is opened onto the stair may be found to be dangerous. (*Skidd v. Quattrochi* (1939); 304 Mass. 438, 23 N.E.2d 1009; *Giliberto v. Yellow Cab Co.* (7th Cir. 1949), 177 F.2d 237.) Likewise, an owner or occupier may be negligent where a step is masked in some way so a person might not notice it before stepping on it. *Boyle v. Simon* (8th Cir. 1977) 558 F.2d 896; *Hall v. Bakersfield Community Hotel Corp.* (1942), 52 Cal. App. 2d 158, 125 P.2d 889.

"A jury here could find that the absence of a landing or the steepness of the stairs rendered them hazardous. If it did so determine, it could also find that the defendant had a duty to correct the danger or warn plaintiff of it, neither of which it did. A landowner or occupier has a duty to give proper warning of hidden dangers. An invitee may assume others have done their duty to give proper warning of hidden dangers and apart from obvious dangers can assume the premises are reasonably safe. (*Geraghty v. Burr Oak Lanes, Inc.* (1955), 5 Ill. 2d 153, 125 N.E.2d 47; *Mock v. Sears, Roebuck and Co.* (1981), 101 Ill. App. 3d 103, 427 N.E.2d 872, 56 Ill. Dec. 540.) Here the danger was hidden by the door until it was opened and the fact that the stair could be seen for the split second plaintiff was placing her foot on it does not necessarily remove it from the realm of hidden dangers.

"Defendant's contention is that when climbing the stairs plaintiff should have realized that although they were not dangerous to ascend they might be dangerous to descend. Then, having realized this, plaintiff should have remembered that danger some two hours later when leaving the restaurant. Defendant also contends that when leaving the restaurant plaintiff should have stopped and looked at the stairs before she walked through when her husband opened the door. But these contentions do not go to the issue of whether the defendant was required to give warning of the danger. Rather, they concern whether the plaintiff was guilty of contributory negligence. [Footnote omitted.]

"Even if plaintiff was aware of the defective condition, her failure to look at the area would not necessarily constitute contributory negligence as a matter of law. (*Kuhn v. General Parking Co.* (1981), 98 Ill. App. 3d 570, 424 N.E.2d 941, 54 Ill. Dec. 191.) A person may have a general knowledge of a source of danger prior to injury and still not be negligent where his attention was distracted. (*Armagast v. Medici Gallery & Coffee House* (1977), 47 Ill. App. 3d 892, 365 N.E.2d 446, 8 Ill. Dec. 208.) A reasonable instance of momentary forgetfulness is not negligence as a matter of law. (*Armagast v. Medici Gallery & Coffee House* (1977), 47 Ill. App. 3d 892, 365 N.E.2d 446, 8 Ill. Dec. 208.) Furthermore, a jury could reasonably find that plaintiff's observations when climbing the stairs would not necessarily put her on notice of any special dangers when descending since the danger of a sudden step is not present to one ascending the stairs.

"Accordingly, the judgment of the trial court is reversed and the case remanded for further proceedings.

"REVERSED AND REMANDED.

"JOHNSON and JIGANTI, JJ., concur."

ROBERTS V. UNITED STATES
514 F. Supp. 712 (D. D.C. 1981)

GASCH, D.J.: "This Federal Tort Claims Act case was tried before the Court on October 20, 1980. Following the trial the Court with counsel visited the scene of the accident. Pursuant to Rule 52(a), Federal Rules of Civil Procedure, the Court makes the following findings of fact and conclusions of law:

Findings of Fact

"1. Plaintiff is the wife of a retired civilian employee of the Department of the Army. As an incident of his employment, plaintiff's husband was eligible for membership in the Fort McNair Officers' Club. His membership in the Fort McNair Club entitled him to make use of the Bolling Air Force Base Officers' Club.

"2. Plaintiff's husband accompanied by plaintiff and their son went to the Officers' Club at Bolling Air Force Base in the District of Columbia on October 10, 1977, to participate in a 'Cook-Your-Own-Steak' dinner at a club room known as the 'Pub' on the occasion of the son's birthday.

"3. October 10, 1977, was Columbus Day, a holiday. The only dining room in operation on that day was the Pub, which was open from 11:00 A.M. until 10:30 P.M. The Pub is on the Upper Floor of the two-story building.

"4. Sometime after 5:00 P.M. on the date in question, plaintiff's husband drove up to the South Entrance to the Lower Floor of the Club, and plaintiff and her son alighted from the car and entered the building. Plaintiff's husband proceeded to park the car.

"5. Upon entering the South Entrance, plaintiff and her son found themselves in a lobby area.

"6. Plaintiff had been to the Club about three times previously, but those visits were some years earlier, and she was not familiar with the building. She had, however, been given instructions by a friend to turn right upon entering the South Entrance, and follow a hallway toward the 'Cook-Your-Own-Steak' location.

"7. Instead, she turned left toward the Washington Room, which was closed and unlighted.

"8. Plaintiff recalled having been in the Washington Room some years before, and wanted to see the room, and perhaps to show it to her son, while they waited for her husband to park the car.

"9. Having turned left from the lobby, plaintiff walked into a reception area. Entering the reception area, she turned right and walked toward the north end of the reception area, which leads to the entrances of the Washington Room and the Maple Room.

"10. Behind the plaintiff as she walked through the reception area toward the entrances to the Washington Room and the Maple Room was a window, facing South.

"11. There was no artificial lighting in the reception area, and no artificial lighting in the two dining rooms toward which plaintiff was walking.

"12. The Officers' Club makes an effort to conserve electricity and has a practice not to turn on unnecessary lights in unused areas of the Club, and so the reception area and the two unused dining rooms which it serves were darkened.

"13. The management of the Club feels that the darkness of such unused areas of the Club is sufficient notice to visitors that they were not invited to enter those areas, although it was not the policy of the Club to exclude members from any part of the premises. In the words of the Club manager, 'people should know' not to go into the dark recesses of darkened rooms.

"14. Accordingly, when plaintiff walked from the lobby through the reception area, she was walking from a relatively bright area toward a dark area.

"15. Following the conclusion of the trial, the Court visited the Officers' Club, and viewed the scene of plaintiff's fall, with the testimony of the witnesses fresh in mind, and aided by diagrams of the Upper and Lower Floors of the Club, which had been received in evidence by stipulation as plaintiff's Exhibit 4. Counsel for both parties were present.

"16. Testimony at the trial established that the scene of plaintiff's fall as the Court viewed it on the trial date differed from the scene at the time of plaintiff's fall in the following respects:

"(a) Wall hangings in the reception area may have been changed to some extent.

"(b) Daylight illumination (from the South window of the reception area and the three South facing windows of the Washington Room) was considerably less at the time of plaintiff's fall. Plaintiff fell between 5:10 and 5:30 P.M. The Court visited the scene roughly two hours earlier than that, on a bright sunny day at about the same time of year, so the Court can conclude that the sun at the time of plaintiff's fall would have been two hours lower in the sky.

"(c) Window shades on the three South-facing windows in the Maple Room and on the South-facing window in the reception area were always kept at 'half-mast' at the time of plaintiff's fall. At the time of the Court's visit to the scene, one of the shades in the Washington Room was missing. The Court therefore concludes that this factor further decreased the amount of natural illumination in the Washington Room at the time of plaintiff's fall, and that the Washington Room was even darker at the time of plaintiff's fall than at the time of the Court's visit.

"17. The plaintiff failed to appreciate as she walked from the South end of the reception area toward the stairs leading down to the Washington Room and the Maple Room, that she was walking into a gradually darker area. But she did acknowledge that when she reached the end of the reception area, she was standing on a very dark area of the floor. She was aware that the Washington Room was at a lower level than the floor on which she was standing for she testified that she looked down over the banister through the windows to see if the tables were set. She saw and held on to a banister and inched her feet along.

"18. Her son testified that walking the same route that his mother walked he was able to see restaurant tables ahead in the dark, and was able to determine that those tables were on a lower level than the level of the reception area.

"19. The Court finds from the testimony of the witnesses, as well as from its own observations that as the plaintiff walked from the South end of the reception area toward the stairs down to the Washington Room and Maple Room, she was walking through a dimly lit area into an almost completely dark area, and that if plaintiff had looked in the direction of the Maple Room, she would have seen either (a) nothing but darkness, or (b) a change in the floor level in the area ahead. In her testimony she indicated awareness of steps in the direction in which she was going.

"20. At the dining room end of the reception area, one stairway leads down to the Washington Room and one leads down to the Maple Room. The stairway down to the Washington Room consists of about ten steps; to the right of that stairway is a flight of two steps leading down to the Maple Room. The two stairways are separated by a railing or banister.

"21. Plaintiff stood at that railing with her hands on the railing, looking in the direction of the Washington Room, and was apparently unaware that she was standing at the head of the stairs to the Maple Room. There was no artificial light ahead. She heard no voices of persons talking or sounds from dishes.

"22. Despite the fact that she was standing in almost complete darkness, plaintiff admitted that she took no precautionary measures for her own safety in moving toward the banister. She also admitted that she was aware that the area to her immediate right as she looked over the banister was dark, and that she had not sought to determine what lay in that direction. Still without any real concern for her safety, she stepped *sideways* to her right, with her attention directed completely toward the Washington Room, and fell down the stairs to the Maple Room.

"23. Plaintiff believes that she was knocked temporarily unconscious. When she regained consciousness, she called to her son, who had not seen her fall.

"24. Both of plaintiff's arms were broken as a result of the fall.

Conclusions of Law

"1. At the outset, it should be noted that it is to be expected that there will be steps and changes in floor levels in public places. *See, e.g., Trinity Episcopal Church of Vero Beach v. Hoglund*, 222 So.2d 781, 783 (Fla. D.C.A. 1969). Thus it should have been apparent to a reasonably prudent person in plaintiff's position that the dark area into which she had walked might lead to a staircase. In fact, while plaintiff herself said that she had paid no attention to what might lie in the direction of the darkness to her right just before she fell, her son testified that he was able to see restaurant tables some distance ahead in the dark area, and was able to determine that those tables were on a lower level than the level of the reception area. Plaintiff indicated some awareness of the steps and consequent change in floor levels.

"2. In addition, it would be expected that a closed restaurant area might contain other possible obstructions such as chairs and tables.

"3. These factors only serve to emphasize the obvious fact that 'darkness is, in itself, a warning to proceed either with extreme caution or not at all.' *Bredder v. Liedenfrost*, 134 F. Supp. 487, 490 (M.D. Pa. 1955); *Trinity Episcopal Church of Vero Beach v. Hoglund, supra,* 222 So.2d at 783; *Hyde v. Blumenthal,* 136 Md. 445, 450, 110 Atl. 862, 864 (1920).

"4. The leading case in this jurisdiction is *Smith v. Arbaugh's Restaurant, Inc.*, 469 F.2d 97 (D.C. Cir. 1972), *cert. denied,* 412 U.S. 939, 93 S.Ct. 2774, 37 L.Ed.2d 399 (1973). This case did away with the common law distinction between 'invitee' and 'licensee' and established the rule that the duty of a landowner to a visitor on his property is to exercise 'reasonable care under the circumstances.'

"... A landowner must act as a reasonable man in maintaining his property in a reasonably safe condition in view of all the circumstances, including the likelihood of injury to others, the seriousness of the injury, and the burden of avoiding the risk.

"*Id.* at 100. In order to determine whether a landowner has exercised reasonable care under all the circumstances,

"[t]he factors to be weighed in the determination of the degree of care demanded in a specific situation are 'the likelihood that [the landowner's] conduct will injure others, taken with the seriousness of the injury if it happens, and balanced against the interest which [the landowner] must sacrifice to avoid the risk,' . . .

"*Id.* at 105–06. Foreseeability is a key factor:

". . . Foreseeability of the visitor's presence determines in part the likelihood of injury to him, and the extent of the interest which must be sacrificed to avoid the risk of injury.

"*Id.* at 106.

"5. It is noted that the plaintiff Smith in *Arbaugh's* was a District of Columbia health inspector who had been instructed by his superior to make an inspection of the barbecue pit in the basement of the adjacent property which could be reached only by going down greasy, slippery metal steps. Smith clearly had the obligation to descend these steps. Smith's obligation was clearly foreseeable insofar as Arbaugh's was concerned. Arbaugh's duty under the circumstances to exercise reasonable care to maintain the steps in a reasonably safe condition was evident. The trial court had relied upon its interpretation of *Firfer v. United States,* 93 U.S. App. D.C. 216, 219, 208 F.2d 524, 527 (1953).

"6. Applying these principles to the facts of this case we note that the Officers' Club was operating on a holiday schedule and that both the Washington Room and the Maple Room were closed. Neither room was lighted nor was the reception area leading to these rooms artificially lighted. There were no employees, maintenance workers or patrons of the club in these areas. Though plaintiff had been in the club before, she was not familiar with the area. She knew that the area where she was exploring was not the 'Pub' where she was to have dinner. She knew that the Washington Room was down a flight of stairs and that all indications were that that room and that area was not open to patrons on this occasion. She nevertheless entered the darkened area not of necessity nor for the purpose of her visit but out of curiosity.

"7. In the context of the *Arbaugh's* standards, plaintiff's presence in the area in question while not likely was perhaps 'foreseeable'. Extinguishing the lights in unused portions of the Club was not an adequate means of keeping all visitors from entering the darkened portions of those areas. Also in the context of the *Arbaugh's* standard of the interest which the landowner 'must sacrifice to avoid the risk', it would be reasonable to expect defendant either to burn lights in areas not in use, or to erect warning signs or barricades to alert guests that the area was closed.[1]

"8. Plaintiff suggests that the deliberate openness of the Club, as testified to by

[1]But see Restatement (Second) of Torts § 359, Comment f (1965):

"The lessor's liability is limited to those parts of the premises which, under the express or implied terms of the lease, are to be thrown open for the admission of the public. Thus the lessor has no liability under this Section to a customer in a leased restaurant who is injured when he wanders into the kitchen."

the managers of the Club, was construed as an invitation to her to wander throughout the Club, and could only have been revoked by the placing of barriers or signs of some sort. The Club managers felt that aesthetic considerations dictated against placing unsightly signs around the Club. The Club manager also thought that the extinguishment of lights was an adequate warning that the unlighted portion of the Club was not open to the public.

"9. The Court concludes that the United States as the property owner owed a duty to plaintiff under the *Arbaugh's* standards, and negligently failed to discharge that duty to exercise ordinary care under all the circumstances. The question remains whether plaintiff was contributorily negligent [footnote omitted] in entering the darkened area of the Club, and was thus barred from any recovery in this action. *See, e.g., Wingfield v. People's Drug Store, Inc.,* 379 A.2d 685 (D.C. App. 1977).

> "Appellant next contends that the court should have charged that a 'substantial degree' rather than 'some degree' of contributory negligence was required on appellant's part in order for the jury to find that she could not recover for her injuries. The instruction given in the instant case was a correct statement of the law since the District of Columbia does not recognize different degrees of contributory negligence. The *rule is simply that contributory negligence bars a plaintiff's recovery. Karma Construction Co., Inc. v. King,* D.C. App., 296 A.2d 604, 605 (1972).

"*Id.* at 687 (emphasis added).

"10. Again we examine the conduct of the plaintiff, not only to determine, as above, whether the defendant should have foreseen her presence in the darkened area in question, but to determine whether the plaintiff herself exercised ordinary care and prudence for her own safety in the circumstances. We note that the plaintiff was moving in a nearly dark area of the floor, and that she saw at a distance that there were tables in the darkened area of the Maple Room, and that the tables were at a level lower than the level on which she stood. She knew there were steps ahead. She had encountered one barricade. Yet plaintiff testified that, while concentrating her attention not on the dark area in which she was, but on the Washington Room, she stepped *sideways* into the dark void, and fell down the stairs.

"11. Proceeding in the dark under similar circumstances has been found to amount to contributory negligence as a matter of law, even where plaintiff was searching for a ladies' room in a public place, *Burgie v. Muench,* 65 Ohio App. 176, 29 N.E.2d 439 (1940); or was walking through a restaurant on a route which to some extent the defendant restauranteur had invited patrons to take, *Lyman v. Recreational Activities, Inc.,* 286 Minn. 308, 175 N.W.2d 498 (1970).

"12. The fact that plaintiff in this case was merely wandering through the darkened portion of the Officers' Club not for the purpose for which she was invited weighs against her. Proceeding in the dark without a 'compelling reason' or a 'pressing emergency' has been held to amount to contributory negligence as a matter of law. *Brant v. Van Zandt,* 77 So.2d 858 (Fla. 1955); *Polm v. Hession,* 363 Pa. 494, 70 A.2d 311, 312 (1950).

"13. Plaintiff cites three federal cases in support of the proposition that the United States owes a duty of care to visitors to its premises. But these three cases are distinguishable on the facts. *Grant v. United States,* 271 F.2d 651 (2d Cir. 1959) involved a newsboy delivering papers in pre-dawn darkness who fell on dark stairs. He was found free of contributory negligence. He was on the steps on which he was invited to travel in the course of his employment. Plaintiff also cites *Salim v. United States,* 382 F.2d 240 (5th Cir. 1967). In this case a Post Office patron was transacting business and in leaving the Post Office fell on icy stairs. The trial court had found contributory negligence but the circuit court held there was no evidence of this and on the contrary concluded she was on the direct path from the post office door to the railing when she slipped on the ice. *Fournier v. United States,* 220 F. Supp. 752 (D. Miss. 1963), involved a club patron leaving by the front entrance who fell on unlighted dark stairs. She was found by the trial judge to be guilty of contributory negligence as she was intoxicated. In accordance with Mississippi law the recovery was reduced 50%. One guilty of contributory negligence in this district may not recover. *See Wingfield v. People's Drug Stores, Inc., supra.*

"14. The only other 'darkness' cases cited by plaintiff involve hidden hazards not analogous to the situation in the instant case. *Gleason v. Academy of the Holy Cross,* 168 F.2d 561 (D.C. Cir. 1948), involved an unexpected drop-off at the back of a dark platform, which was 'latent and hidden', and which 'reasonably careful people [were] not likely to discover.' *Id.* at 562. In *Muldrow v. Daly,* 329 F.2d 886 (D.C. Cir. 1964), the property owner maintained an unguarded stairwell in an unlighted area adjacent to the public space. Mrs. Daly, still believing herself to be on the public alley, fell into the stairwell and was injured. *Id.* at 889.

"15. Plaintiff did not have a 'compelling reason' for walking toward the closed and darkened areas of the Officers' Club, nor was she reacting to a 'pressing emergency'. *Brant v. Van Zandt, supra; Polm v. Hession, supra.* Nor did she have to abandon any business obligation rather than travel in the darkness. *Grant v. United States, supra.* Nor was she a business invitee using the only route available to her. *Salim v. United States, supra; Fournier v. United States, supra.* The reason for plaintiff's entry into the darkened and closed areas of the Club must be described as curiosity rather than necessity. Under the circumstances, her failure to take proper precautions against being injured by proceeding in the dark without any concern for her own safety must be regarded as contributory negligence which was the proximate cause of her fall.

"Defendant is therefore entitled to judgment. An appropriate order will be entered this date."

Insert immediately before 9:11, p. 196:

In the case to follow, the federal District Court for North Dakota stresses an important, but often ignored, principle of law. Statutory compliance with a building code does not insulate an innkeeper from all liability. A business invitee may nonetheless establish lack of due care on other grounds.

LUXEN V. HOLIDAY INNS, INC.
566 F. Supp. 1484 (N.D. Ill. 1983)

BUA, D.J.: ". . . [Plaintiff brought suit for injuries that occurred in a fall while she was climbing a set of stairs on the hotel premises.]

"Plaintiff's final claim is that defendant's failure to provide a handrail on the wall side of the stairway proximately caused plaintiff's injuries. Defendant counters by asserting that summary judgment is warranted because there is no dispute that the premises were in compliance with the applicable building codes.

"On March 5, 1979, the City of Hazelwood, Missouri passed Bill No. 1350, Ordinance No. 1320–79, thus codifying the 1978 BOCA Basic Building Code. Under the BOCA code, unless an inspector finds the exitways to be 'inadequate for safety,' the exitways in an existing building shall be deemed to be in compliance with the Code. BOCA Basic Building Code (1978), § 604.2-1. Because the inspector did not find the stairway to be inadequate for safety, there can be no issue as to whether the stairway was in compliance with the BOCA code. That the stairway was in compliance with the BOCA code is supported by the deposition testimony of experts for both plaintiff and defendant. Furthermore, because the BOCA code specifically sets out requirements in existence prior to its enactment and because it expressly states that all prior codes are 'hereby repealed and held for naught,' there can be no question that the code as enacted in 1979 was the applicable code at the time of the incident. Therefore, no issue of material fact exists that a violation of the code provision was a proximate cause of plaintiff's injury. This does not, however, end the Court's inquiry.

"Plaintiff alleges that the failure to provide a handrail was the proximate cause of plaintiff's injury. While defendant may well have been in compliance with the applicable building and safety code provisions, such compliance does not preclude a determination that, under the circumstances, defendant was nevertheless negligent. As Prosser notes, compliance with a statute does not necessarily mean that due care was used. W. Prosser, *Law of Torts,* 4th ed., § 36, at 203 (1971). Thus, where specific circumstances present situations beyond those which the statute was designed to meet, a plaintiff may prove that the defendant was negligent in not taking extra measures. [Citations omitted.] Defendant is only entitled to summary judgment on the issue of statutory compliance. Whether defendant was nevertheless negligent remains in issue."

In *Sussman v. Tutelman,* 445 So.2d 1081 (Fla. App. 1984), a hotel resident, after descending from a stairway, tripped over the cane of a hotel guest seated in the lobby. The Florida Court of Appeals reversed a jury verdict for the resident.

The evidence failed to demonstrate that the injury was caused by any violation of a legal duty.

9:11 *Bathroom and Shower*

Insert at end of section, p. 202:

In a similar case, *Bidar v. Amfac, Inc.,* —— Haw. ——, 669 P.2d 154 (1983), a hotel guest was injured when she grabbed a towel rack to aid herself in rising from a sitting position on the toilet. The rack came loose from the wall, and the plaintiff fell. The majority of the court held that a genuine issue of material fact existed with respect to whether a hotel should foresee that guests will grab nearby towel racks to assist themselves in rising from the toilet. In a persuasive dissent, however, Judge Spencer concluded that a reasonable guest knows better than to use a towel rack to support his or her weight. Therefore, the court should find that no material issue of fact exists as to the hotel's use of reasonable care.

9:12 *Furnishings and Equipment*

Insert immediately before Dillman v. Nobles, *p. 204:*

In *Wysong v. Little Creek Hotel Courts, Inc.,* 614 S.W.2d 852 (Tex. Civ. App. 1981), plaintiff suffered carbon monoxide poisoning when a gas heater burned up the oxygen in his room. The appellate court upheld the trial jury's verdict for the defendant, finding that the heater was not defective and that the jury could reasonably find that the sole cause of the accident was the plaintiff's use of the heater at a high setting over an extended period of time.

Insert at end of section, p. 206:

The reasoning of *Jones, supra,* and *Schnitzer, supra,* was reexamined in the following case, in which the plaintiff brought an action alleging negligence and breach of warranty against hotel owners after being burned while showering when the hot-water valve failed to shut off the hot water. The court upheld the negligence count but stated that under Virginia law an innkeeper is not, in fact, to be held liable for an implied warranty of suitability.

Ely v. Blevins
706 F.2d 479 (4th Cir. 1983)

Per Curiam: ". . . The problem arises with respect to the warranty count. Having explained negligence with respect to Count 1, the court charged the jury, succinctly, as follows.

"In order to recover for a breach of the implied warranty of suitability, the plaintiff must prove by a preponderance of the evidence as follows:

One, that the fixtures or equipment were defective and unfit for ordinary purposes for which they were to be used, and, two, that as a proximate result the plaintiff was injured.

"There was no requirement, in other words, of a showing of unreasonable conduct, or lack of care.

"Plaintiff would justify this submission by our holding in *Schnitzer v. Nixon*, 439 F.2d 940 (4th Cir. 1971). There a motel guest sat in what proved to be a defective chair, and was injured when it collapsed. The case was tried without jury. The court found defendants were not negligent, and dismissed the complaint. In reversing we said,

"Since this is a diversity case, we would follow the Supreme Court of Appeals of Virginia but unfortunately it has not explicitly expressed itself on warranty in the instant factual environment.

"Certainly, however, nothing in Virginia's jurisprudence, statutory or decisional, denies the availability of the implied warranty—devoid of negligence—for a guest's recovery from his innkeeper for injuries caused by a weak fixture provided for the guest's use. Such an action lies in Virginia, appellees concede, for breach of implied warranty of merchantability or suitability in the *sale* of goods, *Gleason & Co. v. International Harvester*, 197 Va. 255, 88 S.E.2d 904 (1955), and for the wholesomeness of food and drink in its *sale*, *Levy v. Paul*, 207 Va. 100, 147 S.E.2d 722 (1966). These doctrines in reason and logic dictate recognition of actionable implied warranty on the part of the innkeeper. (Emphasis in orig.) 439 F.2d at 941.

"The *Schnitzer* court then discussed an English case holding an innkeeper to an implied warranty of fitness, and concluded that two Virginia cases were '[i]dentical in principle': *Kirby v. Moehlman*, 182 Va. 876, 30 S.E.2d 548 (1944), and *Crosswhite v. Shelby Operating Corp.*, 182 Va. 713, 30 S.E.2d 673 (1944). With great respect, we cannot help noting that the Virginia court's opinions in both of these cases spoke sufficiently in terms of negligence and reasonable care to leave its views on absolute liability not free from doubt. However, our question is not whether this court was correct in its estimation of Virginia warranty law in 1970, but whether there are indicia today that call for a different resolution.

"We start afield. *Schnitzer* was shortly followed by the Michigan court in *Jones v. Keetch*, 388 Mich. 164, 200 N.W.2d 227 (1972). Again a motel guest was injured by a defective chair. The court stated that it was irrelevant whether the plaintiff was to be considered a bailee or a lessee, and, following *Schnitzer*, held that there was a breach of implied warranty of fitness. It appears, however, that the Virginia court has not followed that route. In *Leake v. Meredith*, 221 Va. 14, 267 S.E.2d 93 (1980), plaintiff rented what proved to be a defective ladder from the defendant and the question of a lessor's liability arose. Plaintiff's suit for breach of warranty was dismissed. The court took the opposite view from *Keetch*, declining to align itself with those courts that apply the Uniform Commercial Code to leases. It is true that the court did not say, in so many words, that there was no common law implied warranty in addition to statutory warranties under the Code, but certainly its failure to find one would seem an eloquent omission.

"We do not feel, under these circumstances, that we should find that the Virginia court would make a special rule in favor of an innkeeper's warranty. We are confirmed in this refusal by the realization that, while an innkeeper is often held to a specially high duty of care, the general rule, nationally, falls short of warranty. *See, e.g., Truett v. Morgan,* 153 Ga. App. 778, 266 S.E.2d 557 (1980); *Rappaport v. Days Inns of America, Inc.,* 296 N.C. 382, 250 S.E.2d 245 (1979); *Bearse v. Fowler,* 347 Mass. 179, 196 N.E.2d 910 (1964); *Early v. Lowe,* 119 W.Va. 690, 195 S.E. 852 (1938).

"Finally, there is no possible merit in defendants' claim that plaintiff was contributorily negligent as matter of law. We have reviewed defendants' other contentions, but find them not to require comment. We trust that plaintiff's extreme jury argument will not be repeated; it was uncalled for to talk about great national hotel tragedies, and the need to teach motel keepers lessons.

"Reversed; new trial on Count 1."

Defective hotel-room chairs have subjected innkeepers to liability in Georgia: *Gary Hotel Courts Inc. v. Perry,* 148 Ga. App. 22, 251 S.E.2d 37 (Ga. App. 1978); and in Oregon: *Weaver v. Flock,* 43 Or. App. 505, 603 P.2d 1194 (1979).

9:13 *Fire Liability*

Insert at end of section, p. 210:

The following case illustrates two issues: (1) the rescue doctrine and (2) what constitutes proof of the rescuer's contributory negligence sufficient to deny recovery.

ALTAMURO V. MILNER HOTEL, INC.
540 F. Supp. 870 (E.D. Pa. 1982)

McGLYNN, D.J.:

Findings of Fact

"1. The Milner Hotel is located at 111 South 10th Street in Philadelphia, Pennsylvania and is owned by the defendant The Milner Hotel, Inc., a corporation maintaining its registered office at 1526 Center Street, Detroit, Michigan.

"2. During the morning of October 11, 1978, Patricia DeLoss, a guest in Room 706 at the Hotel, went to the Hotel's Lobby and there told the Desk Clerk, William T. Wilson, that the television in her room was not receiving a picture and requested that it be repaired. After speaking to Wilson, Ms. DeLoss left the Hotel.

"3. Wilson then summoned Edwin Jennings, the maintenance man employed by the Hotel, and instructed him to proceed to Ms. DeLoss' room on the seventh floor to inspect the television.

"4. Mr. Jennings went to Room 706 and turned the power-switch of the television to the 'on' position, but the switch did not activate the set.

"5. Jennings then moved the television and placed the plug into another receptacle in the same room. When he did this, the television began to emit a 'burning' odor and made a 'popping' or 'crackling' sound. Jennings removed the plug from the receptacle and then placed the television in its former position reinserting the plug into the original receptacle with the power switch still in the 'on' position.

"6. Jennings then returned to the Lobby and reported to Wilson that he thought the television had a 'short' in it. In response, Wilson asked Jennings if he turned the television off. Jennings replied, 'No, I don't think I did.' Wilson then told Jennings to return to Room 706 and turn off the TV set. As Jennings began to ascend the stairs, an unidentified man came in and stated that there was smoke coming out of one of the Hotel's windows on the third floor.

"7. Wilson called the Fire Department and then, using the switchboard, called all the rooms in the Hotel, alerting the residents to the fire.

"8. About fifteen minutes later, Harry E. Vonada, the Manager of the Hotel, entered the Lobby, and after being apprised of the fire by Wilson, he and Jennings went to the third floor but were unable to locate the source of the smoke. Vonada then telephoned Wilson from one of the rooms on the third floor and told him that there was no fire at that level. Wilson then went outside, observed that the fire was on the seventh floor, and so advised Vonada.

"9. About fifteen minutes before Wilson told Vonada that the fire was on the seventh floor, Altamuro, who operated the newsstand in front of the Hotel, and who was known to Wilson, rushed into the Lobby and shouted to Wilson that smoke was pouring out of one of the rooms.

"10. Altamuro then boarded an elevator alone and went to one of the upper floors to alert the residents.

"11. Wilson testified that he warned Altamuro not to go because the Fire Department was called and would be soon arriving.

"12. Wilson also stated that Altamuro came back down to the Lobby, stayed there for approximately ten minutes and then boarded the elevator a second time. Wilson again warned him 'not to go up'.

"13. Wilson testified that Altamuro went up alone the second time and that this is the last time he saw him alive.

"14. At about this time, Officer Edward Markowski of the Philadelphia Police Department noticed the fire while driving in his patrol car. He pulled up in front of the Hotel, went into the Lobby and informed the Clerk at the desk that there was a fire in the Hotel. He then went out to his patrol car and radioed the Fire Department and then returned to the Hotel Lobby.

"15. While there, Officer Markowski met Jennings and Altamuro, with whom the Officer was acquainted. The officer said to Jennings: 'Let's get upstairs and see what's happening.' Altamuro asked if he could also go along to see if 'he could give them a hand.' Officer Markowski said it was all right with him, 'but if anything went wrong, he'd have to get out.'

"16. All three men then boarded the elevator and went to the seventh floor. They were joined by Vonada, the Manager.[1]

"17. All four men went to Room 706 where the fire had started. Officer Markowski tried to open the door but the door was locked. The Officer asked Jennings if he had a key to the room. Jennings said he did. Officer Markowski said: 'Open the door.' Mr. Vonada ordered Jennings to keep it closed in order to keep the fire contained in the room. Officer Markowski countered by telling Jennings: 'I am the law. Open up the door.'[2] Jennings complied with his command. When the door was opened, black smoke poured out of the room and into the hallway and filled the entire corridor. The lights in the hallway then went out.

"18. The men then became nauseous and the police officer began vomiting. Officer Markowski ordered the men downstairs, which order the men obeyed.

"19. While on the seventh floor, Officer Markowski found a woman unconscious on the floor. He picked the woman up and placed her on his shoulder and carried her down to the fifth floor.

"20. When on the fifth floor, Officer Markowski saw Altamuro knocking on doors informing guests of the fire. The police officer asked Altamuro to take the woman down to the Lobby for him. Altamuro carried the woman downstairs and Officer Markowski returned to the seventh floor.

"21. When he returned to the seventh floor, Officer Markowski found a tall slender Black male, assisted him to the Lobby, and then across the street away from the Hotel.

"22. The officer returned to the Lobby, but at this time, the fire was spreading rapidly. Flaming debris had fallen on the Hotel's marquee and consequently the firemen in the Lobby ordered all policemen and civilians out of the building.

"23. Officer Markowski testified that at the time the firemen made this an-

---

[1]Officer Markowski's testimony that he met Edward Jennings in the Lobby and went upstairs with him, see N.T., 11/24/81, at 95–96, appears to be in direct conflict with Jennings' testimony. Jennings testified that the first time he met Officer Markowski was on the elevator on the third floor of the Hotel where he along with Harry Vonada joined the Officer and then together went to the seventh floor. See Vonada Deposition at 6–7; Jennings deposition at 8. However, because this fact is not of crucial importance to the disposition of this case, I will assume that the Officer's account of his first meeting with Jennings is correct.

[2]Officer Markowski later testified that he ordered the door opened because he was told by Mr. Jennings that there was a possibility that the room was occupied. N.T., 11/24/81, at 96. Mr. Vonada expressed his reason for wanting the door to remain closed thus:

"Q.   Why didn't you want Jennings to open the door?

"A.   Any stupid bastard knows you don't open up a door when there is a fire in the room.

Vonada Deposition at 24–25. It was subsequently learned that no one was present in Room 706 during the fire."

nouncement, he observed the presence of Mr. Wilson and Mr. Altamuro in the Lobby and that immediately after this announcement, he escorted these men to the outside of the Hotel.

"24. Officer Markowski testified that this was the last time he saw Altamuro alive and never saw him return to the Hotel.

"25. The decedent's body was found in Room 710 sometime after he had left the Hotel to go across the street with Officer Markowski. The cause of death was 'inhalation of fumes and carbon monoxide poisoning' and there were burns on his body and 'skin slip of the face.' [Footnote omitted.]

"26. The fire at the Milner Hotel had been in progress for an undetermined length of time before the Philadelphia Fire Department arrived.

"27. There were four means of access to the seventh floor from the Lobby: two elevators, a stairway and a fire tower.

"28. Fire Department personnel had no knowledge of the activities of Officer Markowski and/or the decedent and were unaware of the uses to which the elevators and stairwells were put prior to their arrival at the scene.

"29. Fire Department personnel only used the stairway for access to the seventh floor of the Hotel.

"30. The decedent's death occurred after the Philadelphia Police Department and Philadelphia Fire Department arrived at the Milner Hotel and ordered all civilians to vacate the premises.

"31. The fire that occurred at the Hotel on October 11, 1978 originated in the defective television set owned by the Hotel in Room 706. . . .

Discussion

I. Defendant Milner Hotel

"Plaintiff's case against the defendant, Milner Hotel, is based principally on the 'rescue doctrine', which provides that when one person is exposed to peril of life or limb by the negligence of another, the latter will be liable in damages for injuries received by a third person in a reasonable effort to rescue the one so imperiled. *Guca v. Pittsburgh Railways Co.*, 367 Pa. 579, 80 A.2d 779 (1951); *Toner v. Pennsylvania Railroad Co.*, 263 Pa. 438, 106 A. 797 (1919); *Corbin v. City of Philadelphia*, 195 Pa. 461, 45 A. 1070 (1900); *Truitt v. Hays*, 33 Pa.D. & C.2d 453 (C.P. Ven. 1963); W. Prosser, The Law of Torts § 44, at 277 (4th ed. 1971); Annot., 91 A.L.R.3d 1202 (1979).[4]

"Perhaps the most quoted articulation of this doctrine was that by then New York Court of Appeals Justice Cardozo:

"Danger invites rescue. The cry of distress is the summons to relief. The law does not ignore these reactions of the mind in tracing conduct to its consequences. It recognizes them as normal. It places their effects within the range of the natural and probable. The wrong that imperils life is a wrong to

[4]The parties agree that Pennsylvania law is to be applied to the substantive issues in the case.

the imperiled victim; it is a wrong also to his rescuer. The state that leaves an opening in a bridge is liable to the child that falls into the stream, but liable also to the parent who plunges to its aid. . . . The risk of rescue, if only it be not wanton, is born of the occasion. The emergency begets the man. The wrongdoer may not have foreseen the coming of the deliverer. He is accountable as if he had. . . .

"*Wagner v. International Railway Co.,* 232 N.Y. 176, 180, 133 N.E. 437, 438 (1921). Twenty-one years earlier, the Pennsylvania Supreme Court stated:

"A rescuer—one who, from the most unselfish motives, prompted by the noblest impulses that can impel man to deeds of heroism, faces deadly peril—ought not to hear from the law words of condemnation of his bravery, because he rushed into danger, to snatch from it the life of a fellow creature imperiled by the negligence of another; but he should rather listen to words of approval, unless regretfully withheld on account of the unmistakable evidence of his rashness and imprudence. . . .

". . . The law has so high a regard for human life, that it will not impute negligence to an effort to preserve it, unless made under such circumstances as to constitute rashness in the judgment of prudent persons. . . . One who imperils his own life for the sake of rescuing another from imminent danger is not chargeable, as a matter of law, with contributory negligence; and, if the life of the rescued person was endangered by the defendant's negligence, the rescuer may recover for the injuries which he suffered from the defendant in consequence of his intervention.

"*Corbin v. City of Philadelphia,* 195 Pa. 461, 468–472, 45 A. 1070, 1072–1074 (1900) (citations omitted). In applying the rescue doctrine, I must first determine the negligence *vel non* of The Milner Hotel.

A. The Negligence of the Hotel Caused a Peril to Its Guests

"Under Pennsylvania law, a hotel keeper, while not an insurer or guarantor of the safety of his guests, must nonetheless exercise ordinary or reasonable care to keep them from injury. *Lyttle v. Denny,* 222 Pa. 395, 71 A. 841 (1909); *Winkler v. Seven Springs Farm, Inc.,* 240 Pa. Super. Ct. 641, 359 A.2d 440 (1976), *aff'd,* 477 Pa. 445, 384 A.2d 241 (1978); *Hunter v. Hotel Sylvania Co.,* 153 Pa. Super. Ct. 591, 34 A.2d 816 (1943). In *Ritchey v. Cassone,* 296 Pa. 249, 145 A. 822 (1929), the plaintiff's decedent died in a fire at defendant's hotel while he was a guest there. The court spelled out the duty the hotel owed to the decedent as follows:

"[T]here is no presumption of negligence arising merely from the fact that fire breaks out in a hotel. In the present case defendant owned and operated the hotel at the time of the destruction of the building. He was not of course an insurer of the safety of his patrons; but he was bound to exercise such watchfulness and care as would reasonably secure their safety while guests in this hotel. Destruction of a hotel may not be anticipated, but it is generally a possibility. . . . One who negligently creates a dangerous condition cannot escape liability for the natural and probable consequences resulting from his carelessness. . . .

"*Id.* at 255–56, 145 A. at 824 (citations omitted). *See also* Annot., 60 A.L.R.3d 1217 (1974).

"Here, the fire at The Milner Hotel on October 11, 1978 originated in the defective television set in Room 706. The defective condition of the television was known to the Hotel through its employee, Jennings, who nevertheless left the set plugged in, unattended and with the power switch in the 'on' position. I have no difficulty in concluding that, under these circumstances and given the substantial risk of fire resulting from a short-circuited or otherwise faulty television set, Jennings' conduct clearly amounted to negligence and that his negligence was a substantial factor in placing the lives of the Hotel guests in peril. The very least a reasonably prudent person would have done would have been to disconnect the power source by turning the set off or removing the plug. Of course, Jennings' negligence is imputed to his employer under the doctrine of respondeat superior. *Wagaman v. General Finance Co.,* 116 F.2d 254, 257 (3d Cir. 1940).

"That a fire in a ten-story hotel presents an imminent danger to the residents cannot be gainsaid. The Hotel employees, the police and firemen as well as Altamuro recognized the need for immediate action. The prompt action taken by them at considerable risk to themselves was undoubtedly responsible for preventing a catastrophic loss of life.

B. Contributory or Comparative Negligence

"Having decided that the Hotel's negligence placed the lives of the guests in imminent peril, the next question is whether any conduct on the part of Altamuro would bar recovery.

"Defendant Hotel argues that since Altamuro's death occurred after the firemen ordered all civilians out of the Hotel and because it can be inferred from the evidence that the deceased heard the command by his conduct in immediately leaving the Hotel, then his final rescue effort was so unreasonable as to preclude recovery by his administratrix. The test, as enunciated in *Corbin v. Philadelphia,* 195 Pa. 461, 45 A. 1070 (1900), is whether the rescuer 'acted with due regard for his own safety, or so rashly and imprudently' as to bar recovery. *Id.* at 473, 45 A. at 1074. The court stated that 'where another is in great and imminent danger, he who attempts a rescue may be warranted, by surrounding circumstances, in exposing his limbs or life to a very high degree of danger. In such a case, he should not be charged with the consequences of errors of judgments resulting from the excitement and confusion of the moment. . . .'' 195 Pa. at 472, 45 A. at 1074. Similarly, in *Simmons v. Pennsylvania Railroad Co.,* 2 Pa.D.&C.2d 233 (C.P. Dauph. 1955), the court stated:

"While an attempt to rescue a person from a peril created by another's negligence does not charge the negligent person with liability if it was condemned by reason, and a rescuer who has been injured can be deprived of a recovery from the person responsible for the peril, on the ground that the dangers and desperate character of his act rendered him guilty of contributory negligence, *errors of judgment are to be weighed in view of the excitement and confusion of the moment in determining whether the rescuer acted without rashness or imprudence.*

"*Id.* at 238 (emphasis added) (quoting 38 Am. Jur. § 80, at 738).[5] Thus the standard of care for a rescuer is not to act rashly or imprudently.

"In any event, Pennsylvania has abolished the defense of contributory negligence and has replaced it with comparative negligence. See 42 Pa. Cons. Stat. Ann. §7102 (Purdon Supp. 1981). [Footnote omitted.] Although no reported case has applied Pennsylvania's Comparative Negligence Statute to the rescue doctrine, the instant case clearly falls within the literal language of Act, which states that the Act is to be applied to '*all actions* brought to recover damages for negligence resulting in death or injury to person or property. . . .' 42 Pa. Cons. Stat. Ann. § 7102(a) (Purdon Supp. 1981) (emphasis added). Courts in other jurisdictions have applied their comparative negligence schemes in similar circumstances, holding that if 'the trier of fact finds that the rescue is unreasonable or unreasonably carried out the factfinder should then make a comparison of negligence between the rescuer and the one whose negligence created the situation to which the rescue was a response.' *Cords v. Anderson,* 80 Wis.2d 525, 548, 259 N.W.2d 672, 683 (1977). *Accord, Ryder Truck Rental, Inc. v. Korte,* 357 So.2d 228, 230 (Fla. Dist. Ct. App. 1978). While I believe Pennsylvania courts would reach a similar result, it is not necessary for me to decide the issue because I find that Altamuro did not act rashly, imprudently or so unreasonably as to constitute negligence on his part under the rescue doctrine.

"There is no dispute that during the initial phase of the fire, Altamuro busied himself warning guests at the Hotel of the fire, and later he assisted Officer Markowski in helping people out of the building. The last time Altamuro was seen alive was when he left the Hotel after the firemen ordered all civilians out of the building. There was no evidence as to how Altamuro got back into the building. What prompted his return can only be surmised but, having been successful in two prior missions to the upper floors of the Hotel, I am not convinced that it was unreasonable for him to conclude that he could successfully complete another mission without unduly imperiling his own safety even though he disobeyed the order of the firemen by returning to the building.[7]

---

[5]*Cf.* Stebner v. YMCA, 428 Pa. 370, 374, 238 A.2d 19, 21 (1968) ("A building owner responsible for placing an invitee in a dangerous situation cannot escape responsibility for an injury resulting to the invitee, merely because the victim, in fright, frenzy or panic adds to his danger by an act which, in a later serene moment of contemplation, might seem to have been unwise.").

[7]*Cf.* Clayton v. Blair, 254 Iowa 372, 117 N.W.2d 879 (1962) (While plaintiff's decedent was warning others of danger during apartment house fire she was within the doctrine of rescue and, although it did not appear why decedent had returned from second floor of building to third floor, where her apartment was located and her daughter and personal belongings were, jury should have been instructed as to doctrine of rescue.)

II. Third-Party Defendant City of Philadelphia

"The Milner Hotel joined the City of Philadelphia as a third-party defendant alleging that the City took possession and control of the building during the fire-fighting efforts; that the City was negligent in failing to prevent Altamuro from slipping back into the Hotel after the Fire Department personnel ordered all civilians to leave the building; and that this negligence was the proximate cause of Altamuro's death and therefore the Hotel should be entitled to contribution and /or indemnity from the City. The plaintiff has not asserted any claim directly against the City.

"Assuming, without deciding, that the City had a duty to use reasonable care to prevent the plaintiff's decedent from entering the Hotel while it was in flames and thus exposing himself to harm, [footnote omitted] and assuming further that the Political Subdivision Tort Claims Act, 42 Pa. Cons. Stat. Ann. §§ 8541–8564 (Purdon Supp. 1981), would permit an action against the City in these circumstances, nevertheless, I find that the City did not breach this duty, but rather exercised reasonable care under the circumstances. The evidence is clear that once it became apparent to the fire personnel at the scene that the conflagration posed a grave danger, all persons were ordered out and a barricade was erected. There is no evidence that either the firemen or the police became aware that Altamuro had reentered the Hotel. The City is not an insurer or guarantor of a person's safety, *see Chapman v. City of Philadelphia,* 290 Pa. Super. Ct. 281, 434 A.2d 753 (1981), but is liable only for negligent acts which cause him harm. The Hotel's claim against the City must fall simply because it lacks proof. Accordingly, the Hotel is not entitled to recover from the City for contribution and/or indemnity. [Footnote omitted.] . . .

"Accordingly, I arrive at the following

Conclusions of Law

"1. The Court has jurisdiction over the subject matter and the parties.

"2. The defendant, The Milner Hotel, Inc., by the acts of its employees, was negligent, and this negligence placed the lives of the residents in imminent peril. Such negligence was the cause of the death of Joseph S. Altamuro.

"3. The plaintiff's deceased, Joseph S. Altamuro, did not act rashly, imprudently or unreasonably in his efforts to alert the residents of The Milner Hotel to the imminent danger of the fire and in aiding in their removal from the building.

"4. The City of Philadelphia was not negligent and therefore is not liable to the defendant-third party plaintiff.

"5. Plaintiff is entitled to judgment in her favor and against defendant The Milner Hotel, Inc. in the amount of $396,373.

"6. The third-party defendant City of Philadelphia is entitled to judgment in its favor and against third-party plaintiff The Milner Hotel, Inc."

9:15 *Vermin, Insects, Animals*

Insert at end of section, p. 214:

The difference between "causing" and "contributing to" guest injuries relating to the presence of a beehive as a predicate for a finding of innkeeper liability is illustrated by the following case.

BRASSEAUX V. STAND-BY CORPORATION
402 So.2d 140 (La. Ct. App.), *writ denied*, 409 So.2d 617 (La. 1981)

CHIASSON, J.: ". . . We will first consider the question of liability since we pretermitted that issue in the first appeal. The trial court found that the accident occurred as contended by the plaintiff. We find there is a causal relationship between the bees attacking and stinging the plaintiff and his slipping and falling in the shower injuring his left wrist.

"We next consider the duty owed by the motel's personnel toward this plaintiff-guest. The duty owed by an innkeeper to his guests or patrons is that of exercising reasonable and ordinary care including maintaining the premises in a reasonably safe and suitable condition and the warning of guests or patrons of any hidden or concealed perils which are known or reasonably discoverable by the innkeeper. *Brown v. Southern Ventures Corporation*, 331 So.2d 207 (La. App. 3d Cir. 1976), writ refused 344 So.2d 211 (La. 1976), and *Jarvis v. Prout*, 247 So.2d 244 (La. App. 4th Cir. 1971).

"The trial court found that the defendants breached this duty in failing to remove the bees and in failing to warn the plaintiff that there were bees about the premises. We agree with this finding. The bees were known to be on the outside of the building for a sufficient amount of time that the defendants could have had them removed. In addition, the defendants should have warned occupants of the rooms in the immediate vicinity of the existence of bees in the area and the possibility of the bees entering the rooms. We find the risk involved in this case, plaintiff slipping in a shower from warding off bees, would be encompassed within the duty to keep the premises reasonably safe and warning him of this hidden peril.

"Defendants argue that they had no control over the bees and that they were not the insurer of safety of their guests under the theory of strict liability. Because we hold defendants are liable under the negligence theory we need not address the theory of strict liability. With reference to not having control over 'Mother Nature's' insects, we agree with defendants but that does not relieve them of the duty to inspect their premises and rid it of any perils that might confront their patrons or guests. In this case the defendants, knowing of the presence of the beehive, should have had the hive removed or at least warned their patrons of its presence. Additionally, we find no merit in defendants' contention that plaintiff was contributorily negligent or that he assumed the risk."

9:16 *Condition of Areas outside the Inn*

Insert at end of section, p. 219:

In the following case, a lawsuit predicated on an innkeeper's failure to remove unnatural shrubbery from its driveway, resulting in an automobile accident that injured a hotel guest, was held to state a cause of action.

DESCHAMPS V. HERTZ CORP. [AND THE RAMADA INN]
429 So.2d. 75 (Fla. App. 1983)

PER CURIAM: "This appeal arises from a judgment on the pleadings in favor of appellees/third party defendants, Charles and Nancy Thornburgh, owners of the Key West Ramada Inn. Alexanda Stefaniw, a guest at the Ramada, was involved in an automobile accident with Richard Deschamps while attempting to exit the motel's driveway. Plaintiff, Deschamps, sued Stefaniw and Hertz Corporation, owner of the car Stefaniw was driving, in an action grounded in negligence. The defendants then impleaded the Thornburghs as third party defendants alleging that they failed to maintain their property in a safe condition in that unnatural shrubbery was positioned so as to obstruct the view of Stefaniw as he attempted to exit. Furthermore, the defendants alleged that the Thornburghs violated certain county and municipal ordinances. Plaintiff, Deschamps, also filed a direct action against the Thornburghs as defendants. The defendants/third party defendants moved for judgment on the pleadings contending there was no legal liability on their part to any of the parties. The trial court granted this motion and this appeal follows.

"Although we affirm the trial court's determination that the county and municipal ordinances were inapplicable to this case, we are compelled to reverse its decision on the remainder of the complaint. We hold that the plaintiff and the defendants stated a cause of action in their respective complaints against the Thornburghs. *See Cook v. Martin,* 330 So.2d 498 (Fla. 4th D.C.A. 1976). Accordingly, this matter is remanded to the trial court for further proceedings consistent with this opinion.

"AFFIRMED IN PART; REVERSED IN PART; AND REMANDED.

"LETTS, C.J., and BERANEK and DELL, JJ., concur."

Chapter 10. Liability of Resort Facilities

10:1 *General Rule*

Insert at end of section, p. 227:

In *Blanc v. Windham Mountain Club, Inc.,* 115 Misc. 2d 404, 454 N.Y.S.2d 383 (Sup. Ct. 1982), *aff'd,* 92 A.D.2d 529, 459 N.Y.S.2d 447 (1st Dep't 1983), a member of a private club and his wife sued the club to recover for injuries she had sustained while using the club's skiing facilities. The club counterclaimed for indemnification from the husband on the basis of an exculpatory clause in the club's bylaws wherein members agreed to hold the club harmless from claims of any kind, including employee negligence, which the plaintiffs alleged in this action. The club's motion for summary judgment dismissing the complaint was denied; the plaintiffs' cross-motion striking the affirmative defense and counterclaim was granted.

The court found first that the plaintiff wife, not being a member of the club, could not be held to any covenant barring her recovery arising out of the alleged incident relating to such membership. Second, the club's defense was insufficient as against the plaintiff husband, a member of the club, because there was no proof that the members had ever been notified of the exculpatory clause. Finally, the court held that the club was a "place of . . . recreation, or similar establishment" within the scope of the General Obligations Law, section 5–326, which prohibits such organizations, where the owner or operator receives a fee for the use of its facilities, from making covenants, agreements, or understandings that exempt the owner or operator from liability caused by or resulting from the negligence of the owner, the operator, or their agents, servants, or employees, as void against public policy. As such, the club's exculpatory clause was invalid as against public policy. The court stated that General Obligations Law, section 5–326, applied to both public and private organizations.

10:3 *Constructive Notice of Concealed Perils*

Insert at end of section, p. 232:

The following case stresses the importance courts attach to constructive notice, i.e., what the resort operator ought to have known, where the risk of harm to users of recreational equipment is concealed rather than obvious.

PAUL v. KAGAN
92 A.D.2d 988, 461 N.Y.S.2d 489 (3d Dep't 1983)

MEMORANDUM DECISION: "Cross-appeals (1) from a judgment of the Supreme Court in favor of plaintiffs, entered January 13, 1982 in Sullivan County, upon a verdict rendered at Trial Term, and (2) from an order of said court, entered January 22, 1982 in Sullivan County, which dismissed the third-party action.

"Plaintiff Geraldine Paul sustained a compression fracture of a vertebra and back strain while she was a passenger on a snowmobile rented from, and operated on a course owned by, defendant Ramada Hotel Operating Company, d/b/a Homowack Lodge, Inc. Her cause of action based on breach of implied warranty and the third-party complaint over against the operator of the machine (plaintiff's son) were dismissed by the court. There should be an affirmance.

"Initially, defendant argues that plaintiffs failed to prove a prima facie case of common-law negligence and that the court erred in its instructions to the jury concerning notice. We find that the court specifically instructed the jury to disregard and not consider any references to actual notice which was not pleaded. Although use of the words 'knew or should have known' in the jury charge might better have been otherwise phrased, it is clear that the court meticulously instructed the jury to dismiss from their minds any theory of actual notice. Moreover, it does not appear that defendant made timely or specific exception to that part of the charge and is thus bound by the charge (*Miles v. R & M Appliance Sales,* 26 N.Y.2d 451, 311 N.Y.S.2d 491, 259 N.E.2d 913).

"The record shows that the snowmobile course was examined twice daily by the employee in charge, who, after plaintiff's accident, remarked '[T]hat's a problem area. We've had problems in that area'. A landowner owes a single duty of reasonable care in all the circumstances to foresee the use of his land and the possibility of injury resulting therefrom (*Basso v. Miller,* 40 N.Y.2d 233, 386 N.Y.S.2d 564, 352 N.E.2d 868). A landowner is not an insurer of the safety of those using the property for recreational purposes so long as it does not present inherently dangerous conditions (*Scaduto v. State of New York,* 86 A.D.2d 682, 446 N.Y.S.2d 529; *Luftig v. Steinhorn,* 21 A.D.2d 760, 250 N.Y.S.2d 354, *aff'd* 16 N.Y.2d 568, 260 N.Y.S.2d 840, 208 N.E.2d 784). Before a jury may consider whether reasonable care was exercised by a landowner, a plaintiff must pass the threshold question to be determined by a court, i.e., whether the evidence presented was adequate to prove a case sufficient at law to support a favorable jury verdict, which requires proof of an existing duty, a breach of such duty, and, injury to a plaintiff as a result of the breach (*Akins v. Glens Falls City School Dist.,* 53 N.Y.2d 325, 441 N.Y.S.2d 644, 424 N.E.2d 531). Central to this appeal is the question of whether defendant had constructive notice of the defect in the snowmobile course which caused the accident, sufficient to support a finding of negligence. 'Constructive notice in this respect means such notice as the law imputes from the circumstances of the case, so that where a defective condition has existed for such a length of time that knowledge thereof should have been acquired in the exercise of reasonable care by a landlord, then such a party will be held to have known what he should have known as a result of such care' (*Batton v. Elghanayan,* 43 N.Y.2d 898, 901, 403 N.Y.S.2d 717, 374 N.E.2d 611 [COOKE, J., dissenting]). Since defendant inspected the course twice daily, the trial court, in evaluating the evidence, correctly found that plaintiffs established the elements necessary to a cause of action in negligence to entitle the case to be submitted to the jury (*Akins v. Glens Falls City School Dist.,* 53 N.Y.2d 325, 332–333, 441 N.Y.S.2d 644, 424 N.E.2d 531, *supra*). It was sufficient that the condition was a dangerous one and that defendant should reasonably have foreseen that injury could result therefrom (*Rivera v. City of New York,* 10 A.D.2d 72, 73, 197 N.Y.S.2d 261). We find no reason to disturb the jury verdict on the issue of liability. . . .

"[Affirmed.]"

10:3a   *(New Section) Tortious Breach of Contract*

Insert immediately before 10:4, p. 232:

In general, courts do not authorize recovery of punitive damages arising out of contract claims (see Chapter 7, Sec. 7:6, *supra*). In the following case, a federal circuit court of appeals distinguished between Alabama's statutory wrongful death action, which cannot arise out of a breach of contract claim because of its punitive damage basis, and an independent wrong based upon a violation of a contractual duty, which authorizes a wrongful death claim.

BAROCO v. ARASERV, INC.
621 F.2d 189 (5th Cir. 1980)

KRAVITCH, C.J.: "In this wrongful death action the jury returned a verdict for the appellee in the amount of $500,000. Appellants claim errors below including instructions to the jury, denial of a motion for directed verdict and failure to reverse as excessive the jury's award. We find these claims to be without merit; therefore, we affirm.

"On April 10, 1973 the appellant Araserv and its subsidiary entered into a contract with the state of Alabama for the operation of a recreation facility at Gulf Shores, Alabama. The contract expressly provided that it was entered into for the benefit of the public. Specifically, the contract required that Araserv operate a pavilion at the Gulf Shores beach area. Pursuant to § 16 of the contract, the appellants were obligated to provide two lifeguards for the pavilion area and to furnish all necessary life-saving equipment. Moreover, the appellants were required to take all proper safeguards for the prevention of injuries or damage to the public. The contract was scheduled to terminate five years from the opening of the Gulf Shores Park in 1974, although the precise date for the opening was not provided. Only one lifeguard was hired, however, and he was not advised of the availability of any life-saving equipment, nor had such equipment been purchased at the time of the death involved here. The lifeguard reported for work on May 12, 1974.

"May 12, 1974 was also the day on which Anthony Baroco, appellee's decedent, took his wife and family to the Gulf Shores Beach. Upon their arrival at the beach, Baroco noticed two teenagers at play in the water. Later, one of the teenagers approached Mr. Baroco and informed him that her playmate was in danger and asked for his assistance. Although the water was choppy and the waves were high, Baroco, after instructing the teenager to summon the lifeguard, went to the young girl's aid. As soon as the lifeguard was informed of the plight of the teenaged swimmer and the rescue attempt of Mr. Baroco, he also attempted a rescue. Although the lifeguard was able to swim the nearly 150 yards to the pair, he was unable to save either: the teenager already appeared dead and Baroco had panicked preventing rescue. Because the rescue attempts failed, Baroco drowned.

"Appellee filed a wrongful death action in a two-count complaint charging tortious breach of contract and negligence. At trial, this claim was submitted to the jury, which returned a vredict against the appellants, awarding appellee $500,000.

"The appellants urge several grounds for reversal: *inter alia* [footnote omitted] (1) that a breach of contract claim cannot support a wrongful death action. . . .

"Appellants first argue that the court erred in submitting the tortious breach of contract claim to the jury. Appellants base their argument on the punitive nature of Alabama's wrongful death statute: damages recoverable are punitive rather than compensatory, and because punitive damages are not recoverable in contract actions in Alabama, then a wrongful death action may not be maintained in a breach of contract claim. As the appellants contend, the Supreme Court of Alabama has specifically held that a contract claim cannot support a wrongful death action. *Clinton Geohagan v. General Motors Corp.,* 291 Ala. 167, 279 So.2d 436 (1973). The appellants are correct as far as the argument goes. The appellants have failed to focus, however, on the *tortious* nature of the instant breach of contract action. Here, the appellee did not claim that the death occurred as a result of a breach of contract, but rather the death resulted from the nonperformance of a duty *established* by the contract. In *Thaggard v. Vafes,* 218 Ala. 609, 119 So. 647 (1929), the Supreme Court of Alabama expressly held that a wrongful death action may be maintained for such tortious breach of contract. In the instant case, as provided in the contract, appellant Araserv owed a duty to patrons of the beach as third party beneficiaries of the contract to provide two lifeguards and life-saving equipment. The appellants failed to observe this duty and testimony established that the failure proximately caused the death of Baroco. [Footnote omitted.] Thus, the court was correct in submitting this claim to the jury. . . .

"[Affirmed.]"

10:7   *Violation of Statutory Duty*

Insert at end of section, p. 251:

In *Utesch v. Atlas Motor Inns, Inc.,* 687 F.2d 20 (3d Cir. 1982), plaintiff suffered a spinal injury resulting in partial quadriplegia after diving into defendant motel's swimming pool. A jury verdict for the plaintiff was reversed and the case remanded for a new trial, in part because of the trial judge's instruction about the defendant's violation of the Virgin Islands' Building Code. After getting plans for the pool approved by the Department of Public Works of the Virgin Islands, the defendant altered the plans and did not resubmit them as required by the code. The trial judge told the jury that if it found that there was a violation of the Building Code, such act raised a presumption of negligence, which the jury could find to have been a proximate cause of the accident. On appeal, this statement was held to be a reversible error because there was no evidence that the violation—the failure to resubmit the plans—was the proximate cause of the accident. An inspector for the Department of Public Works testified that the original plans for the swimming pool were inspected not for depth and type of diving board but for safety of electrical and plumbing components. Had the altered plans been submitted, a similar inspection would have been given, leaving the inference that if the Building Code had been fully complied with, there would have been no change in depth or diving board, the two characteristics that the plaintiff claimed were defective. There must be a legal or proximate cause between the statutory violation and the accident in question.

In the following case, the plaintiff brought an action to recover for injuries sustained when the plaintiff collided with snow-grooming equipment at the defendant ski resort.

PHILLIPS V. MONARCH RECREATION CORPORATION
668 P.2d 982 (Colo. App. 1983)

STERNBURG, J.: ". . .

I

"Monarch argues that the jury should not have been instructed on the statutory duty to post warning signs when snow grooming equipment is in use because the sno-cat was not grooming when the accident occurred. We disagree.

"The threshold determination of admissibility of a statute is one of relevancy. *Sego v. Mains,* 41 Colo. App. 1, 578 P.2d 1069 (1978). When the General Assembly has expressly designated the violation of a statute to be negligence, the statute is relevant if: (1) there is evidence that the alleged violation was the proximate cause of the injury, *Lambotte v. Payton,* 147 Colo. 207, 363 P.2d 167 (1961); (2) the party injured is a member of the class of persons to be protected by the statute, *Hamilton v. Gravinsky,* 28 Colo. App. 408, 474 P.2d 185 (1970); and (3) the statute can be construed to apply to the facts at issue. *Restatement (Second) of Torts* § 285 (1976).

"On its face the Ski Safety Act reveals that its purpose is to require warnings to skiers that their path may be obstructed by heavy machinery. The sno-cat involved carried the same equipment and was being operated in the same manner as if it were grooming the Catwalk. The hazard of colliding with equipment on a blind corner was the same whether or not the sno-cat was grooming. Indeed, the sno-cat would have been 'grooming' had the Catwalk not been groomed earlier that morning.

"The rule of strict construction is relaxed in the interpretation of an act designed to declare and enforce a principle of public policy. *Rinnander v. Denver Milk Producers, Inc.,* 114 Colo. 506, 166 P.2d 984 (1946). Although the act only requires a sign when equipment is 'grooming and maintaining' a ski slope, we hold that a warning sign must also be posted when a sno-cat is present on the ski slopes for those purposes but is not actively 'grooming' in that particular location. . . .

V

"As additional grounds for reversal Monarch argues that it was error to exclude language on the back of Phillips' lift ticket by which a skier was purported to have agreed that he understood and assumed the risk of skiing, and that the evidence did not support an instruction on future medical expenses and lost earning capacity. We find no error.

"Statutory provisions may not be modified by private agreement if doing so would violate the public policy expressed in the statute. *In re Marriage of Johnson,* 42 Colo. App. 198, 591 P.2d 1043 (1979). The statutes at issue here allocate the parties' respective duties with regard to the safety of those around them, and the trial court correctly excluded a purported agreement intended to alter those duties. . . .

"[Affirmed.]"

In *Grass v. Catamount Development Corporation,* 390 Mass. 551, 457 N.E.2d 627 (1983), the court interpreted section 71–P of the Massachusetts Ski Act, which requires that an action for recovery of an injury be brought within one year of the date of the injury, as not applying to wrongful-death actions, for which there is a three-year statute of limitations. The court stated that although the enactment of the Ski Act was to provide greater protection to the ski industry, its language indicates that it does not extend to the extreme and relatively rare death claim, and had the legislature so intended it would have specifically set that forth in the act.

10:10 *Contributory Negligence of Patron*

Insert immediately after Mullery v. Ro-Mill Construction Corp., *p. 262:*
   The Court of Appeals reversed the Appellate Division in *Mullary v. Ro-Mill Construction Corp.,* 54 N.Y.2d 888, 429 N.E.2d 419 (1981), holding:

MEMORANDUM.
   The order of the Appellate Division, 76 A.D.2d 802, 429 N.Y.S.2d 200, should be reversed, with costs, and the matter remitted to that court for review of the facts (C.P.L.R. 5613). Under the charge given by the trial court the jury was instructed to determine whether the decedent was so intoxicated as to be rendered incapable of understanding or appreciating the danger which confronted him. In view of this charge, to which no exception was taken, and on the evidence adduced at trial, it cannot be said, as a matter of law, that the decedent was contributorily negligent.

Chapter 11. Responsibility for Conduct of Persons in the Inn

11:1 *Protection against Injury by Third Parties: The Trend toward*
       Stricter Standards

Insert immediately after second paragraph, p. 274:

In addition to evidence with respect to a hotel's "social milieu," a court can
hear evidence concerning security measures taken at substantially similar area
hotels and motels for the purpose of determining whether the hotel at issue adequately protects its guests from third-party misconduct. In the Missouri case of
Anderson v. Malloy, 700 F.2d 1208 (8th Cir. 1983), plaintiff was raped while
she was staying at defendant hotel. The court held that differences in the physical
layout between the defendant hotel and area hotels notwithstanding, evidence
concerning security measures at similar area hotels was relevant to the adequacy
of the defendant's security measures.

Insert immediately after Peters v. Holiday Inns, Inc., *p. 283:*

The case to follow illustrates the judicial trend toward relating standards of
reasonable care for the physical safety of hotel guests from third-party criminal
misconduct to the size, class, and quality of services represented to the public.
Moreover, and of equal importance, the case disallows the defense that the industry, lacking any standards, thus immunizes itself from liability. The jury is
permitted reasonable latitude to set its own standards in such cases.

ORLANDO EXECUTIVE PARK, INC., v. P.D.R.
402 So.2d 442 (Fla. Dist. Ct. App. 1981)
pet. for rev. denied,
411 So.2d 384 (1981), *decision approved, Orlando Executive Park, Inc. v. Rob-
bins,* 433 So.2d 491 (Fla. 1983)

ORFINGER, J.: ". . . "On October 22, 1975, [plaintiff] was in Orlando performing the duties of her employment. She telephoned the Howard Johnson's
Motor Lodge involved in this action at approximately 9:30 P.M. and made a room
reservation. [Footnote omitted.] Approximately ten minutes later she left the restaurant and drove directly to the motor lodge. When she arrived, she signed the
registration form which had already been filled out by the desk clerk and was directed to her room which was located on the ground level in building 'A', the
first building behind the registration office. Plaintiff parked her car, went to her
room and left her suitcase there. She then went back to her car to get some papers
and when starting back to her room, she noticed a man standing in a walkway behind the registration office. Having reentered the building and while proceeding
back along the interior hallway to her room, she was accosted by the man she had
seen behind the registration office, who struck her very hard in the throat and on
the back of her neck and then choked her until she became unconscious. When
consciousness returned, plaintiff found herself lying on the floor of the hallway

with her assailant sitting on top of her, grabbing her throat. Plaintiff was physically unable to speak and lapsed into an unconscious or semi-conscious state. Her assailant stripped her jewelry from her and then dragged her down the hallway to a place beneath a secluded stairwell, where he kicked her and brutally forced her to perform an unnatural sex act. He then disappeared in the night and has never been identified.

"Plaintiff's action for damages was based on her claim that defendants owed her the legal duty to exercise reasonable care for her safety while she was a guest on the premises. And she alleged that this duty had been breached by, *inter alia,* allowing the building to remain open and available to anyone who cared to enter, by failing to have adequate security on the premises either on the night in question or prior thereto so as to deter criminal activity against guests which had occurred before and which could foreseeably occur again, failing to install TV monitoring equipment in the public areas of the motel to deter criminal activity, failing to establish and enforce standards of operation at the lodge which would protect guests from physical attack and theft of property, and failure to warn plaintiff that there had been prior criminal activity on the premises and that such activity would or might constitute a threat to her safety on the premises. . . .

"There was evidence submitted tending to show serious physical and psychological injury as a result of this assault which was susceptible of the conclusion that within a year following the assault, plaintiff lost her job because of memory lapses, mental confusion and inability to tolerate and communicate with people. There was evidence from which the jury could conclude that this injury was permanent and that she would require expensive, long-term medical and psychiatric treatment, and that she had suffered a great loss in her earning capacity. . . .

"There was no regular security force at the motor lodge, nor were there other security devices such as TV monitors in hallways or other common areas. One security guard was employed from time to time, on a sporadic basis. For the six-month period prior to the incident in question, management of the motor lodge was aware of approximately thirty criminal incidents occurring on the premises. While most of these involved burglary, some of them involved direct attacks upon the guests. Following one of the attacks, approximately ten weeks prior to the incident in question, the motor lodge owners had hired a full-time security guard, but he was terminated a short time later. Anticipating high occupancy, one security guard had been employed for the evening in question commencing at 10:00 P.M. While it is not clear whether the attack occurred during the period this guard was on duty, the jury could have concluded that he was not on duty at the time, although he was on the premises becoming familiar with the layout because he had never been on the property before. Additionally, the evidence indicated that the guard had been employed to patrol the parking areas, and not the motor lodge buildings. The security service which provided the guards from time to time, had recommended the employment of two to three guards on a full-time basis. Plaintiff's security expert testified that three guards on staggered shifts would be necessary to deter criminal activity, although he agreed that there were no industry standards for security guards and that it was impossible to say that the assault would not have occurred if three guards had been on the premises. He did, however, testify that in his opinion, a proper security force would serve as a deterrent to this type of activity and the chance of this happening would be slight.

I. Liability of Orlando Executive Park, Inc.

"It seems clear in Florida registered guests in a hotel or motel are business invitees to whom the hotel or motel owes a duty of reasonable care for their safety. *Phillips Petroleum Company of Bartlesville, Oklahoma v. Dorn*, 292 So.2d 429 (Fla. 4th D.C.A. 1974). While recognizing this principle and conceding this duty, appellants say, nevertheless, that there is no evidence of a breach of their duty, since the injury to appellee was caused by the criminal act of a stranger, thus acting as an intervening efficient cause for which they are not responsible.

"The evidence clearly shows numerous criminal activities on the premises in the six-month period immediately prior to this occurrence. [Footnote omitted.] The testimony of a security expert produced by plaintiff indicated adequate security at this motor lodge required the presence of at least three full-time security guards. Thus the question becomes one of foreseeability. Could a jury, under the facts of this case reasonably conclude that the absence of adequate security would lead to the robbery and attack here? [Footnote omitted.] Such is ordinarily a question for the jury. *Rosier v. Gainesville Inns Associates, Ltd.*, 347 So.2d 1100 (Fla. 1st D.C.A. 1977). . . . We first reject, as entirely fallacious, the defendant's claim that the brutal and deliberate act of the rapist-murderer constituted an 'independent intervening cause' which served to insulate it from liability. It is well-established that if the reasonable possibility of the intervention, criminal or otherwise, of a third party is the avoidable risk of harm which itself causes one to be deemed negligent, the occurrence of that very conduct cannot be a superseding cause of a subsequent misadventure. . . .

"Appellant continues, however, with its argument that there was no evidence that security was inadequate or more to the point, that any specific quantity of security guards or other measures would have prevented this robbery and attack. They say that since there are no standards for security in the motel industry, there is no way for a jury to determine the reasonableness (or unreasonableness) of any particular security measure. The absence of industry standards does not insulate the defendants from liability when there is credible evidence presented to the jury pointing to measures reasonably available to deter incidents of this kind, against which the jury can judge the reasonableness of the measures taken *in this case*.

"Obviously, a six-unit, one building 'Mom and Pop' motel will not have the same security problems as a large highrise thousand room hotel, or of a three hundred room motor lodge spread out over six buildings. Each presents a peculiar security problem of its own. How the means necessary to fulfill the duty of care varies with the peculiar circumstances of each case is explained by the Wisconsin Supreme Court in *Peters v. Holiday Inns, Inc.,* 89 Wis. 2d 115, 278 N.W.2d 208 (1979). . . .

"Here, the jury had the right to consider that the size and layout of the complex, its various accessory uses and the apparent ease of entrance into the motel buildings, and could have concluded that these factors required *some* security measures. They could also conclude from the evidence that the type of activity within the complex increased the security risk and that no security was provided at the time of this attack.

"And while appellant suggests plaintiff was required to show the attack would have been prevented had reasonable measures been taken, this is not the test. Causation, like any other element of plaintiff's case, need not be demonstrated by conclusive proof:

"and it is enough that [plaintiff] introduces evidence from which reasonable men may conclude that it is more probable that the event was caused by the defendant, than that it was not. The fact of causation is incapable of mathematical proof, since no man can say with absolute certainty what would have occurred if the defendant had acted otherwise.

"W. Prosser, *Law of Torts,* § 41 at 242 (4th ed. 1977). Plaintiff adduced evidence that reasonable measures were not taken. Expert testimony, as well as reasonable inferences from the suggested measures, allowed a conclusion that the chance of this attack was 'slight' had reasonable measures been taken. Thus the question of whether defendant's negligence was the proximate cause of plaintiff's injury was properly a jury question. *See Helman v. Seaboard Coast Line Railroad Co.,* 349 So.2d 1187, 1189 (Fla. 1977); *Yamada v. Hilton Hotel Corp.,* 17 Ill. Dec. at 233, 376 N.E.2d at 232.

"Plaintiff also proved that the area under the stairwell where she was dragged was dark and secluded and was in itself a security hazard which should have been boarded up as had other similar stairwells in the motel. OEP management actively discouraged criminal investigations by sheriff's deputies, minimizing any deterrent effect they may have had. Thus, the totality of the circumstances presented a jury question regarding causation. . . . It cannot be said that there was a complete absence of probative facts to support the jury's conclusion. *See Yamada v. Hilton Hotel Corp.,* 17 Ill. Dec. at 233, 376 N.E.2d at 232. . . .

"The judgment appealed from is affirmed."

Insert after second full paragraph, p. 283:

In *Davenport v. Nixon,* 434 So.2d 1203 (La. Ct. App. 1983), the defendant innkeeper's check-in window was located in the hotel parking lot. The plaintiff was assaulted and robbed in the parking lot, immediately in front of the check-in window, by an assailant who had watched plaintiff expose a large quantity of money while paying the desk clerk. The court held that the defendant's check-in method unreasonably increased the risk of attacks on patrons.

Insert immediately before 11:2, p. 283:

Recently, courts have increased innkeepers' duty of care by expanding the scope of "constructive notice." In particular, a court will charge an innkeeper with constructive notice of a criminal incident even if previous criminal incidents that have occurred on the inn's premises have differed both in kind and in location from the incident at bar.[a]

In *Urbanov v. Days Inns of America, Inc.*, 58 N.C. App. 795, 295 S.E.2d 40 (1982), the court held that the existence of twelve criminal episodes on the motel premises, including one armed robbery and several illegal entries during the three months preceding the assault at issue, was sufficient to give the innkeeper constructive notice that security measures in the parking lot where plaintiff was assaulted were inadequate.

In the following case, the Missouri Supreme Court charged the defendants with possessing sufficient constructive notice of a criminal attack on the basis of a few, dissimilar prior acts of misconduct.

VIRGINIA D. v. MADESCO INVESTMENT CORP.
648 S.W.2d 881 (Mo. 1983)

BLACKMAR, J.: "Bel Air Hilton is a first class motor hotel located just across the street from Mansion House Center in the easternmost portion of downtown St. Louis, near the two downtown bus stations and Interstate 70. It has 17 stories, with an attached parking garage having access to the hotel elevators on six levels. The hotel has an upper lobby at street level containing the registration and cashiers windows, a small gift shop, and the entrances to the two restaurants. There are two revolving doors on the west side facing Fourth Street, one near the registration area and the other opposite the entrance to Trader Vic's, one of the restaurants in the hotel. Each of the revolving doors has a hinged door on each side. There is also a rear entrance used by employees, and for making deliveries. The lower lobby may be reached by a flight of stairs from the main floor or by elevator from any level of the hotel. The hotel offices are located off the lower lobby, as are men's and ladies' restrooms, the latter being the scene of the events involved in this case. The lower level also contains banquet and meeting rooms.

"Besides Trader Vic's, the hotel has a Miss Hullings restaurant. The restaurants are apparently under separate ownership, utilizing leased space, but the evidence would support a finding that they are integral parts of the hotel complex. Both restaurants serve liquor.

"After work on September 24, 1976 the plaintiff and some friends went to the Miss Hullings restaurant intending to eat dinner. They arrived before the dinner hour and ordered beer. One of the plaintiff's companions left to use the restroom

[a]But *cf.* Highlands Insurance Co. v. Gilday, 398 So.2d 834 (Fla. Dist. Ct. App. 1981), *petition for rev. denied*, 411 So.2d 382 (Fla. 1981) (previous misconduct, including disgruntled employee's threat and a breaking and entering, held not to give hotel sufficient constructive notice that guests were inadequately protected against criminal attacks); McCoy v. Gay, 165 Ga. App. 590, 302 S.E.2d 130 (1983) (previous purse-snatching and robbery on hotel premises not sufficient to give hotel constructive notice that parking lot was inadequately secured).

and returned after about five minutes. Miss Hullings has no public restrooms. Patrons of Miss Hullings could use the restrooms in Trader Vic's or those on the lower level of the hotel. After her companion returned the plaintiff went to the restroom, deciding to use the lower level facilities because Trader Vic's restrooms can be reached only through a noisy bar.

"The plaintiff probably visited the restroom at about 5:30 P.M. She testified that she saw nobody in the lower lobby or in the ladies' restroom before entering the cubicle. There had been a meeting on the lower level during the day but it had adjourned and the banquet room was being set up for an evening affair for the same group, with six to eight people working there. The doors from the lower lobby to the banquet room were open. The usual quitting hour for employees in the office was 5:00 P.M. Operations Manager Raymond Baddock was still there, and he testified that three other employees were also. The restroom consists of a toilet room and a lavatory room, separated by walls, with a rather narrow passage. As the plaintiff was leaving the cubicle she was grabbed from behind by a man, threatened, and sexually abused. Since the defendant does not deny the attack, and does not challenge the amount of the verdict, further detail is not necessary. The attacker ran out of the restroom, pursued by a bellhop who had gone to the lower level to move some suitcases and heard the plaintiff's screams. Baddock also heard the screams and joined the chase, as did other employees. The bellhop made the capture and the plaintiff noted the hour as 5:48 P.M.

"The assailant was arrested, identified, and eventually sentenced on a plea of guilty. There is some variation in the evidence as to his manner of dress, but all witnesses agreed that nothing in his appearance would have caused any hotel employee to detain or question him if he had been seen to enter the hotel by one of the street level doors and then to enter the elevator or go down the stairs to the lower lobby. Any person who presented a reasonably neat appearance and was not obviously intoxicated or otherwise disorderly would be allowed to enter the hotel for the purpose of using the lower level restrooms. Nor would it be difficult to enter the garage on foot, since there was only one attendant and he would often be involved in checking cars out.

"There was substantial evidence that persons having no proper business in the hotel and not scrupulous about respect for law and property entered with some regularity and were a cause of concern to the hotel authorities. Management was on the alert for prostitutes. Former manager Charles Powers testified that they would sometimes take the elevators to the upper floors, while Baddock said that they operated in the restaurants and bars. Vandalism and 'burglary' of automobiles occurred in the garage. Young boys created problems by gathering in the lower lobby, sometimes two or three times a week. There had been vandalism in the men's restroom and coins were removed from the 'wishing pool' at the foot of the stairs. A person who had worked at the hotel as a security guard expressed concern about thefts from the gift shop. On one occasion an 'arsenal' was found in a room, apparently brought in by registered guests. There was, however, no evidence of recent incidents of rape, assault, robbery or other violent crime in or near the hotel.[3] Nor was there any evidence of previous criminal activity or violence in the lower level ladies' room.

"No employees of the hotel were regularly stationed in the lower lobby, in positions from which they could observe the lobby and the adjoining restroom area. The four to six women who worked in the hotel offices used this restroom, and it may be assumed that it would have been in heavy use during a banquet or meeting on the lower level. The hotel had no television monitor in the lower lobby but did maintain one at the back door. There was a single security officer on duty 24 hours a day, supplied under contract by a private agency. This agency had recommended that an additional guard or guards be employed. The security officer's regular rounds took him elsewhere at the time the plaintiff was attacked, and he did not regularly visit the lower lobby. There was evidence that the downstairs restrooms had been locked after 5:00 P.M. in the past as a security measure, when there were no evening functions scheduled in the banquet rooms. [Footnote omitted.] The manager of Miss Hullings complained and the practice was abandoned.

"Any suggestion that crime is not foreseeable is particularly inappropriate when a downtown metropolitan area is involved especially when the case involves a hotel. [Footnote omitted.] Our traditional innkeeper statutes, in providing that an innkeeper may provide a safe for valuables and may avoid extraordinary liabilities by posting notice of its availability, recognize that hotels are very public places and that guests may be the victims of crime. §§ 419.010–020, R.S. Mo. 1978. Colonel Warren, in saying that there is some crime everywhere, and Manager Baddock, in testifying that rape was a possibility, simply reflect common experience, as did the trial judge in his statement that 'rape can occur anywhere.' Certain people, for reasons we do not fully understand, are disposed toward violent crime, and act without apparent motive. Some men subject women who are strangers to atrocious physical indignities. The operator of a hotel to which the public has easy access, in the discharge of the duties imposed on account of the innkeeper's special relationship to the guests, should not be heard to say that he had no inkling that crime of the kind here involved might occur on his premises simply because there had been none in the past. There is no requirement that there be at least one mugging or rape before the innkeeper is obliged to consider the possibility. The duty is one of the appropriate degree of care under the circumstances.

"The defendant cites some of the numerous cases holding that a hotel operator, or other owner of premises to which the public is invited, is not liable for the consequences of a sudden and unanticipated assault, committed by a person who has given no prior reason for suspicion. [Footnote omitted.] We agree that the defendant could not be found negligent on the basis of the assailant's presence in

---

[3]The trial court excluded evidence of an assault in 1971 and a reported rape in a guest room in 1973 as too remote.

the hotel, but only up to the point at which he entered the ladies' room. Had his entry there been observed by a hotel employee, an immediate duty to take action would have arisen. [Footnote omitted.] But the entry was not observed. Nothing in the record shows where the attacker came from or when he went into the ladies' room. The plaintiff would have a case for the jury, then, only on the basis that security measures suggested in the evidence could increase the likelihood that the attacker would have been discovered by the plaintiff or somebody else in time to prevent the assault. We must determine whether there is substantial evidence to support such a finding.

"There is ample evidence that persons on the fringe of the law, and some quite over the border, could enter, remain, and misbehave in the hotel without great difficulty. There were continuing problems with prostitutes. 'Burglaries' of cars, and thefts, took place in the garage. We do not agree that incidents in the garage are necessarily insufficient to provide warning with regard to the hotel proper, since persons in the garage could easily enter the hotel and could go to any level on the elevator. *See Murphy v. Penn Fruit Co.*, 274 Pa. Super. 427, 418 A.2d 480 (1980). A former security guard at the hotel testified about thefts in the gift shop, off the upper lobby. Then there were problems with young men or boys who gathered in the lower lobby as often as two or three times a week and who probably vandalized the men's room. Colonel Warren testified that persons so assembling would pose potential danger. The jury could find that this evidence of past incidents was sufficient to alert management to the possibility of crime on the premises, so as to invoke the duty of exercising an appropriate degree of care to protect hotel guests from criminal victimization.

"Nor can it be said that the duty of anticipation extends only to crimes similar in nature and seriousness to those that have occurred in the past. *See Orlando Executive Park, Inc. v. P.D.R.*, 402 So.2d 442 (Fla. Dist. Ct. App. 1981), (burglaries sufficient to alert hotel operator to possibility of attack); *Mozlak v. Ettinger*, 25 Ill. App. 3d 706, 323 N.E.2d 796 (1975), (attempted break-ins at women's residence indicated possibility of assault); *Jenness v. Sheraton-Cadillac Properties, Inc.*, 48 Mich. App. 723, 211 N.W.2d 106 (1973), (in which hotel employees allowed a prostitute to loiter and she assaulted a guest who refused her solicitations); *Morgan v. Bucks Associates*, 428 F. Supp. 546 (E.D. Pa. 1977), (holding that auto thefts on parking lot should alert owner to danger of assaults, citing Restatement (Second) of Torts § 281, Comment (j) (1965)). . . .

"The jury might have sensed that the lower lobby was quite a lonely place after 5 P.M. on September 24, 1977. The meeting participants had departed and most of the employees in the office had left. The employees in the large banquet room, setting up for an evening affair, undoubtedly gave very little attention to the lobby area. Former Manager Powers considered the lower lobby an area of concern, and had tried or suggested various security measures. The jury well might have felt that criminal types might enter the hotel from the street, or even take out rooms, and might gravitate to the lower lobby at a time when traffic was at a minimum, creating the potential for severe harassment or violence directed against guests.

"The evidence suggests a variety of possibilities for improving security on the lower level, including a television monitor in the lobby, locking the restrooms or a gate which might be placed at the head of the stairs when there are no activities downstairs, detail of an employee who could observe the lower lobby and restroom entrances or of a matron for the ladies' room, and an increase in the security force.

"It is not for us to decide whether any one or more of these measures would be necessary, practical, or effective. All we need say is that the jury might have concluded that precautions were available which might have increased the chances of dissuading the attacker from entering the ladies' room, of discovering his entry, or of interrupting him before he caused substantial harm to the plaintiff. The plaintiff is not obliged to prove that the utilization of security measures would surely have prevented the assault. *Mayer v. Housing Authority of Jersey City*, 84 N.J. Super. 411, 202 A.2d 439, 447 (1964); *Orlando Executive Park, Inc. v. P.D.R.*, 402 So.2d 442 (Fla. Dist. Ct. App. 1981) (plaintiff does not have the burden of showing that the security measures would necessarily have been effective). . . .

"Evidence of feasibility and cost could also have been presented to the jury. The manager testified that there was a program of security training for employees, but the employee who made the capture, although described as having an important position, said that he had no security training. The jury might well have felt that there had been insufficient attention to security, and that added security precautions might have increased the chances for avoiding the incident.

"The evidence of the witness claiming to be a security expert, to the effect that the ladies' room could have been so designed as to increase the possibility that an intruder would have been discovered, was also before the jury. We do not have to decide whether this evidence, in and of itself, would have been sufficient to support a finding of negligent design giving rise to a submissible case. The jury could properly consider her testimony along with the other evidence.

"We conclude that the question whether the defendant exercised the proper degree of care under the circumstances, and the question of causation, were issues to be decided by the jury and should not have been preempted by the court. The jury was certainly not obliged to find negligence under the circumstances, but there was substantial evidence on which it could have made this finding. It follows that the judgment must be reversed and the cause remanded with directions to reinstate the judgment on the verdict for the plaintiff."

11:2 *Liability of Occupiers of Premises Other than Hotels*

Insert at end of section, p. 284:

Illustrative of a trend toward subjecting shopping centers and malls to higher standards of care is the decision of the North Carolina Supreme Court in *Foster v. Winston-Salem Joint Venture*, 303 N.C. 636, 281 S.E.2d 36 (1981). In *Foster*, plaintiff was assaulted in the parking lot of defendant's mall during the Christmas season. The evidence showed that defendant had only one guard assigned to the large mall parking lot during the busy season and that thirty-one incidents of crime, including four or five assaults, had occurred in the lot during the previous year. Consequently, the court reversed a summary judgment granted in the lower court in favor of the defendant and concluded that a reasonable jury could find that the defendant could have foreseen the assault upon the plaintiff at bar.

11:3 *Liability in Landlord-Tenant Relationships*

Insert after Totten v. More Oakland Residential Housing, Inc., *p. 287:*

Since *Kline v. 1500 Massachusetts Avenue Apartment Corp.*, courts have approached the issue of landlords' liability for criminal attacks upon tenants in two different ways. Some courts, like the *Kline* court, find an implied warranty of habitability running in favor of tenants. *Trentacost v. Brussel*, 82 N.J. 214, 412 A.2d 436 (1980). Other courts, also like the *Kline* court, deem the landlord-tenant relationship a "special relationship" in which the landlord owes the duty to protect the tenant from third-party misconduct. *Kwaitkowski v. Superior Trading Co.*, 123 Cal. App. 3d 324, 176 Cal. Rptr. 494 (1981).[b]

In *Feld v. Merriam*, —— Pa. ——, 485 A.2d 742 (1984), the Supreme Court of Pennsylvania held that a landlord is under no duty to protect tenants from foreseeable criminal acts by third parties. In that case, the plaintiff was robbed and raped in the defendant's apartment-building garage. The court stated that a duty to protect tenants from criminal intrusion could only be incurred by a landlord voluntarily by a specific agreement, or by providing a program of security.

11:4a *(New Section) Protection against Injury to Employees*

Insert immediately before 11:5, p. 290:

Whether an employer has a "special relationship" with the employees that creates a duty on the employer to provide adequate protection from third-party misconduct has not been clearly decided by any court. In a recent Illinois decision dealing with innkeepers, however, the court "assumed" such a special relationship when it analyzed the facts, although it did not specifically hold that such a relationship existed. *Ozment v. Lance,* 107 Ill. App. 3d 348, 437 N.E.2d 930 (1982). The plaintiff, a seventeen-year-old boy, was assaulted by two guests while he was delivering beer to their room. The court held that even if a duty

[b]But *cf.* Riley v. Marcus, 125 Cal. App. 3d 103, 177 Cal. Rptr. 827 (1981), and King v. Ilikai Properties, Inc., 2 Hawaii Ct. App. 359, 632 P.2d 657 (1981), in which the ordinary negligence standard was used.

existed on the part of the innkeeper to protect its employees from third-party misconduct, the hotel was not liable here because there had been no previous criminal attacks of any kind in the hotel; this attack, therefore, was completely unforeseeable.

11:6   *Employee's Abusive Conduct*

Insert at end of section, p. 292:

But compare *Pollock v. Holsa Corp.*, 114 Misc. 2d 1076, 454 N.Y.S.2d 582 (App. Term. 1st Dep't 1982), *aff'd as modified*, 98 A.D.2d 265, 470 N.Y.S. 2d 151 (1st Dep't 1984), in which an employee was held not to be "discourteous" or "abusive" when he mistakenly terminated plaintiff's stay one day early, preventing plaintiff from returning to room during early-morning hours. On appeal, the trial court's dismissal of the plaintiff's claim for damages resulting from emotional harm was affirmed. The appellate court, however, reversed the trial court's dismissal of the plaintiff's clam of physical harm. See sec. 8:7, *supra*, pp. 56–57. Compare *Eckhart v. Robert E. Lee Motel,* 20 Ohio App. 3d 80, 440 N.E.2d 824 (1981): sleeping guest not entitled to a refund after a man had entered her motel doorway, apparently by mistake.

11:8   *Employer's Liability under the Doctrine of* Respondeat Superior

Insert at end of section, p. 299:

When the nature of an employee's duties are such that the employer necessarily contemplates that the employee will occasionally be required to use force, the employer is not necessarily relieved of liability merely because the employee uses more force than is necessary in the performance of a particular job.

In *Sage Club v. Hunt,* 638 P.2d 161 (Wyo. 1981), the bartender at the defendant's club assaulted a patron who disagreed with him over the amount that the patron owed for drinks. The court affirmed the holding of the lower court that the bartender was acting within the scope of his duties when he assaulted the plaintiff. The court said:

> Here Mr. Thyfault's [the bartender's] duties included collecting money for drinks, and he lost his temper over that matter. His duties also included keeping order in the bar and removing disruptive customers which Thyfault apparently tried to do by pushing appellee down the stairs. . . . Appellant evidently allowed Thyfault to use force at his discretion, and he was performing work of the kind he was employed to perform. . . . This Court will therefore not indulge in nice distinctions to determine whether excessive force was motivated by personal reasons. *Id.* at 163.

In *Cappo v. Vinson Guard Services Inc.,* 60 A.D.2d 615, 400 N.Y.S. 2d 148 (1981), the court held that the defendant restaurant was liable for the acts of its parking-lot guard when the guard struck the plaintiff during a dispute over parking privileges. The court found that the dispute occurred in the course of the guard's duties in enforcing parking regulations. *Id.* at 151.

11:10 *Duty to Rescue and Aid Guests*

Insert after excerpt from Stahlin v. Hilton Hotels Corporation, *p. 307:*

In *Boles v. La Quinta Motor Inns, Inc.*, 680 F.2d 1077 (5th Cir. 1982), a Texas decision, plaintiff, Mrs. Boles, was bound, gagged, and raped in her room while a guest at the defendant motel. She managed to telephone the motel's front desk but was forced to speak to several different motel employees before one of them, a desk clerk, would contact the police. Plaintiff claimed that the desk clerk spoke sarcastically to her and refused to send motel employees to help her, though plaintiff told the clerk that she feared the rapist's return. Unknown to the plaintiff, two relief managers stood outside her door, listening to her terrified screams but failing to comfort her, while they waited for the police to arrive.

The court of appeals found the defendant negligent in failing to respond more quickly to the plaintiff's peril. Plaintiff was awarded $43,000 in damages for the mental anxiety she suffered while waiting for the hotel employees to respond to her situation.

Insert at the end of section, p. 307:

The following case reiterates a basic rule of the law of negligence in the delivery of medical aid to a hotel guest. The delay in rendering such aid, no matter how unreasonable, must be the proximate cause of the guest's injuries, including pain and suffering, to be actionable.

ROOM v. CARIBE HILTON HOTEL
659 F.2d 5 (1st Cir. 1981)

CAMPBELL, C.J.: "Plaintiff Herbert Room commenced this diversity action to recover damages allegedly arising out of a heart attack he suffered on November 24, 1976, while a guest at defendant Caribe Hilton Hotel. At the close of plaintiff's case-in-chief, the district court granted a directed verdict for defendant and plaintiff appeals. We affirm.

"The facts as viewed in the light most favorable to plaintiff, *see, e.g., Carlson v. American Safety Equipment Corp.*, 528 F.2d 384, 385 (1st Cir. 1976), are as follows. Herbert Room arrived in Puerto Rico on November 24, 1976 and registered as a guest at the Caribe Hilton Hotel in San Juan. That evening, Room gambled at the hotel casino. As he was leaving the casino, he began to feel weak and returned to his room. Upon arriving there, he felt nauseous, and therefore called the hotel operator, after reading the following section in the hotel service directory:

"A registered nurse is on duty, and a qualified physician is available at all times. Call doctor's office for appointment 8:30 A.M. to 5:00 P.M., Monday through Friday. After hours and Saturdays and Sundays, call: Telephone operator. Nurse will be glad to make dental appointments. Call: Ext. 1740.

"This first call to the operator took place, according to Room, at 7:30 P.M. He requested a doctor, although he did not describe his symptoms, and testified that the operator told him she would get him one. At 11:30 P.M., he called the operator and again requested a doctor, again making no mention of his symptoms. The operator tried to call one of three doctors listed on a hotel roster as available to treat guests, but his line was busy. She then called Room, who told her to keep trying. Five or ten minutes later she tried again to call the doctor, but his line was still busy. She informed Room, who again asked her to keep trying. She tried to call the other doctors on the list, but was unable to make contact with any of them. Once again, she called Room, who again asked her to keep trying. At no time did she call the 24-hour emergency number of the San Jorge Hospital, although that number was also listed on her roster. Eventually, Room called some friends in Puerto Rico, who advised him to take a cab to the Presbyterian Hospital, which he did. They also called the hotel operator and informed her that she could stop trying to call the doctor.

"Room arrived at the hospital at approximately 1:15 A.M. His condition was diagnosed as a myocardial infarction, or heart attack. He remained hospitalized for almost a month. In the course of that time, he suffered two more serious incidents involving his heart, acute cardiac failure on November 30, and paroxysmal tachycardia on December 8.

"After being released from the hospital, Room returned to his home in New York and took a job as a converter in the textile industry. He quit approximately nine months later because he was unable to keep enough information in his head to do his job satisfactorily. He now suffers from a poor memory and head pains, complaints he never had before his heart attack.

"Room sued the hotel, alleging that it had breached a duty under Puerto Rico law to provide him with adequate medical care by failing to put him in touch with a doctor from the time he first called the operator until he left for the hospital. Room alleged that this delay caused him permanent brain damage, and claimed $1 million in damages for hospital and medical expenses, loss of earnings, and pain and suffering. In directing a verdict for the defendant, the district court found, *inter alia,* that the delay in providing plaintiff with medical attention was not a proximate cause of his injuries. [Footnote omitted.]

"Assuming *arguendo* that the defendant breached a duty to exercise reasonable care in providing medical care to its guests,[2] the plaintiff must still establish a causal relation between the defendant's negligence and the plaintiff's injury. *See, e.g., Portilla v. Carreras Schira,* 95 P.R.R. 785, 793 (1968). In discussing this issue, it is necessary to distinguish the plaintiff's permanent brain damage from any pain and mental anguish he may have suffered during the time when the defendant failed to provide him with a doctor. We shall address the permanent injuries first.

"The plaintiff's sole expert testimony concerning his medical condition was given by Dr. Jose Luis Freyre, a clinical neurologist. Dr. Freyre examined the

---

[2]We do not decide whether such a duty actually existed or whether it was breached in this case.

plaintiff on November 1, 1978. He had no contact with plaintiff at any time prior to this; specifically, he did not treat plaintiff during his hospitalization in 1976.

"Dr. Freyre testified as to plaintiff's loss of some cerebral function, and testified further that the heart attack of November 24 could have caused this condition. On cross-examination, however, he admitted that the hospital's records of plaintiff's condition at the time of his admission were not complete enough to determine with any degree of certainty whether the November 24 attack did indeed cause any brain damage. In particular, the lack of any information as to plaintiff's blood pressure at the time of admission made it impossible for Dr. Freyre to ascertain whether the attack had resulted in any significant decrease in blood flow to the brain.

"Most significantly, Dr. Freyre was unable to determine which of the three heart-related incidents suffered by plaintiff caused the brain damage. The following colloquy took place between the court and Dr. Freyre:
"THE COURT: [C]ould the second [heart failure] have been the cause of [plaintiff's] condition?
"THE WITNESS: It could have.
"THE COURT: Is there any way of telling whether it was the second or the first?
"THE WITNESS: No way of telling whether it was the first, second or third.

"It is not disputed that the delay in rendering medical assistance on November 24 was not a cause of the two subsequent cardiac incidents. There was no evidence that the delay on November 24 was a more likely cause of plaintiff's condition than were the other two incidents. In such a situation, any determination by the jury that the delay did cause the injury would be pure speculation and conjecture. Such speculation is not permitted. *Widow of Delgado v. Boston Insurance Co.,* 99 P.R.R. 693, 702–04 (1971); W. Prosser, Handbook of the Law of Torts § 41, at 241 (4th ed. 1971). The directed verdict for defendant as to plaintiff's permanent brain damage was therefore proper.

"The evidence of any mental anguish[3] that plaintiff may have suffered during the delay in obtaining medical treatment was also insufficient to overcome defendant's motion for a directed verdict. Plaintiff's sole evidence on this issue is as follows. He testified that during the time he was in the hotel room waiting for the operator to contact a doctor, he was weak and had few lucid moments. He said he had some pains in his back and arms, and that at one point they became very severe, at which time he felt that he was going to die.

"There was, however, no evidence that the delay alone caused any pain or mental suffering. Defendant quite rightly points out that the heart attack itself —an event for which defendant was not responsible—would be accompanied by some pain, regardless of the speed with which help arrived. There was no attempt by plaintiff to show the extent to which prompt medical attention would

---

[3]Under Puerto Rico law, a plaintiff may recover damages for mental suffering, even without any physical injury being alleged or proven. *See Compagnia Nationale Air France v. Castano,* 358 F.2d 203 (1st Cir. 1966); *Muriel v. Suazo,* 72 P.R.R. 348 (1951); *Rivera v. Rossi,* 64 P.R.R. 683 (1945).

have alleviated his pain, if at all. Given this failure even to attempt to apportion the damages between the delay and the heart attack,[4] no reasonable jury could conclude that the delay alone caused any pain or mental suffering.

"Similarly, the proof of mental anguish based on plaintiff's fear that he was going to die was insufficient. Again, there is no evidence that he would not have feared for his life even after receiving medical attention. The fact that he suffered two more cardiac-related crises while in the hospital certainly suggests that he was not out of danger even after his hospitalization. Moreover, plaintiff did not describe how long he feared for his life or how great that fear was. Any attempt by the jury to assign a dollar value to this injury based on the testimony described above could only be the result of speculation and conjecture. While plaintiff's testimony may amount to a scintilla of evidence that the delay caused him substantial mental anguish, that is not sufficient to overcome a motion for a directed verdict. *See, e.g., Trinidad v. Pan American World Airways, Inc.,* 575 F.2d 983, 985 (1st Cir. 1978).

"*Affirmed.*"

In a single California case, the court even went so far as to hold a tavern liable for the wrongful death of a patron in a tavern *across the street.* In *Soldano v. O'Daniels,* 141 Cal. App. 3d 443, 190 Cal. Rptr. 310 (1983), plaintiff's husband was shot and killed in a bar across the street from the defendant's bar (the Circle Inn). A patron of the other bar came into the Circle Inn and asked the bartender if he could use the phone to call the police to break up a fight that was going on at the other bar. The bartender refused, and plaintiff's husband was subsequently shot and killed during the fight in the other bar. The court held that the bartender at the Circle Inn was negligent in refusing the use of the phone to the patron. While the court acknowledged that no "special relationship" existed between the bartender at the Circle Inn and plaintiff's husband, the court viewed its holding as a natural extension of the principle that people are liable for negligent interference with a person attempting to render necessary aid.

11:13 *Restaurant Keeper's Duty to Protect Patrons*

Insert at end of section, p. 322:

Restaurants, like hotels, are subject to increasingly higher standards of care with respect to protecting guests from third-party misconduct.

In *Jones v. Oberg,* 52 Or. Ct. App. 601, 628 P.2d 773, *pet. for rev. denied,* 639 P.2d 1280 (1981), plaintiff, immediately after exiting defendant's tavern, was struck by a beer bottle thrown in defendant's parking lot. The court held the defendant negligent for requiring the plaintiff to leave the tavern at closing time when the defendant was aware that a crowd of unruly persons were gathered in the parking lot.

---

[4]Defendant is not, of course, responsible for that portion of the injury resulting solely from the heart attack. *See generally* W. Prosser, *Handbook of the Law of Torts* § 52, at 317–20.

ALLEN V. BABRAB, INC.
438 So.2d 356 (Fla. 1983)

McDONALD, J.: "The petitioner, Pearl Allen, and a companion were patrons of the Gemini Club on the evening of October 1, 1977. As the two women left the club in the early morning hours and proceeded to their car in the Gemini Club's parking lot, a male patron of the club, Leroy Allen (not related to the plaintiff), approached them. Pearl Allen and her companion rebuffed Leroy Allen's advances, and the trio exchanged harsh words. After pouring his drink on the companion, Leroy Allen hurled the empty glass, which struck Ms. Allen in the face and permanently blinded her in the left eye. . . .

". . . Implicit in the district court opinion is the view that a tavern owner may be liable for injuries to its patrons caused by the tortious conduct of third parties only if the tavern owner knew or should have known of the dangerous propensities of that specific assailant. This is the very proposition we recently rejected in *Stevens*. [Stevens v. Lankard, 254 N.E.2d 339] The proprietor of a place of public entertainment will not be held liable for the unforeseeable acts of third persons, but, as we emphasized in *Stevens,* specific knowledge of an individual's dangerous propensities is not the exclusive method of proving foreseeability. It can be shown by proving that, based on past experience, a proprietor knew of or should have recognized the likelihood of disorderly conduct by third persons in general which might endanger the safety of the proprietor's patrons. Foreseeability of an intervening cause is a question for the trier of fact. *Gibson v. Avis Rent-a-Car System, Inc.,* 386 So.2d 520 (Fla. 1980).

"The Gemini Club had a history of fighting and other disturbances. Prior to October 1, 1977 Babrab had employed a 'bouncer' to maintain security on the premises. The bouncer's duties included patrolling the parking lot and preventing patrons from removing glasses from the bar. [Footnote omitted.] Despite urgings to the corporate officers by the bartenders that such security was needed, no such employee was on duty the night of Pearl Allen's assault.

"The evidence was sufficient for the jury reasonably to find that Babrab should have known of the likelihood of injury to patrons caused by disorderly conduct on the part of third parties in general and failed to do anything about it. It is a close question as to whether this failure caused or contributed to the plaintiff's injuries, but the jury could have reasonably concluded that, if Babrab had continued its previous policy of hiring security personnel to take glasses from patrons as they left the club and to patrol the parking lot, the injury suffered by Pearl Allen would have been prevented. This being so, the jury verdict should stand.

"The decision below is quashed, and the district court is ordered to reinstate the judgment rendered by the trial court in favor of Ms. Allen.

"It is so ordered.

"ALDERMAN, C.J., and ADKINS, OVERTON and EHRLICH, JJ., concur.

"BOYD, J., dissents."

The importance of proof of adequate notice to a tavernkeeper of the likelihood of a patron assaulting another patron on a dance floor is illustrated by *Harvey v. Van Aelstyn,* 211 Neb. 607, 319 N.W.2d 725 (1982). In that case, the Supreme Court of Nebraska found no liability to exist because the injured patron failed to establish that the tavernkeeper knew or should have known of such a risk.

11:15 *Anticipated Future Standards of Care*

Addendum to footnote 54, p. 326:

Possibly, Louisiana is joining Illinois in holding hotels to a "high standard of care" with respect to providing adequate protection to patrons. In *Kraaz v. La Quinta Motor Inns, Inc.,* 410 So.2d 1048 (La. 1982), the court said: "The innkeeper's position vis-a-vis his guests is similar to that of a common carrier toward its passengers. [Citation omitted.] Thus a guest is entitled to a high degree of care and protection. *Id.* at 1053. Whether the court in *Kraaz* actually applied a stricter standard of care, however, is not clear for two reasons. First, the court later said: "The innkeeper has a duty to take reasonable precautions against criminals." *Id.* Second, the result in the case—holding the defendant liable because the desk clerk negligently gave a hotel passkey to a stranger—would certainly have been reached under either standard of care.

Insert after line (g), p. 326:

In *Margreiter v. New Hotel Monteleone, Inc.,* 640 F.2d 508 (5th Cir. 1981), the court held that under applicable Louisiana law, the defendant hotel had inadequately protected plaintiff from a criminal attack. The court noted that the hotel had no security cameras, no heat-sensing devices, and no adequate alarm system.

Insert at end of section, p. 327:

Effective January 1, 1982, the New York legislature added the following to section 204 of the New York General Business Law (governing hotel registration records): "204–a. Safety chain latches required. Every person, firm or corporation engaged in the business of furnishing public lodging accommodations in hotels, motels or motor courts shall install and maintain, on the inside of each entrance door to every rental unit for which there is a duplicate or master key which would afford entry to said unit by one other than the occupant, a safety chain latch."

Although no New York court decision imposing liability for a failure to provide such a device, thereby causing personal injury or loss of guest property, has been found, the new requirement manifests a significant legislative concern for guests' safety in their rooms. At the very least, failure to install such devices could be interpreted as violating the growing stricter standard of care for the person of a guest who, as a result, is assaulted by an intruder whose access to the room is facilitated by the absence of such devices. See also section 11:1.

In *Montgomery v. Royal Motel,* 98 Nev. 240, 645 P.2d 968 (Nev. 1982), the Nevada Supreme Court ruled that a Las Vegas municipal ordinance requiring deadbolt locks, but not self-locking doors, at residential housing units applied also to motel guest rooms, but also that the motelkeeper had not violated that statute. An unknown assailant had entered the guests' room and assaulted the plaintiffs. It was established that the door was not locked, but deadbolt locks were provided. Absent proof that the motelkeeper could reasonably foresee or anticipate a criminal act under these circumstances and injury resulting therefrom, summary judgment granted by the trial court as a matter of law was affirmed.

The most recent decision reflecting the increased standard of care required of innkeepers for guests' safety from the criminal misconduct of third parties is *Banks v. Hyatt Corporation*. That Louisiana case involved the death of a guest who was shot by an armed robber four feet from the doors to the hotel entranceway and underneath an overhang that formed the second floor of the New Orleans Hyatt–Superdome complex. At trial, in affirming the judgment that imposed liability upon the innkeeper, the Court of Appeals for the Fifth Circuit set forth the public-policy arguments supporting innkeeper liability (722 F.2d at 226–227):

BANKS V. HYATT CORPORATION
722 F.2d 214 (5th Cir.)
rehearing denied 731 F.2d 888 (1984)

WINTER, C.J.: "Tort law has become increasingly concerned with placing liability upon the party that is best able to determine the cost-justified level of accident prevention. *See* G. Calabresi, *The Costs of Accidents: A Legal and Economic Analysis* (1970); Calabresi & Hirschoff, *Toward a Test for Strict Liability in Torts,* 81 Yale L.J. 1055, 1060 (1972); Posner, *A Theory of Negligence,* 1 J. Legal Stud. 29, 33 (1972). Holding a negligent innkeeper liable when there is a third-party assault on the premises is sensible, not because of some abstract conceptual notion about the risk arising within 'the course of the relation', but because the innkeeper is able to identify and carry out cost-justified ('reasonable') preventive measures on the premises. If the innkeeper has sufficient control of property adjacent to his premises so that he is capable of taking reasonable actions to reduce the risk of injury to guests present on the adjacent property, the innkeeper should not be immune from liability when his failure to take such actions results in an injury to a guest. As between innkeeper and guest, the innkeeper is the only one in the position to take the reasonably necessary acts to guard against the predictable risk of assaults. He is not an insurer, but he is obligated to take reasonable steps to minimize the risk to his guests within his sphere of control.

"The security measures adopted by Hyatt, especially the 'perimeter patrol', demonstrate that Hyatt had the power to take preventive action within the immediate surrounding area. As noted above, the jury found that Hyatt did not go far

enough. Allowing the jury's finding of negligence to stand should induce Hyatt
to determine and to put in effect cost-justified preventive measures covering both
the premises of the hotel and such adjacent areas as are sufficiently within its
control to permit reasonable preventive action. . . .

"Our decision in this case is strongly influenced by the peculiar facts with
which we are presented. Dr. Banks's death occurred only four feet from the entrance doors to the mall and hotel, underneath an overhang that is actually the
second floor of the complex. The defendants were aware of the crime problem in
the plaza complex and its immediate environs, and were capable of taking reasonable action to reduce the risk to guests and invitees in these areas.

"We affirm the judgment n.o.v. [notwithstanding the verdict] in favor of
Refco [the owner of the Superdome complex], because that defendant's duty of
care to invitees does not include a duty to adopt precautionary measures to reduce the general risk of criminal assault. Hyatt's duty to its guests, however,
does embrace a responsibility to take reasonable precautionary measures. We reject Hyatt's argument that its duty cannot, as a matter of law, extend to the location of Dr. Banks's death. Dr. Banks did not make it through the entrance doors
to the complex. We refuse to transform those doors into an impregnable legal
wall of immunity.

"The judgment of the district court is AFFIRMED."

Chapter 12. Civil and Criminal Responsibility for Anticompetitive Marketing Activities

12:5 Per Se *Illegality: Price Fixing*

Insert at end of section, p. 334:
The following case illustrates the treatment of a variety of antitrust problems
in a typical fast-food franchise. The franchisees sought certification for class-
action status. All references to that procedural issue are omitted.

KREHL V. BASKIN-ROBBINS ICE CREAM CO.
78 F.R.D. 108 (C.D. Cal. 1978)

WILLIAMS D.J.: "Twenty store franchise owners have brought this antitrust action against Baskin-Robbins Ice Cream Co., its subsidiaries and its area franchisors alleging violations of § 1 of the Sherman Act (15 U.S.C. § 1) and § 3 of the
Clayton Act (15 U.S.C. § 14). . . .The complaint was filed on June 4, 1976. A
first amended complaint was filed August 3, 1976, alleging that the defendants
conspired to restrain trade by: (1) tying sales of ice cream products, store leases,
equipment, supplies and advertising to the sale of the Baskin-Robbins trademark;
(2) by fixing the wholesale prices of ice cream products; and (3) by maintaining

the resale price of ice cream products. Plaintiffs have raised an additional allegation of territorial market division and propose to amend their complaint appropriately to include this allegation. As to each of the claims, the plaintiffs pray for treble damages, injunctive relief, costs and reasonable attorneys' fees. . . .

1. The Tying Claim

"Plaintiffs have alleged that the following products have been illegally tied to the sale of the Baskin-Robbins trademark: (1) ice cream products, (2) store leases, (3) equipment package, (4) supplies, (5) advertising. The prima facie case is the same for each of these claims. There are five elements of a per se tying violation: (1) there must be a tying arrangement between two distinct products or services, (2) the defendant must have sufficient economic power in the tying market to impose significant restrictions in the tied product market, (3) the amount of commerce in the tied product market must not be insubstantial, (4) the seller of the tying product must have an interest in the tied product, and (5) there must be a modicum of coercion shown. *Moore v. Jas. H. Matthews & Co.*, 550 F.2d 1207, 1212 and 1216-17 (9th Cir. 1977). In addition to showing the tie, plaintiffs must demonstrate fact of damage as an element of the prima facie case. *Windham v. American Brands, Inc.*, 565 F.2d 59 (4th Cir. 1977). The final element of proof is the quantum of damages. The defendants contest the predominance of common questions as to each element except the third; it is conceded that a substantial amount of commerce in the tied products is involved.

a. Existence of the Tie and Coercion

"The existence of the tie and proof of coercion can be addressed together since they are functionally linked. In the typical franchise case there are two ways in which a tying arrangement can be demonstrated. The first is by express provision in the franchise agreement conditioning the sale of one product, the tying product, on the sale of the second, or tied product. When the tie is a term of the franchise agreement, the plaintiff does not need to show that he was coerced, coercion is implied. *See Siegel v. Chicken Delight, Inc.*, 448 F.2d 43, 46 (9th Cir. 1971), *cert. denied,* 405 U.S. 955, 92 S.Ct. 1172, 31 L.Ed.2d 232 (1972). The second method of showing the tie, in the absence of an express agreement, is by proving a course of conduct. *Abercrombie v. Lum's Inc.*, 345 F. Supp. 387, 391 (S.D. Fla. 1972). In this second instance the buyer must show that he was coerced into purchasing the tied item.

"As to the first claim, that the sale of Baskin-Robbins ice cream products was tied to the purchase of the franchise trademark, this term appears in the franchise agreements. The terms of the Store Franchise Agreement specify that the franchisee may sell only Baskin-Robbins ice cream products. By virtue of the Area Franchise Agreement, the area franchisor is the exclusive source of Baskin-Robbins products in his region. Reading the terms together, the store owner is compelled to buy his ice cream products from his area franchisor as a condition of his franchise. The defendants do not challenge this conclusion, but argue that the trademark and the ice cream are not separate products. Even if such a contention is plausible after *Siegel v. Chicken Delight, Inc., supra*, it is a legal question common to the class.

"The alleged tie of the store lease and the equipment package can be aggregated since, upon aquisition of a franchise, the store owner obtains both a sublease from 31 Flavors Realty Inc., and the full equipment package. Neither the lease nor the equipment package are expressly tied to the trademark in the franchise agreements. Plaintiff's support for this tie is provided by documents submitted by BRICO [Baskin-Robbins Ice Cream Co.] to the Security Exchange Commission and the Federal Trade Commission in which it is admitted that 31 Flavors Realty Inc. is the prime lessor on all stores and that each store is fully equipped and ready for operation before it is turned over to the franchisee. *See* Plaintiffs' exhibits 1 and 2. These documents are offered as proof of coercion . . .

"The standard for showing coercion in a tying case is established by *Moore v. Jas. H. Matthews & Co., supra* at 1216–1217.

> "Although some cases in other circuits have required a showing of actual coercion, . . . our reading of the Supreme Court's opinions supports the view that coercion may be implied from a showing that an appreciable number of buyers have accepted burdensome terms, such as a tie-in, and there exists sufficient economic power in the tying product market . . . . Coercion occurs when the buyer must accept the tied item and forego possibly desirable substitutes . . . (citations omitted).

"BRICO possesses sufficient economic power in its trademark, as will be discussed in more detail *infra*, that, coupled with a showing of 100% franchise adherence, . . . coercion is conclusively demonstrated by the BRICO documents supplied to the SEC and FTC. "Plaintiffs have attempted to include equipment replacement within the ambit of the tie of the initial equipment package sold to new store owners. Neither the SEC nor the FTC documents demonstrate a tie of replacement equipment. . . .

"There is dispute over whether the fourth alleged tie, that relating to supplies is explicit in the franchise agreements. The term which arguably constitutes the tie is contained in paragraph ten of the Store Franchise Agreement.

> "RETAILOR agrees, in the conduct of the business of said store, to use only supplies, materials and accessories . . . of such quality, design and standard or brands as are currently approved in writing by BASKIN-ROBBINS.

"BRICO implements this provision by maintaining a list of approved supplies and suppliers who carry these items. BRICO also has arrangements with Martin-Brower, Benchmark Group, and Halper Bros., independent distribution companies, which enable them to service orders by the store owners by maintaining inventories of the approved supplies.

"The supply provision of paragraph ten is almost identical to a term addressed in *Smith v. Denny's Restaurant, Inc.*, 62 F.R.D. 459, at 461 (N.D. Cal. 1974). The *Smith* Court concluded as a matter of law, that the supply term did not constitute a tying arrangement without reference to external proof of coercion. . . . The same conclusion obtains in this case, particularly in light of the fact that Halper Bros. was added as a distributor at the insistence of some of these plaintiffs. This latter fact demonstrates that BRICO was amenable to some suggestions from its franchisees in adding approved distributors. "The final tie, that involving forced contributions of one cent per gallon by the franchisees to the advertising fund, appears in the franchise agreement at paragraph five. The existence of this tie is shown without recourse to proof of coercion.

b. Economic Power

"A per se showing of tying violations requires that defendants have sufficient economic power in the tying market to impose restrictions in the tied product market. The focus in determining economic power is whether the seller has sufficient power to raise prices or to impose onerous terms that could not be expected in a completely competitive market. See *Moore v. Jas. H. Matthews, supra*, at 1215. One cannot look at the tied product in isolation to determine if the terms are onerous; one must look at the attractiveness of the package. *See United States Steel Corp. v. Fortner Enterprises, Inc.* 429 U.S. 610, 97 S.Ct. 861, 51 L.Ed.2d 80 (1977) (*Fortner II*). As in the *Fortner* case in which supracompetitive credit was tied to marginally competitive prefabricated housing, the package can be viewed as a legitimate form of price competition. *Id.*, 429 U.S. at 618-619, 97 S.Ct. at 867, 51 L.Ed.2d at 88-89 n. 10.

"The difficulties of proving that the tying packages in this case were burdensome in accordance with *Fortner II* standard can be avoided if the Baskin-Robbins trademark itself is sufficiently unique that economic power can be inferred. It has long been recognized that in the cases of patents and copyrights economic power is presumed. *United States v. Loew's Inc.*, 371 U.S. 38, 83 S.Ct. 97, 9 L.Ed.2d 11 (1962); *United States v. Paramount Pictures, Inc.*, 334 U.S. 131, 68 S.Ct. 915, 92 L.Ed. 1260 (1948); *International Salt Co. v. United States*, 332 U.S. 392, 68 S.Ct. 12, 92 L.Ed. 20 (1947). The Ninth Circuit has extended the presumption that exists in the case of patents and copyrights to trademarks. *Siegel v. Chicken Delight, Inc., supra* at 50. . . .

". . . [T]his Court finds that the Baskin-Robbins trademark is coupled with such nationwide preeminence in the retail sale of ice cream market that . . . sufficient economic power is present as a matter of law. . . .

d. Damages

". . . Fact of damage requires proof that the alleged tying violation caused actual injury. In the case of the tie of ice cream products, plaintiffs will be required to show that alternate sources of comparable quality products would have been available, but for the tie. It is possible that such a showing will require proof of the conditions of the wholesale ice cream market in each locality in which there is a franchise. It is, however, more likely that potential competitors to the Baskin-Robbins area franchisors will themselves have to operate on a comparable scale if they are to supply the variety and volume demanded by the Baskin-Robbins franchisee. It is reasonable to assume that such a competitor would, in many cases, compete not only as to individual stores, but as to regions. If this is the case, the Court's burden as to fact of damage will be reduced considerably. . . .

"The situation is quite different as to proving fact of damage with respect to the other tying claims. Plaintiffs have suggested that fact of damage can be shown as to the alleged tie of the sublease by virtue of the $10 per month administrative surcharge imposed on each franchisee by 31 Flavors Realty, Inc. The surcharge does not, taken by itself, assist the plaintiffs in showing fact of damage. The intermediate step in reaching the conclusion that the franchisee was damaged by the surcharge is a showing that each franchisee could have obtained the same or an equivalent site at the rental rate at which 31 Flavors Realty, Inc. secured the prime lease. The size and reputation of a tenant is a vitally important factor in determining the terms of a commercial lease. A case by case comparison of the lease that a store owner might have gotten with the terms of the sublease written by 31 Flavors Realty, Inc. would bury this Court in a consideration of intangibles. . . .

"The equipment package and the supply tying claims are afflicted by the same problem with respect to fact of damage: because they involve numerous products and suppliers, proof of fact of damage would be unmanageable. The equipment package would pose the further difficulty that plaintiffs would have to show that the total price charged for the entire package was noncompetitive. It would not be sufficient for each franchisee to accept the good buys in the package and to reject the balance. *See Siegel v. Chicken Delight,Inc., supra* at 52-53.

"Assuming that plaintiffs could show that advertising was a separate product from the trademark for purposes of a tying claim, [Footnote omitted] proof of fact of damage would be elusive. Plaintiffs have not suggested how the individual franchisees might have used their advertising dollars more efficiently.

"An individual franchisee will have a considerable task to show damage in view of the fact that BRICO invested seven times the total contribution of store owners in advertising during 1975, the last year of the penny-per-gallon program. . . .

2. Price-Fixing

"Plaintiffs allege that BRICO, its subsidiaries, and its area franchisors conspired among themselves and with various suppliers and distributors to fix the wholesale prices at which ice cream products, the equipment package and other supplies were sold to the franchisees. To prove such a price-fixing allegation, plaintiffs must show: (1) an agreement to set prices at a noncompetitive level, (2) fact of damage, and (3) quantum of damage. *See United States v. Socony-Vacuum Oil Co.*, 310 U.S. 150, 60 S.Ct. 811, 84 L.Ed. 1129 (1940); *Windham v. American Brands, Inc., supra*, 565 F.2d at 59.

"As noted in *In re Sugar Antitrust Litigation*, 1977-1 Trade Cases ¶ 61,373 at 71,329 (N.D. Cal. 1977) class action petitions on wholesale price-fixing claims have generally been given favorable treatment.

"Courts have consistently held that antitrust price-fixing conspiracy litigations, by their nature, involve common legal and factual questions concerning the existence, scope and effect of the alleged conspiracy.

". . . It appears that proof of the conspiratorial agreement to fix prices in the sale of ice cream products at its most complex, would involve only nine agreements and proof of a common objective. Proof of fact of damage as to the price-fixing claim of ice cream products would not be sufficiently complex to justify the *Windham* type exception. It may be possible to prove fact of damage as to ice cream products by relating increases in prices to increases in costs for each of the area franchisors. If this type of common proof does not work, then individualized proof of the competitive prices in each ice cream product may be necessary.

3. Resale Price Maintenance

"Plaintiffs allege that BRICO and the area franchisors conspired to fix the maximum price at which the franchisees could sell ice cream products. The crucial element of a resale price maintenance claim is an agreement between a manufacturer and the retailer to restrict the resale price to a maximum level. *Santa Clara Valley Dist. Co. v. Pabst Brewing Co.*, 556 F.2d 942 n.3 (9th Cir. 1977). That agreement may be demonstrated by contract or by a course of conduct. In the absence of a contractual term evidencing the retailer's commitment to maintain prices, there must be a showing that the retailer's participation was involuntary for the scheme to be actionable. *Gray v. Shell Oil Co.*, 469 F.2d 742, 747-48 (9th Cir. 1972). As stated in *Hanson v. Shell Oil Co.*, 541 F.2d 1352, 1357 n.4 (9th Cir. 1976), *cert. denied*, 429 U.S. 1074, 97 S.Ct. 813, 50 L.Ed. 2d 792 (1977):

"[A] supplier may suggest retail prices to its dealers and use 'persuasion' to get them to adopt the suggested prices. No violation is made out unless plaintiff can show that the supplier's conduct rose to the level of coercion to deprive the dealers of their free choice.

"Plaintiffs claim that the resale price maintenance program was conducted by the area franchisors through indirect restrictions on the store owners in the Store Franchise Agreement. The Agreement provides that store owners may post only those signs supplied by the company. Among the approved signs are price stickers designed to be affixed on the wall behind the ice cream counter. Along with the list of suggested retail prices which the store owner is supplied from time to time, the new franchisee is given the back board with the price stickers already affixed. Plaintiffs have adduced testimony that some franchises were not given any price stickers in addition to those initially affixed to the back board and that they were denied permission to raise their retail prices above the suggested prices.

"It appears that any resale price maintenance practices that might have existed were limited to the McDonald area in Michigan. Other than in Michigan, there was little price uniformity among franchisees in the same franchise area. . . .

4. Territorial Market Division Claim

"In presenting this motion, plaintiffs have introduced a claim that was not stated in the first amended complaint—that defendants violated the antitrust laws by horizontal market division. Plaintiffs stated at oral argument that they would move to amend their complaint to include this claim. . . .

"The essence of the claim is that the Baskin-Robbins franchise system which divides the country into nine different regions and appoints each area franchisor as the exclusive supplier of ice cream products in his region violates § 1 of the Sherman Act.

"Defendants contend that the territorial market division is vertical in character and that such agreements are governed by the 'Rule of Reason.' *Continental TV, Inc. v. GTE Sylvania Inc.*, 433 U.S. 36, 97 S.Ct. 2549, 53 L.Ed.2d 568 (1977). Defendants argue that proof under a Rule of Reason test would necessarily be so individual as to each alleged restriction that class procedures would be unmanageable. The Court need not decide whether individual questions would predominate under a Rule of Reason test since the challenged territorial restriction is horizontal in nature.

"Horizontal restrictions on competition are per se illegal. This includes territorial market allocations between competitors, *Timken Roller Bearing Co. v. United States*, 341 U.S. 593, 71 S.Ct. 971, 95 L.Ed. 1199 (1951) and territorial market allocations as part of a franchising system when the allocatur is controlled by the franchisees, *United States v. Sealey, Inc.*, 388 U.S. 350, 87 S.Ct. 1847, 18 L.Ed.2d 1238 (1967). Defendants contend that *Sealey* and the similar holding in *United States v. Topco Associates, Inc.*, 405 U.S. 596, 92 S.Ct. 1126, 31 L.Ed.2d 515 (1972) are inapposite since the area franchisees do not own or control BRICO and it is BRICO that makes the territorial allocations. If BRICO were the franchisor and nothing more, this system would indeed be vertical. *Tomac, Inc. v. The Coca Cola Co.*, 418 F. Supp. 359 (C.D. Cal. 1976). BRICO is not, however, strictly a franchisor. It is connected to the manufacture and supply of Baskin-Robbins ice cream products through its subsidiary, Baskin-Robbins, Inc. which is the area franchisor for much of the country. An entity occupying such a dual role is forbidden per se from imposing territorial market restrictions. *American Motor Inns, Inc. v. Holiday Inns, Inc.*, 521 F.2d 1230, 1254 (5th Cir. 1975). In the latter case, Holiday Inns, Inc. was acting both as a franchisor of its trademark and as an operator of inns. The Court found that restrictions in its franchise agreements prohibiting franchisees from establishing competing Holiday Inns or competing non-Holiday Inns in cities in which Holiday Inn, Inc. operated an establishment, unless done with Holiday Inn, Inc.'s permission, constituted market allocation agreements among competitors and was per se illegal. Except for the absence of a clause waiving the territorial restrictions on the area franchisor's with BRICO's permission, the territorial allocation provision of BRICO is indistinguishable from that of Holiday Inn.

"The only possible individual issue with reference to the horizontal territorial restriction claim is fact of damage. Plaintiffs may be able to show fact of damage as to this claim by demonstrating that a neighboring area franchisor is a potential competitor. If it could be shown that a neighboring area franchisor had sufficient capacity to handle excess demand at lower prices, fact of damage would be proven. If transportation problems do not prevent such a showing, proof of fact of damages could be relatively mechanical. Even if fact of damage must be demonstrated by other means, the showing will be no more involved than that required to prove the price-fixing or tying claim as to ice cream products. . . ."

12:19 *Monopoly Updated in New York*

Insert at end of section, p. 347:
The interplay between the Sherman and Donnelly acts is reviewed in the following case.

BUSINESS FOOD SERVICE V. FOOD CONCEPTS CORP.
533 F. Supp. 992 (E.D.N.Y. 1982)

MCLAUGHLIN, D.J.: "The parties to this antitrust action compete in the employee or commissary catering business in the States of New York and New Jersey. They supply their respective customers with daily deliveries of a wide variety of food, except for items such as milk, eggs, and bread, and they do almost no on-premises cooking. In the overall cafeteria service industry, commissary catering lies somewhere between vending machines and extensive on-premises cooking.

"Plaintiff has moved for summary judgment alleging that the defendant utilizes a restrictive covenant that is both an unreasonable restraint of trade under Section 1 of the Sherman Act, 15 U.S.C. § 1, and a violation of Section 340 of the New York General Business Law. Since there are disputes as to the size of the geographic market and the scope of the relevant product market, the reasonableness of the alleged restraint cannot be presently assessed. Accordingly, summary judgment is denied.

I. The Covenant

"The restrictive covenant [footnote omitted] in question is atypical. It is a hybrid provision incorporating aspects of both a traditional employer-employee covenant not to compete and an exclusive dealing arrangement. While the covenant restricts the employment opportunities of former employees of the defendant, the covenant itself appears in contracts entered into by the defendant and its customers, rather than in contracts between the defendant and its employees. If a competitor of the defendant hires a former employee of the defendant, the controversial covenant bars the defendant's customers from using the services of the defendant's competitor for one year after the termination of the service contract between that customer and the defendant.

II. The Companies and Their Employees

". . . The plaintiff alleges that the covenant goes beyond what is necessary to protect the defendant's business. It claims that the duration of the provision's restriction is potentially infinite. The plaintiff also notes that the employees involved were not privy to business secrets nor did they hold unique positions while employed by the defendant.

"Furthermore, plaintiff claims that it has lost at least three customers directly as a result of the restrictive covenant in question. According to the plaintiff, these customers failed to make contracts with the plaintiff because they feared that the defendant would start litigation over the restrictive covenant. Indeed, since the commencement of this action, the defendant has in fact brought two lawsuits against several of its customers and in each case has joined the plaintiff in order to enforce the provision.

"The defendant counters by asserting that the covenant is fair, reasonably warranted, and necessary for its protection. It asserts that the purpose of the restrictive covenant is to prevent the unfair use of information (e.g., business secrets) gleaned by employees while in the employ of the defendant. . . .

III. The Law

A. The Sherman Act

"Although the reasonableness of employee covenants not to compete is seldom raised in the federal courts, such restrictive covenants are 'proper subjects for scrutiny under section 1 of the Sherman Act.' *Newburger, Loeb & Co. v. Gross,* 563 F.2d 1057, 1082 (2d Cir. 1977). [Citations omitted.] So too, the reasonableness of an exclusive dealing contract may also be measured against Section 1. [Footnote and citations omitted.]

"While Section I applies both to covenants not to compete and to exclusive dealing arrangements, neither of these potentially anticompetitive contractual provisions is per se illegal. The per se rule has not been extended to restrictive covenants primarily because of the limited experience courts have had in judging the competitive impact of such covenants within the rubric of Section 1 of the Sherman Act. *Bradford v. New York Times Co.,* 501 F.2d 51, 59-60 (2d Cir. 1974). *See also, United States v. Topco Assoc., Inc.,* 405 U.S. 596, 607-08, 92 S.Ct. 1126, 1133-34, 31 L.Ed.2d 515 (1972). Similarly, the benefits to sellers and buyers as well as to society from exclusive dealing arrangements must be balanced against possible anticompetitive effects. [Citations omitted.]

"Thus, the legality of restrictive covenants and exclusive dealing contracts turns on the reasonableness of the provision in question. Consideration must, therefore, be directed to the nature of the business in which the restraint is used as well as the reasons for and the competitive impact of the restraint. [Citations omitted.]

"The rule of reason has recently been revitalized in Section 1 cases. *See Continental T.V., Inc. v. GTE Sylvania, Inc.*, 433 U.S. 36, 97 S.Ct. 2549, 53 L.Ed.2d 568 (1977); 2 Von Kalinowski, Antitrust Laws and Trade Regulation, § 6.02(3) (1981). In light of this resurgence, identifying the relevant market and isolating the effect of the challenged restraint on that market become essential since these are the dominant considerations in determining whether the restraint is reasonable. [Citations omitted.] Without market analysis, the competitive impact of the challenged restraint cannot be assessed. [Citations omitted.]

"Although the parties concur that they complete in the commissary catering business in the Greater New York Metropolitan Area ('GNYMA'), and that the number of people employed by a customer determines the type of cafeteria service chosen, they disagree over the geographic and product markets. . . .

"The plaintiff contends that the provision is overbroad and therefore unreasonable. It argues, for one thing, that the duration of the restriction is potentially infinite. Considering that the ban against competition lasts until one year after the termination of the contract between the defendant and its customer, the provision obviously restricts the employment opportunities of defendant's former employees long after their employment with the defendant has ended. While the plaintiff's argument has appeal, 'the duration of the restriction is not the essential inquiry here. . . . Of primary importance is the "market impact" of the alleged restraint and "the challenged restraint's impact on competitive conditions."' *Lektro-Vend Corp. v. Vendo Corp.*, 500 F. Supp. [332] at 354-55, *quoting GTE Sylvania*, 433 U.S. at 50, 97 S.Ct. at 2557 (footnotes omitted). *See National Society of Professional Engineers v. United States*, 435 U.S. at 688, 98 S.Ct. at 1363. Since there is a dispute as to the boundaries of the relevant product and geographic markets, summary judgment under Section 1 of the Sherman Act is inappropriate.

B. The Donnelly Act

"Although the Court has determined that summary judgment is inappropriate with respect to the Sherman Act claim, this does not end the inquiry. The plaintiff has also alleged a violation of New York law, specifically the Donnelly Act, [footnote omitted] and this issue may be reached under the Court's pendent jurisdiction. [Citation omitted.]

"Whether summary judgment should be granted on the Donnelly Act claim is problematic. The clear public policy of New York, as reflected in the Donnelly

Act, [footnote omitted] is against restrictive covenants in the employment contract. [Citations omitted.] To constitute a violation of the Donnelly Act, however, the provision must still be found to be unreasonable. [Citation omitted.]

"Although the duration of a covenant not to compete may be a more important factor under New York law than under the Sherman Act, [citation omitted] the covenant's effect on competition and the business justification for the restraint must still be assessed.[Footnote omitted.] *Horne v. Radiological Health Services, P.C.*, 83 Misc. 2d 446, 371 N.Y.S.2d 948, 958, *aff'd*, 379 N.Y.S.2d 374 (1975). The harm to the general public cannot be assessed in a vacuum; it must be weighed on the scales of the relevant market. Moreover, it is significant that this case does not strictly involve a covenant not to compete. As already noted, the restrictive covenant is incorporated into contracts entered into by the defendant with its customers rather than contracts between the defendants and its employees. As stated by the plaintiff's own economist, 'by restricting the choices of some customers, the restrictive covenant is equivalent to targeted exclusive dealing.' . . .

"Even if the competitive impact of the restraint is not the crucial consideration in weighing the reasonableness of a restrictive covenant under New York law, it is clear that such an assessment is of primary importance when determining the legality of an exclusive dealing arrangement. *See, e.g., Big Top Stores, Inc. v. Ardsley Toy Shoppe*, 64 Misc. 2d 894, 315 N.Y.S.2d 897, *aff'd*, 36 A.D.2d 582, 318 N.Y.S.2d 924 (1971). Considering that the restrictive covenant in this case is actually a hybrid of these two types of contractual arrangements, the dispute as to the relevant market again precludes the granting of the plaintiff's motion for summary judgment. . . .

"The reasonableness of the challenged restraint must be viewed in the light of its competitive impact on the relevant market. Because the parties disagree as to the product and geographic markets, these material issues must be resolved at trial. Plaintiff's motion for summary judgment is, therefore, denied.

"SO ORDERED."

Chapter 13. Franchise Agreements: Legal Rights and Responsibilities of Franchisor and Franchisee

13:4 *Derelictions Imputable to Franchisor: Factors Creating Liability*

Insert at end of section, p. 350:

The Supreme Court of Virginia reached the contrary conclusion in *Murphy v. Holiday Inns*, 216 Va. 490, 219 S.E.2d 874 (1975). To the same effect, see *Slates v. International House of Pancakes, Inc.*, 90 Ill. App. 3d 716, 413 N.E.2d 457 (1980).

Chapter 14. Regulation Governing the Sale of Food, Beverages, and Intoxicants

14:6 *Penalties*

Insert between two paragraphs of section, p. 359:

In *United States v. Park*, 421 U.S. 658 (1975), the United States Supreme Court reaffirmed and amplified its holding in *United States v. Dotterweich*, 320 U.S. 277 (1943), cited at footnote 12. The president of a national supermarket chain was held criminally responsible under the Federal Food, Drug and Cosmetic Act for unsanitary conditions (rodent infestation) found to exist in one of the chain's food warehouses. The high court ruled that the act requires every corporate officer exercising authority and supervisory responsibility not only to seek out and remedy violations but also, indeed primarily, to implement measures that will ensure that violations do not occur. The court held that the strictest standard governs the merchandise of food distributors.

The following Texas case, another typical adulteration situation, illustrates the recurring problem of the constitutional validity of the health inspector's search of the premises.

JEAN PIERRE, INC. v. STATE
635 S.W.2d 548 (Tex. Crim. App. 1982)

DALLY, J.: ". . .The appellant, Jean Pierre, Inc., is a wholesale and retail bakery. On November 14, 1978, Charles Palmer, an inspector for the Texas Department of Health went to the premises of the company for the purpose of making a routine sanitation inspection. On arrival, Palmer was directed to the back room of the bakery where François Goodhuys, the proprietor of the bakery, was working. Palmer, who made four previous inspections of the bakery and who was acquainted with Goodhuys, stated he was there to do an FDA inspection, to which Goodhuys replied, 'Fine.' Palmer did not ask permission or present any authority to inspect. Their conversation was at all times friendly and businesslike. Goodhuys did not object to the entry into the bakery or the subsequent gathering of samples and taking of photographs. In fact, he accompanied Mr. Palmer 'on and off' during the inspection, which lasted approximately four hours, and the two talked over some of the alleged violations at that time. There is nothing in the record to suggest any coercion.

"Prior to trial, appellant filed a Motion to Suppress, contending that the warrantless search violated appellant's rights under the Fourth and Fourteenth Amendments to the United States Constitution and under Article I, Section 9 of the Texas Constitution. However, the record amply indicates that Mr. Goodhuys gave his consent to the search. A similar inspection was upheld in *United States v. Hammond Milling Co.*, 413 F.3d 608 (5th Cir. 1969), *cert. denied*, 396 U.S.

1002, 90 S.Ct. 552, 24 L.Ed.2d 494 (1970). The court there additionally held that there was no requirement that the appellant be aware of the right to refuse the inspection order to give valid consent to the inspection. *Id.* at 611. Although the consent to inspect was tacit or implied, it was no less valid. The inspection was lawful. *United States v. Hammond Milling Co., supra; United States v. Del Campo Baking Mfg. Co.*, 345 F. Supp. 1371 (D. Del. 1972); *United States v. Thriftmart*, 429 F.2d 106 (9th Cir. 1970), *cert. denied*, 400 U.S. 926, 91 S.Ct. 188, 27 L.Ed.2d 185 (1970). The samples and photographs taken as part of the inspection are thus admissible. *United States v. Acri Wholesale Grocery Co.*, 409 F. Supp. 529 (S.D. Iowa 1976). This ground of error is overruled.

"Appellant attacks the sufficiency of the evidence to sustain the conviction. Specifically he contends that the evidence is insufficient to prove the elements of 'selling an adulterated product' and the required culpable mental state. The elements of the offense as alleged are:

"(1) a person

"(2) in the course of business

"(3) intentionally or knowingly

"(4) sells an adulterated product.

"V.T.C.A. Penal Code, Section 32.42(a)(1) defines 'adulterated' as 'varying from the standard of composition or quality prescribed by law or set by established commercial usage' and the Texas Food, Drug, and Cosmetic Act, supra, deems food to be adulterated 'if it has been produced, prepared, packaged or held under unsanitary conditions whereby it may have been rendered injurious to health.'

"Inspector Palmer testified he found several violations of sanitary standards at the Jean Pierre bakery including weevil infestation of flour, rodent feces, urine, and hair in and around flour sacks and cooking utensils, dirty and unsanitized cooking utensils, and a dead rat near the oven. He further testified that he observed actual sales of bakery goods take place during his inspection. The record also indicates that Mr. Goodhuys was stipulated as the owner of the bakery. Palmer testified that Goodhuys was present during this and previous inspections, and that Goodhuys indicated to Palmer that he was aware of the rodent problem in the bakery.

"Upon these facts there was sufficient proof of each element of the offense, and the evidence supports the trial court's judgment that the appellant is guilty of committing a deceptive trade practice beyond a reasonable doubt. This ground of error is overrruled.

"The judgment is affirmed."

14:8 *False Advertising*

Insert between third and fourth paragraphs, p. 360:

In the following case a federal district court construed the Food, Drug and Cosmetic Act to make starchblockers subject to regulation as a drug. In so doing the court differentiated between the treatment of foods and drugs under the act.

AMERICAN HEALTH PRODUCTS CO., INC. V. HAYES
574 F. Supp. 1498 (S.D.N.Y. 1983) *aff'd*, 744 F.2d 912 (2d Cir. 1984)

SOFAER, D.J.: ". . . Finally, a court's responsibility to construe the statute in accord with its protective purposes does not confer a license to ignore congressional judgments reflected in the classification scheme. *See 62 Cases of Jam v. United States*, 340 U.S. 593 600, 71 S.Ct. 515, 520, 95 L.Ed. 566 (1951); *NNFA v. Mathews*, 557 F.2d at 336-37. Items classified as foods by no means escape regulations. Though food manufacturers need not obtain premarketing approval for their products, they are still subject to the Act's provisions on adulteration and misbranding. 21 U.S.C. §§ 342, 343. To enforce these provisions, the FDA may inspect factories, *id*.§ 374; commerce seizures of adulterated foods, *id*. § 334; seek injunctions against the sale of adulterated or misbranded food, *id*. § 332; and seek criminal penalties in appropriate cases, *id*. § 333. Though these provisions do not bear directly on the threshold question whether an item is a food or a drug, they do support the inference that Congress determined that a different level of regulation was adequate to protect the public in the case of an article commonly used for food, even though marketers of the product claim that it produces specific physiological effects. . . .

"Thus if an article affects bodily structure or function by way of its consumption as a food, the parenthetical [§ 321 (g) (1) (C)] precludes its regulation as a drug notwithstanding a manufacturer's representations as to physiological effect. The Act evidences throughout an objective to guarantee accurate information to consumers of foods, drugs, and cosmetics. *See, e.g.*, 21 U.S.C. § 343. The presence of the parenthetical in part (C) suggests that Congress did not want to inhibit the dissemination of useful information concerning a food's physiological properties by subjecting foods to drug regulation on the basis of representations in this regard. . . .

"The Seventh Circuit recently considered the identical question of the status of starchblockers . . . and concluded that they are drugs. *Nutrilab, Inc. v. Schweiker*, 713 F.2d 335 (7th Cir. 1983), *aff'g* 547 F. Supp. 880 (N.D. Ill. 1982). The *Nutrilab* district court had treated the issue as one of intended use, and held that ' "food" refers only to those items actually and solely . . . consumed either for taste, aroma, or nutritional value.' 547 F. Supp. at 883. The Circuit Court found this definition 'unduly restrictive' because, it observed, 'some products such as coffee or prune juice are undoubtedly food but may be consumed on occasion for reasons other than taste, aroma, or nutritive value.' 713 F.2d at 338. It instead defined food as articles used '*primarily* for taste, aroma, or nutritive value.' *id*. (emphasis added), properly rejecting also any suggestion that the source of the product makes it a food, *id*. at 337.

"Here the manufacturers contend that starchblockers must be deemed a food because their biochemical composition varies from that of the bean flour used for making bread—a paradigmatic food—only by the percentage of each component and the addition of excipients and binders. This argument fails for the same reasons articulated in *Nutrilab*. The concentration of certain components during processing effects a significant physical change. The Supreme Court recently ruled in fact that the marketing of an established drug with different excipients and binders will necessitate submission of an application for approval as a new drug. *See United States v. Generix Drug Corp.*, [460] U.S. [453], 103 S.Ct. 1298, 75 L.Ed.2d 198 (1983). Most fundamentally, the argument fails to address the Act's focus on usage."

In *State v. Glassman*, 109 Misc. 2d 1088, 441 N.Y.S.2d 346 (N.Y. Co. Ct. 1981), the court interpreted New York's food-service deceptive advertising law to require proof of intention (*scienter*) to sustain a conviction of both a hotel coffee-shop operator and the owner of the hotel premises. The fact that Kosher food items purchased and advertised as Kosher were non-Kosher when offered to the public because they were not prepared in accordance with Orthodox Hebrew religious requirements did not constitute intent to defraud.

14:10   *Emergence of Truth-in-Menu Acts*

Insert at end of first (partial) paragraph, p. 363:

In a recent decision, the California Supreme Court applied its own consumer-protection statutes, including California's Sherman Food, Drug and Cosmetic Law, to allow consumer organizations to sue food manufacturers, retailers, and advertising agencies to halt deceptive trade practices in the sale of sugared cereals as nutritive food rather than as confections. In so doing, the court interpreted the statutes broadly to protect the public interest.

COMMITTEE ON CHILDREN'S TELEVISION, INC. v. GENERAL FOODS CORP.
35 Cal. 3d 197, 197 Cal. Rptr. 783, 673 P.2d 660 (1983)

BROUSSARD, J.: "The Plaintiffs appeal from a judgment of dismissal following a trial court order sustaining demurrers without leave to amend to their fourth amended complaint. The complaint essentially charges defendants—General Foods Corporation, Safeway Stores, and two advertising agencies—with fraudulent, misleading and deceptive advertising in the marketing of sugared breakfast cereals. The trial court found its allegations insufficient because they fail to state with specificity the advertisements containing the alleged misrepresentations. We review the allegations of the complaint and conclude that the trial court erred in sustaining demurrers without leave to amend to plaintiffs' causes of action charging fraud and violation of laws against unfair competition and deceptive advertising. . . .

Causes of Action Based on Consumer Protection Statutes

"Plaintiffs' first cause of action in the fourth amended complaint seeks injunctive relief and restitution under Business and Professions Code section 17200 and subsequent sections (the unfair competition law). The operative language appears in section 17203: 'Any person performing or proposing to perform an act of unfair competition within this state may be enjoined in any court of competent jurisdiction. The court may make such orders or judgments . . . as may be necessary to prevent the use or employment by any person of any practice which constitutes unfair competition . . . or as may be necessary to restore to any person in interest any money or property, real or personal, which may have been acquired by means of such unfair competition.'

"The term 'unfair competition' receives a broad definition. A recent Court of Appeal decision summarized its breadth. 'Historically, the tort of unfair business competition required a *competitive* injury. However the language of section 17200 . . . "demonstrates a clear design to protect consumers as well as competitors by its final clause, permitting inter alia, any member of the public to sue on his own behalf or on behalf of the public generally." (*Barquis v. Merchants Collection Assn.* (1972) 7 Cal. 3d 94, 110 [101 Cal. Rptr. 745, 496 P.2d 817].) Thus, section 17200 is not confined to anti-competitive business practice but is equally directed toward " 'the right of the *public* to protection from fraud and deceit.' " (*Ibid.*) Furthermore, the section 17200 proscription of "unfair competition" is not restricted to deceptive or fraudulent conduct but extends to any *unlawful* business practice (id., at p. 111 [101 Cal. Rptr. 745, 496 P.2d 817]). The Legislature apparently intended to permit courts to enjoin ongoing wrongful business conduct in whatever context such activity might occur (*id.*, at p. 111 [101 Cal. Rptr. 745, 496 P.2d 817]; *People v. McKale* (1979) 25 Cal. 3d 626, 632 [159 Cal. Rptr. 811, 602 P.2d 731]; see also Howard, *Former Civil Code, Section 3369: A Study in Judicial Interpretation* (1979) 30 Hastings L.J. 705. Note, *Unlawful Agricultural Working Conditions as Nuisance or Unfair Competition* (1968) 19 Hastings L.J. 398, 408-409). (*Stoiber v. Honeychuck* (1980) 101 Cal. App. 3d 903, 927, 162 Cal. Rptr. 194.)

"Plaintiffs' second cause of action is based on Business and Professions Code section 17500 and subsequent sections (the false advertising law), which prohibits the dissemination in any advertising media of any 'statement' concerning real or personal property offered for sale, 'which is untrue or misleading, and which is unknown, or which by the exercise of reasonable care should be known, to be untrue or misleading.' (Bus. & Prof. Code, § 17500.) Section 17535 authorizes injunctive relief and restitution. (See *Fletcher v. Security Pacific National Bank* (1979) 23 Cal. 3d 442, 450, 153 Cal. Rptr. 28, 591 P.2d 51.) Any violation of the false advertising law, moreover, necessarily violates the unfair competition law. [Footnote omitted.]

"In addition to the causes of action asserted in the fourth amended complaint, plaintiffs' second amended complaint also asserted a cause of action based on the Sherman Food, Drug and Cosmetic Law (Health & Saf. Code, § 26000 *et seq.*). Section 26460 provides that '[i]t is unlawful for any person to disseminate any false advertising of any food, drug, device, or cosmetic. an advertisement is false if it is false or misleading in any particular.' Unlike the Business and Professions Code provisions cited earlier, this act does not expressly provide for private enforcement. The parties vigorously dispute whether a private right of action should be implied under this statute, [footnote omitted] but the question is immaterial since any unlawful business practice, including violations of the Sherman Law, may be redressed by a private action charging unfair competition in violation of Business and Professions Code sections 17200 and 17203. [Footnote omitted.]

"In sum, plaintiffs rely on three statutes—the unfair competition law, the false advertising law, and the Sherman Food, Drug and Cosmetic Law—all of which in similar language prohibit false, unfair, misleading, or deceptive advertising. In the present context we discern no difference in the scope of these enactments (apart from the fact that the Sherman law is limited to food, drugs, and cosmetics) or the meaning of their provisions. We proceed, therefore, on the basis that any advertising scheme involving false, unfair, misleading or deceptive advertising of food products equally violates all three statutes.

"To state a cause of action under these statutes for injunctive relief, it is necessary only to show that 'members of the public are likely to be deceived.' (*Chern v. Bank of America*, (1976) 15 Cal. 3d 866, 876, 127 Cal. Rptr. 110, 544 P.2d 1310; see Payne v. United California Bank (1972) 23 Cal. App. 3d 850, 856, 100 Cal. Rptr. 672 and cases there cited.) Allegations of actual deception, reasonable reliance, and damage are unnecessary. The court may also order restitution without individualized proof of deception, reliance, and injury if it 'determines that such a remedy is necessary "to prevent the use or employment" of the unfair practice. . . .' (*Fletcher v. Security Pacific National Bank, supra,* 23 Cal. 3d 442, 453, 158 Cal. Rptr. 28, 591 P.2d 51.)

"Insofar as plaintiffs seek injunctive relief and restitution under the cited consumer protection statutes, defendants' principal basis for demurrer is the charge that the complaint fails to describe the alleged deceptive practices with sufficient particularity. Defendants assert that plaintiffs should not merely describe the substance of the misrepresentations, but should state the specific deceptive language employed, identify the persons making the misrepresentations and those to whom they were made, and indicate the date, time and place of the deception . . .

"The fourth amended complaint in the present case describes the alleged deceptive scheme in considerable detail. Paragraph 35 alleges some 19 misrepresentations—some general, others relatively specific. Paragraph 42 lists material facts which are not disclosed. Finally, plaintiffs allege that each misrepresentation appears (and every listed material fact is concealed) in every advertisement for the specified product during the period in question. [Footnote omitted.] There is thus no doubt as to what advertisements are at issue, nor as to what deceptive practices are called into question. [Footnote omitted.] We believe these allegations are sufficient to notify the defendants of the claim made against them, and to frame the issues for litigation. [Footnote omitted.] . . ."

14:11   *Regulation of Smoking in Restaurants and Similar Public Places*

Insert at end of section, p. 371:

In a related context, a federal circuit court of appeals has rejected the claim that the federal Constitution sanctions federal courts to impose no-smoking rules in the workplace.

KENSELL v. STATE OF OKLAHOMA
716 F.2d 1350 (10th Cir. 1983)

LOGAN, C.J.: "After examining the briefs and the appellate record, this three-judge panel has determined unanimously that oral argument would not be of material assistance in the determination of this appeal. *See* Fed. R. App. P. 34(a); Tenth Cir. R. 10(e). The cause is therefore ordered submitted without oral argument.

"Plaintiff L. Anthony Kensell appeals a judgment granting a motion to dismiss his amended complaint for failure to state a claim upon which relief can be granted. Fed. R. Civ. P. 12(b)(6). Alleging that he suffers from respiratory and cardiovascular ailments, the plaintiff brought suit under 42 U.S.C. § 1983, claiming that the State of Oklahoma and various officers and employees of the State of Oklahoma violated his constitutional rights under the First, Fifth, Ninth, and Fourteenth Amendments by failing to prohibit smoking in the area where plaintiff worked at the Oklahoma Department of Human Services. He sought damages and injunctive relief. [Footnote omitted.]

"A complaint should not be dismissed for failure to state a claim unless it appears beyond doubt that the plaintiff can prove no set of facts that would entitle him to recover. *Conley v. Gibson*, 355 U.S. 41, 78 S.Ct. 99, 2 L.Ed.2d 80 (1957). We affirm the district court's dismissal of the complaint; clearly the plaintiff could not prove that he was deprived of a federal right.

"The plaintiff asserts that the defendants' failure to provide a smoke-free workplace violated his First Amendment rights because the smoke interfered with his ability to think. In support of that argument, appellant cites only *Rogers v. Okin*, 478 F. Supp. 1342 (D. Mass. 1979), *aff'd in part, rev'd in part*, 634 F.2d 650 (1st Cir. 1980), *vacated sub nom. Mills v. Rogers*, 457 U.S. 291, 102 S.Ct. 2442, 73 L.Ed.2d 16(1982), a class action brought by patients at a Massachusetts state mental institution. Part of the relief those patients sought was an injunction against the forcible injection of psychotrophic drugs. The district court held that the right to think was an aspect of the right of privacy, with its roots in the First Amendment, and that, absent an emergency, forcible injections of such drugs violated the patients' right to think. *Id.* at 1367.

"The plaintiff also claims that by allowing smoking in his workplace the defendants assaulted him and thereby deprived him of his constitutional rights. In support he cites cases in which police and prison personnel have been held liable under section 1983 for assaults against persons in their custody. Finally, the plaintiff alleges that he was deprived of a property right in his state job because his only options were to endure cigarette smoke or quit. We note that the plaintiff still is an employee of the Department of Human Resources; thus, he has no constructive discharge claim. His contention that he must quit his job or endure the smoke is legally indistinguishable from his claim that his constitutional rights are violated by his being assaulted on the job by cigarette smoke.

"The intrusions upon the plaintiff's person resulting from working with fellow servants who smoke is a far cry from forcible injections of mind altering drugs and assaults committed by police or prison officials to intimidate or punish persons in their custody. This is not a case in which governmental officers are abusing power they possess only because the government is sovereign. In essence, the plaintiff has voluntarily accepted employment in an office in which he knew or should have known other employees smoke. Upon discovering that he is allergic to smoke or that it exacerbates his health problems, instead of quiting or transferring he seeks to force his employer to install a no-smoking rule in the office or to segregate smokers from nonsmokers. The state as his employer no doubt has the power to grant his request. As sovereign, it can make exposing him to smoke a tort, *see Shimp v. New Jersey Bell Telephone Co.*, 145 N.J. Super. 516, 368 A.2d 408 (1976), or a crime. *See* Okla. Stat. Ann. tit. 21, § 1247. We are certain, however, that the United States Constitution does not empower the federal judiciary, upon the plaintiff's application, to impose no-smoking rules in the plaintiff's workplace. To do so would support the most extreme expectations of the critics who fear the federal judiciary as a superlegislature promulgating social change under the guise of securing constitutional rights. *Accord Fed. Employees for Nonsmokers' Rights (FENSR) v. United States*, 446 F. Supp. 181 (D.D.C. 1978), *aff'd mem.*, 598 F.2d 310 (D.C. Cir. 1979); *Gasper v. Louisiana Stadium and Exposition Dist.*, 418 F. Supp. 716 (E.D. La 1976), *aff'd*, 577 F.2d 897 (5th Cir. 1978). . . .

"AFFIRMED."

The District of Columbia Court of Appeals has likewise ruled that no common-law duty exists to require an employer to provide a smoke-free environment for an employee who is especially sensitive to tobacco smoke. *Gordon v. Raven Systems & Research, Inc.*, 462 A.2d 10 (D.C. App. 1983).

14:11a   *(New Section) Public Health Provisions Regarding*
           Emergency First Aid to Food-Service Patrons Choking
           on Food

Insert immediately before 14:12, p. 371:

In 1980, New York adopted Public Health Law 1352–b, requiring all public food-service establishments to post first-aid instructions regarding assistance to patrons choking on food lodged in their throats. Failure to post the instructions, known as the Heimlich maneuver, does not itself impose liability upon the operator or the employees in any civil lawsuit brought by a patron injured in a choking emergency. Nor does the statute impose any legal duty on any operator, employee, or other person to remove or assist in removing food from the throat of a choking victim. Regardless of any contrary local law or ordinance, any operator, employee, or other person who voluntarily and without expectation of compensation removes, assists in removing or attempts to remove food from a choking victim in accordance with the instructions adopted by the Department of Public Health may not be held liable for personal injuries or for the wrongful death of the victim by reason of any act or failure to act in the rendering of emergency assistance unless the resulting injuries or death was caused by gross negligence of the operator, employee, or other person. Local counsel should be consulted to determine whether or not similar laws have been adopted in other states and, if so, what requirements must be met.

14:17   *Sexual Misconduct in General*

Insert at end of section, p. 382:

The New York Court of Appeals has set limits on the traditional rule that exonerates a licensee from license revocation because of a lack of any pattern of conduct or actual knowledge of an employee's misconduct in tolerating prostitutes on the premises. A critical factor noted by the court was the numerous warning letters sent to the licensee by the authority about the problem.

AWRICH RESTAURANT, INC. v. NEW YORK STATE LIQUOR AUTHORITY
60 N.Y.2d 645, 454 N.E.2d 1307 (1983)

MEMORANDUM: "The judgment of the Appellate Division should be affirmed, with costs. 92 A.D.2d 925, 460 N.Y.S.2d 347.

"Where an employee is found to have been vested with managerial authority over the operation of premises licensed to serve liquor and the conduct of the licensed activity thereon on other than a casual or temporary basis, his conduct may be imputed to the licensee in establishing a violation of subdivision 6 of section 106 of the Alcoholic Beverage Control Law despite the lack of a pattern of conduct or any actual knowledge by the licensee of the bartender's conduct (*Mat-*

ter of Falso v. State Liq. Auth., 43 N.Y.2d 721, 401 N.Y.S.2d 484, 372 N.E.2d 325). Here the licensee testified that the bartender left in charge was responsible for, among other things, dealing with any disorder which might come up on the premises and making sure that the premises were operating in orderly fashion. Based on this testimony, there was substantial evidence to support the hearing officer's determination that the bartender had been delegated sufficient managerial authority to hold the licensee responsible for his conduct. Moreover, the licensee admitted that he had been aware of problems with prostitues coming on the premises, and he had been sent numerous warning letters by the authority with regard to subdivision 6 of section 106 violations. This evidence provides further support for the hearing officer's ruling that the licensee should, with due diligence and proper supervision, have known of the events that took place on the premises which give rise to the violation.

"COOKE, C.J., and JASEN, JONES, WACHTLER, MEYER and SIMONS, JJ., concur."

14:18 *Sexually Explicit Entertainment*

Insert immediately after Bellanca v. New York State Liquor Authority, p. 388:

The *Bellanca* case found in the revised edition is now *Bellanca I*. *Bellanca II* and *Bellanca III*, which follow chronologically, appear in this supplement. The trilogy of decisions is important as it represents a conflict between federal and state constitutional interpretations over the issue of regulation of entertainment within licensed premises.

BELLANCA V. NEW YORK STATE LIQUOR AUTHORITY [BELLANCA II]
452 U.S. 714, 101 S.Ct. 2599, 69 L.E.2d 357 (1980)

PER CURIAM: "The question presented in this case is the power of a State to prohibit topless dancing in an establishment licensed by the State to serve liquor. In 1977, the State of New York amended its Alcoholic Beverage Control Law to prohibit nude dancing in establishments licensed by the State to sell liquor for on-premises consumption. N.Y. Alco. Bev. Cont. Law, § 106 (subd. 6a) (1977). [Footnote omitted.] The statute does not provide for criminal penalties, but its violation may cause an establishment to lose its liquor license.

"Respondents, owners of nightclubs, bars, and restaurants which had for a number of years offered topless dancing, brought a declaratory judgment action in state court, alleging that the statute violates the First Amendment of the U.S. Constitution insofar as it prohibits all topless dancing in all licensed premises. The New York Supreme Court declared the statute unconstitutional and the New York Court of Appeals affirmed by a divided vote. It reasoned that topless dancing was a form of protected expression under the First Amendment and that 'the State had not demonstrated a need for prohibiting licensees from presenting nonobscene topless dancing performances to willing customers.' The dissent contended that the statute was well within the State's power, conferred by the Twenty-first Amendment, to regulate the sale of liquor within its boundaries. [Footnote omitted.] We agree with the reasoning of the dissent and now reverse the decision of the New York Court of Appeals. This Court has long recognized that a State has absolute power under the Twenty-first Amendment to prohibit totally the sale of liquor within its boundaries. *Ziffrin, Inc. v. Reeves*, 308 U.S. 132, 138, 84 L. Ed. 128, 60 S. Ct. 163 (1939). It is equally well established that a State has broad power under the Twenty-first Amendment to regulate the times, places and circumstances under which liquor may be sold. In *California v. LaRue*, 409 U.S. 109, 34 L.Ed.2d 342, 93 S.Ct. 390 (1972), we upheld the facial constitutionality of a statute prohibiting acts of 'gross sexuality,' including the display of the genitals and live or filmed performances of sexual acts, in establishments licensed by the State to serve liquor. Although we recognized that not all of the prohibited acts would be found obscene and were therefore entitled to some measure of First Amendment protection, we reasoned that the statute was within the State's broad power under the Twenty-first Amendment to regulate the sale of liquor.

"In *Doran v. Salem Inn, Inc.*, 422 U.S. 922, 45 L.Ed. 648, 95 S.Ct. 2561 (1975), we considered a First Amendment challenge to a local ordinance which prohibited females from appearing topless not just in bars, but 'any public place.' Though we concluded that the District Court had not abused its discretion in granting a preliminary injunction against enforcement of the ordinance, that decision does not limit our holding in *LaRue*. First, because *Doran* arose in the context of a preliminary injunction, we limited our standard of review to whether the District Court abused its discretion in concluding that plaintiffs were *likely* to prevail on the merits of their claim, not whether the ordinance actually violated the First Amendment. Thus, the decision may not be considered a 'final judicial decision based on the actual merits of the controversy.' *University of Texas v. Camenisch*, —— U.S. ——, 68 L.Ed.2d 175, 101 S.Ct. 1830 (1981). Second, the ordinance involved either in *LaRue* or here, since it proscribed conduct at 'any public place,' a term that 'could include the theatre, town hall, opera place, as well as a marketplace, street or any place of assembly indoors or outdoors.' 422 U.S. at 933, 45 L.Ed.2d 648, 95 S.Ct. 2561. Here, in contrast, the State has not attempted to ban topless dancing in 'any public place': As in *LaRue*, the statute's prohibition applies only to establishments which are licensed by the State to serve liquor. Indeed, we explicitly recognized in *Doran* that a more narrowly drawn statute would survive judicial scrutiny:

"Although the customary 'barroom' type of nude dancing may involve only the barest minimum of protected expression, we recognized in *California v. LaRue*, 409 U.S. 109, [34 L.Ed.2d 342, 93 S.Ct. 390] (1972), that this form of entertainment might be entitled to First and Fourteenth Amendment protection under some circumstances. In *LaRue*, however, we concluded that the broad powers of the States to regulate the sale of liquors conferred by the Twenty-first Amendment, outweighed any First Amendment interest in nude dancing and that a State could therefore ban such dancing as part of its liquor license control program. 422 U.S., at 932–933, 45 L.Ed.2d 648, 95 S.Ct. 2561.

"Judged by the standards announced in *LaRue* and *Doran*, the statute at issue here is not unconstitutional. What the NewYork Legislature has done in this case is precisely what this Court has said a State may do in *Doran*. Pursuant to its power to regulate the sale of liquor within its boundaries, it has banned topless dancing in establishments granted a license to serve liquor. The State's power to ban the sale of alcoholic beverages entirely includes the lesser power to ban the sale of liquor on premises where topless dancing occurs.

"Respondents nonetheless insist that *LaRue* is distinguishable from this case, since the statute there prohibited acts of 'gross sexuality' and was well-supported by legislative findings demonstrating a need for the rule. They argue that the statute here is unconstitutional as applied to topless dancing because there is no legislative finding that topless dancing poses anywhere near the problem posed by acts of 'gross sexuality.' But even if explicit legislative findings were required to uphold the constitutionality of this statute as applied to topless dancing, those findings exist in this case. The purposes of the statute have been set forth in an accompanying legislative memorandum, N.Y. State Legislative Annual, 150 (1977).

"Nudity is the kind of conduct that is a proper subject of legislative action as well as regulation by the State Liquor Authority as a phase of liquor licensing. It has long been held that sexual acts and performances may constitute disorderly behavior within the meaning of the Alcoholic Beverage Control Law. . . .

"Common sense indicates that any form of nudity coupled with alcohol in public place begets undesirable behavior. This legislation prohibiting nudity in public will once and for all, outlaw conduct which is now quite out of hand.

"In short, the elected representatives of the State of New York have chosen to avoid the disturbances associated with mixing alcohol and nude dancing by means of a reasonable restriction upon establishments which sell liquor for on-premises consumption. Given the 'added presumption in favor of the state regulation' conferred by the Twenty-first Amendment, *California v. LaRue, supra,* at 118, 34 L.Ed.2d 342, 93 S.Ct. 390, we cannot agree with the New York Court of Appeals that the statute violates the United States Constitution. Whatever artistic or communicative value may attach to topless dancing is overcome by the State's exercise of its broad powers arising under the Twenty-first Amendment. Although some may quarrel with the wisdom of such legislation and may consider topless dancing a harmless diversion, the Twenty-first Amendment makes that a policy judgment for the state legislature, not the courts.

"Accordingly, the petition for certiorari is granted and the judgment of the New York Court of Appeals is reversed for further proceedings not inconsistent with this opinion.

"Justice MARSHALL concurs in the judgment."

On remand, the New York Court of Appeals held that some forms of topless dancing are constitutionally protected under the New York Constitution, in spite of the validity of the state ban on such activities permitted under the Twenty-first Amendment to the United States Constitution.

BELLANCA V. NEW YORK STATE LIQUOR AUTHORITY [BELLANCA III]
54 N.Y.2d 228, 429 N.E.2d 765 (1981)
cert. denied, 456 U.S. 1006 (1982)

JONES, J.: "The guarantee of freedom of expression declared in our State Constitution mandates invalidation of the blanket proscription against all topless dancing in premises licensed by the State Liquor Authority presently stated in subdivision 6–a of section 106 of the Alcoholic Beverage Control Law. Although that statutory ban has been held to be valid under the Federal Constitution in consequence of the provisions of its Twenty-first Amendment, it is invalid under the guarantee of freedom of expression of our State Constitution, as to which the Twenty-first Amendment has no application.

"This case is now before us on remand from the Supreme Court of the United States (——— U.S. ———, 101 S.Ct. 2599, 69 L.Ed.2d 357). On our prior consideration a majority in our court held that subdivision 6–a of section 106 of the Alcoholic Beverage Control Law [footnote omitted] was unconstitutional under the First Amendment of the United States Constitution insofar as it prohibits topless dancing at premises licensed by the State Liquor Authority (50 N.Y.2d 524, 429 N.Y.S.2d 616, 407 N.E.2d 360, rearg. and amdt. of remittitur den. 51 N.Y.2d 879). On that occasion we found it unnecessary to consider the parallel contention that the statute was unconstitutional under section 8 of article I of our State Constitution (50 N.Y.2d 524, 528, n. 5, 429 N.Y.S.2d 616, 407 N.E.2d 460, *supra*).

"The rationale of the majority then was that the Supreme Court had recognized dancing as a form of expression and had held that topless dancing, like nudity in art and sculpture, was to be accorded at least limited protection under the First Amendment (*Doran v. Salem Inn*, 422 U.S. 922, 95 S.Ct. 2561, 45 L.Ed.2d 648). We explicitly took note of what we considered a critical circumstance in the case, namely, that the statutory provision under scrutiny barred *all* topless dancing—'The only question before us is whether the statute is constitutional to the extent that it absolutely prohibits liquor licensees from presenting nonobscene topless dancing performances to willing customers under all circumstances' (50 N.Y.2d 524, 529, 429 N.Y.S.2d 616, 407 N.E.2d 460, *supra*). We then recognized, as we do now, the right of the Legislature or the State Liquor Authority without infringement of the constitutional proscriptions to prohibit or to regulate topless dancing on either of two bases. If the dancing is itself found to be obscene there can be no question but what it falls outside the shelter of any constitutional right of expression. Or, topless dancing although not obscene may be regulated, even to the extent of its prohibition, in circumstances so functionally related to the exercise of the State's authority to regulate the sale and consumption of alcoholic beverages as to overcome the applicable constitutional guarantee of freedom of expression, as for instance, by a rule, such as that of the State Liquor Authority in effect prior to the legislative enactment of subdivision 6–a, prohibiting topless dancing performed on a stage or platform less than 18 inches above the immediate floor level or removed by less than 6 feet from the nearest patron (9 N.Y.C.R.R. 53.1[s] prior to its amendment [footnote omitted]).

"The determinative infirmity in the enactment of subdivision 6–a by the Legislature was the total absence of any findings by the Legislature or by the State Liquor Authority to support a rationally based factual justification for the blanket prohibition. Chapter 321 of the Laws of 1977 was predicated on no legislative finding and it included no declaration of legislative intent. [Footnote omitted.] It was merely a straightforward, unembellished amendment of section 106 to add a new subdivision. Nor was the amending bill introduced by the State Liquor Authority or accompanied by any memorandum from the authority in support of its enactment. Presumably the authority had been content with the adequacy, for purposes of the discharge of its supervisory responsibility, of its own existing 18-inch 6-foot rule.

"The dissenters in our court expressed the view, corresponding to that of the majority in the Supreme Court, that even if it were to be concluded that subdivision 6–a would otherwise be unconstitutional under the First Amendment its enactment by the State would be authorized under the provisions of the Twenty-first Amendment of the Federal Constitution. [Footnote omitted.]

"The Supreme Court expressly upheld the validity of subdivision 6–a against attack under the Federal Constitution on the ground that its adoption was permitted under the provisions of the Twenty-first Amendment. 'This Court has long recognized that a State has absolute power under the Twenty-first Amendment to prohibit totally the sale of liquor within its boundaries. . . . It is equally well established that a State has broad power under the Twenty-first Amendment to regulate the times, places and circumstances under which liquor may be sold. . . . Pursuant to its power to regulate the sale of liquor within its boundaries, it has banned topless dancing in establishments granted a license to serve liquor. The State's power to ban the sale of alcoholic beverages entirely includes the lesser power to ban the sale of liquor on premises where topless dancing occurs. . . . Whatever artistic or communicative value may attach to topless dancing is overcome by the State's exercise of its broad powers arising under the Twenty-first

Amendment.' (—— U.S. ——, ——, 101 S.Ct. 2599, 2600, 69 L.Ed.2d 357 *supra*.)

"The posture in which we confront this case on remand can thus be summarized as follows. When the case was previously before us the majority held subdivision 6–a unconstitutional as violative of the First Amendment of the United States Constitution; the dissenters would have held that in view of the authority granted the States by the Twenty-first Amendment to regulate the sale and use of liquor, the provision of subdivision 6–a was not irrational and accordingly should be upheld. The Supreme Court similarly upheld subdivision 6–a against challenge under the Federal Constitution on the ground that the broad provisions of the Twenty-first Amendment substantially curtailed the operative scope of the First Amendment. Nothing in its opinion intimates, however, that it would have upheld the subdivision against First Amendment challenge had there been no Twenty-first Amendment.

"We are, of course, bound by the decision of the Supreme Court as to the validity of subdivision 6–a under the provisions of the Federal Constitution. We are now called on to consider the validity of the subdivision under the provisions of our State Constitution, an issue which we did not address when the case was before us on the prior occasion and which, of course, was not within the scope of the Supreme Court's review.

"We perceive no reason to depart from our conclusion, reached before, that subdivision 6–a in its present form is violative of a constitutional guarantee of freedom of expression. In arriving at this result we have no occasion to consider whether our State constitutional guarantee is broader than the guarantee of the Federal Constitution. [Footnote omitted.] For present purposes it suffices to observe that, at the very least, the guarantee of freedom of expression set forth in our State Constitution is of no lesser vitality than the set forth in the Federal Constitution (considered without reference to the curtailing effect of its Twenty-first Amendment). Our State Constitution contains no provision modifying the State guarantee of freedom of expression corresponding to what the Supreme Court has held is the diminishing effect of the Twenty-first Amendment with respect to the Federal guarantee of freedom of expression. We therefore hold that subdivision 6–a is unconstitutional under the provisions of our State Constitution.

"Nor is there anything in the Twenty-first Amendment itself which inhibits or modifies the right of freedom of expression assured by our State Constitution. As read by the Supreme Court, the Twenty-first Amendment recognizes, so far as the restrictive provisions of the Federal Constitution are concerned, the absolute power of a State to prohibit totally, and consequently to regulate, the sale of alcoholic beverages. Appellants do not assert, however, that the source of the State's authority to regulate the sale and consumption of alcoholic beverages is to be found in the Twenty-first Amendment. Contrary to the position now advanced by one of the dissenters, the authority of our State in this respect stems not from any grant to be found in the Federal Constitution but derives from the inherent

police power of the State as a sovereign (see 9 N.Y. Jur., Constitutional Law, §
143; U.S. Const., 10th Amdt.). [Footnote omitted.] The exercise of the police
power by the State Legislature is necessarily subject to the strictures of our State
Constitution, of which the guarantee of freedom of expression found in section 8
of article I is controlling in this instance. [Footnote omitted.] The Supreme Court
has never espoused the proposition that the Twenty-first Amendment of the Federal Constitution confers a power on the States which is superior to or free from
the constraints of their own Constitutions, and nothing cited by the dissenters is
to the contrary.

"Accordingly, we hold that the present statutory ban against topless dancing in
premises licensed by the State Liquor Authority is prohibited by the guarantee of
freedom of expression declared in section 8 of article I, there being no legislative
findings or declaration in this instance providing warrant for the judicial conclusion that the categorical ban is sufficiently functionally related to the exercise of
the State's police power in the discharge of the responsibilities vested in the State
Liquor Authority. [Footnote omitted.]

"For the reasons stated, the judgment of Supreme Court should be affirmed,
with costs.

"FUCHSBERG, J. (concurring).

"Because Judge JONES' analysis of the controlling constitutional and procedural issues—with all of which I agree—does not focus on the practical nature
of the imposition on freedom of expression which we strike down anew today, I
add this additional comment for myself:

"Licensed liquor establishments, regardless of whether they provide nonobscene topless dancing entertainment, may not dispense alcoholic beverages to
minors (Alcoholic Beverage Control Law, § 65).

"As to adults, such performances are not thrust upon the patrons. Those who,
understandably, do not choose to attend, should be, and are, perfectly free to stay
away, and, presumably, they exercise that right. Our profound commitment to
personal liberty demands not only that we respect their right to do so, but, correl-
atively, that we evince like respect for the right of adults who elect to attend. In a
free society, one such right could not long exist without the other.

"The protection of both is implicit in section 8 of article I of our State Constitution. Its guarantee is not confined to the expression of ideas that are conventional or those shared by a majority.

"[Dissenting opinions of GABRIELLI, J., and JASEN, J., omitted.]"

The state supreme courts that have adopted the rationale of the New York
Court of Appeals are Alaska: *Mickens v. City of Kodiak*, 640 P.2d 818 (1982);
California: *Morris v. Municipal Court for San Jose–Milipitas*, 32 Cal. 3d 553,
652 P.2d 51 (1982); and Maine: *Gabriele v. Town of Old Orchard Beach*, 420
A.2d 252 (1980). Massachusetts had done so prior to *Bellanca III*: *Common-
wealth v. Sees*, 374 Mass. 532, 373 N.E.2d 1151 (1978).

14:20 *Trafficking in Narcotics*

Insert at end of section, p. 396:

The seriousness with which violations of the New York Alcoholic Beverage Control laws concerning supervision of licensed premises are viewed is illustrated dramatically by the following case. The views expressed are representative of judicial thinking in regard to strict regulation of licensees by the states.

17 CAMERON ST. RESTAURANT CORP. v. NEW YORK STATE LIQUOR AUTHORITY
48 N.Y.2d 509, 399 N.E.2d 907 (1979)

JASEN, J.: "On this appeal, the sole issue presented for our consideration is whether the penalty imposed on a corporate licensee by the State Liquor Authority is excessive.

"On June 1, 1974, respondent State Liquor Authority issued petitioner 17 Cameron St. Restaurant Corp., doing business as Dillons, a restaurant liquor license for the on-premises consumption of alcoholic beverages. That license was renewed annually, the last such renewal having been made for the license period expiring February 28, 1979. However, on June 26, 1978, respondent commenced a proceeding pursuant to sections 118 and 119 of the Alcoholic Beverage Control Law to revoke petitioner's license upon the ground that one of petitioner's coprincipals, Howard Kolbenhayer, a 50% shareholder of petitioner, had been convicted of a felony, to wit: criminal sale of a controlled substance in the fifth degree. Petitioner entered a plea of no contest and offered evidence of mitigating circumstances. Thereafter, on November 1, 1978, respondent ordered that petitioner's license be revoked, that petitioner forfeit a $1,000 bond which had been given to ensure compliance with the Alcoholic Beverage Control Law and that a two-year proscription against the sale of alcoholic beverages be entered on the premises at 17 Cameron Street, Southampton, New York.

"Petitioner commenced the instant CPLR article 78 proceeding contending that the penalty ordered by respondent was excessive. Upon transfer from Supreme Court, the Appellate Division granted the petition to the extent that it modified, on the law, the determination of the State Liquor Authority by reducing the penalty to the bond forfeiture alone. As so modified, the determination of respondent was affirmed. Respondent appeals from this judgment. There should be a reversal.

"It should be noted at the outset that petitioner does not deny the existence of the facts underlying the revocation proceeding, nor does it now contend that a disciplinary proceeding could not properly be based upon these facts. Rather, petitioner's sole contention is that the sanction imposed by respondent was excessive. In this situation, the role of the courts in reviewing the penalty imposed by an administrative agency is extremely limited. Indeed, it is well settled that 'where the finding of guilt is confirmed and punishment has been imposed, the test is whether such punishment is "'so disproportionate to the offense, in light of all the circumstances, as to be shocking to one's sense of fairness'." *'Matter of Pell v. Board of Educ.*, 34 N.Y.2d 222, 233, 356 N.Y.S.2d 833, 841, 313 N.E.2d 321, 327; *Matter of Stolz v. Board of Regents of Univ. of State of N.Y.*, 4 A.D.2d 361, 165 N.Y.S.2d 179.) We cannot say, as a matter of law, that the penalty imposed was excessive in this case.

"It is beyond dispute that the liquor industry has a significant impact upon the health, welfare and morals of the people of this State and that it must, of necessity, be strictly controlled. Further, the power of the State to regulate every facet of this industry has long been recognized by the courts. (See, e.g., *Seagram & Sons v. Hostetter*, 16 N.Y.2d 47, 56, 262 N.Y.S.2d 75, 79, 209 N.E.2d 701, 704, *aff'd* 384 U.S. 35, 86 S.Ct. 1254, 16 L.Ed.2d 336.) As a result, those who engage in the sale of intoxicants do so with the knowledge that their business conduct will be subject to constant scrutiny and that any violation of the law governing their trade is subject to a penalty commensurate with the nature of the offense. Thus, where it has been shown that a coprincipal of a corporate licensee has engaged feloniously in the sale of illegal drugs, it cannot be said that the penalty of license revocation and the entry of a two-year proscription against the premises formerly operated by the guilty coprincipal is so disproportionate as to be shocking to one's sense of fairness. Trafficking in narcotics is a serious national problem and the authority, in imposing the sanctions, took cognizance of this fact.

"Nor can it be said that the inability of the remaining coprincipal to do business under the corporate license requires us to reach a contrary conclusion. As we have noted in a case involving the operation of a nursing home, another regulated industry, the disqualification of only one of two partners authorized to operate the nursing home does not oblige the licensing agency to continue such authorization for the benefit of the remaining partner alone. (*Matter of Spiegel v. Whalen*, 44 N.Y.2d 745, 405 N.Y.S.2d 679, 376 N.E.2d 1323.) The innocence of one co-owner of petitioner does not diminish the wrongdoing of his associate, nor does it obviate the necessity of penalizing this corporate petitioner where its president, who held 50% of its stock, has been shown to have engaged feloniously in the sale of illegal drugs. In our view, this penalty against the corporate licensee does not become excessive merely because it may have a financial effect upon a shareholder of the guilty corporation. This is a risk any shareholder assumes when a corporation operates a licensed premises.

"For the above reasons, the judgment of the Appellate Division should be reversed, with costs, and the determination of the State Liquor Authority reinstated."

Chapter 15. Responsibility Arising from the Sale of Food, Beverages, and Intoxicants

15:4 *What Is "Fit to Eat"?*

Insert at end of section, p. 410:

The case to follow is significant in that the Supreme Court of Alabama ruled that the presence of a one-centimerter bone in a fish fillet did not render the fish unfit or unreasonably dangerous, as a matter of law. Thus the restaurant keeper was held not liable to a patron under a reasonable expectations warranty theory of liability, contrary to a jury verdict for the patron.

Ex Parte Morrison's Cafeteria of Montgomery, Inc.
431 So.2d 975 (Ala. 1983)

Shores, J.: "This case presents a question of first impression in this state. Morrison's Cafeteria of Montgomery, Inc., petitioned this Court for a writ of certiorari to the Court of Civil Appeals following that court's affirmance of the trial court's judgment entered on a jury verdict totalling $6,000.78 against Morrison's for injuries sustained when Rodney Haddox, a minor, choked on a fishbone while dining at the restaurant.

"The facts as found by the Court of Civil Appeals and by which we are bound are as follows:

"Mrs. Haddox testified that around 2:00 or 3:00 P.M. one afternoon in May 1980, she and her three-year-old son Rodney went to Morrison's Cafeteria. Rodney wanted some fish. Mrs. Haddox took one tray and she and Rodney proceeded down the food line. Mrs. Haddox's testimony as to how she received a portion of fish almondine is conflicting. At one point in her testimony she stated that she pointed to a piece of fish and told the man behind the counter that she would take that piece of fish. At another point she stated that she asked for fried fish. At yet another point she stated that she asked for fried fish fillet. She received a portion of the fish and put it on her tray, together with another food and drink. She saw no signs advertising the fish dish. No one told her that it was a fillet or that it was boneless. She subjectively believed it to be a fillet because of its shape and her prior experience with eating fish dishes at Morrison's. When she and Rodney were seated, Mrs. Haddox cut off a portion of the fish and put it on a plate for Rodney. She testified that she pulled it apart with her knife and fork into very small pieces. At one point Mrs. Haddox testified that she pulled Rodney's portion apart to check for bones. Later in her testimony she stated that she was merely cutting it into bite-sized pieces and not checking for bones. Rodney apparently became choked on the first bit of fish. When Rodney was taken to the hospital, it was discovered that a fishbone approximately one centimeter in length was lodged in his tonsil. The bone was removed after Rodney stayed in the hospital overnight. He suffered no permanent physical injury as a result of the incident. Mrs. Haddox stated that she did not know how Morrison's could have known there was a small bone in the fish. She testified however, that the manager and other personnel at Morrison's were extremely rude to her during the course of Rodney's difficulty. She could not persuade anyone to take her to the hospital and was told at the checkout counter that she must pay her bill before she left.

"The manager of Morrison's at the time of Rodney's injury testified that the fish which Mrs. Haddox bought was Spanish Mackerel fillet. Morrison's bought the fish from Pinellas Seafood Company, Inc. (Pinellas). Pinellas ships the fish to Morrison's in five- to ten-pound boxes. Morrison's uses this fish to prepare a dish they advertise as Fish Almondine. It is not advertised as boneless and employees are instructed not to tell customers that the dish is boneless. Morrison's does not offer the fish on a child's plate because the fish does sometimes contain bones.

"An employee of Pinellas at the time of Rodney's injury testified that Pinellas used machines to fillet the Spanish Mackerel bought by Morrison's. Such machines are commonly used by other wholesale fish processors. Machine filleting strips the sides of the fish away from the backbone. Using this method it is impossible to prevent the occasional presence of small bones in the fillets. Government regulations allow for the presence of small bones in fillets. The employee stated that Morrison's had not been told that Pinellas's fillets were boneless. Approximately ninety-nine percent of the fillets which Pinellas produces are sold to Morrison's, and Pinellas is aware that Morrison's in turn sells the fillets to its customers. He further testified that in order for Pinellas or Morrison's to check for bones in the fillets they would have to cut them into tiny pieces. This would destroy the fillets.

"Another witness, an employee of a fish wholesaler and retailer, stated that a whole fillet of Spanish Mackerel could be recognized by its shape.

"Mrs. Haddox brought suit on behalf of Rodney and herself against Morrison's and Pinellas to recover medical expenses and to compensate Rodney for his pain and suffering. . . . Morrison's filed a cross claim against Pinellas. . . .

"The trial court submitted the case to the jury on the theories of implied warranty of fitness for human consumption and the Alabama Extended Manufacturer's Liability Doctrine (AEMLD) against Morrison's; the AEMLD as against Pinellas; and implied warranty as to Morrison's cross claim against Pinellas.

"The jury returned a verdict in favor of Mrs. Haddox and against Morrison's in the amount of $1,000.78. Rodney was awarded a verdict against Morrison's for $5,000.00. The jury found in favor of Pinellas on the cross claim. . . .

"Morrison's appealed to the Court of Civil Appeals. . . . Morrison's urged the

Court of Civil Appeals to adopt the so-called 'foreign-natural' rule and determine as a matter of law that a bone in a piece of fish does not breach the implied warranty of fitness.

"A divided Court of Civil Appeals, in affirming the trial court's decision, rejected the 'foreign-natural' rule in favor of the 'reasonable expectation' test. Judge Holmes, dissenting in part, agreed with the majority's adoption of the reasonable expectation test, but did not agree that the test under the present facts mandated an affirmance of the trial court.

"This Court granted Morrison's petition for certiorari on October 19, 1982. We reverse.

"The issue concerns the interpretation to be given Ala. Code 1975, § 7-2-314, which provides in part:

"(1) Unless excluded or modified (section 7-2-316), a warranty that the goods shall be merchantable is implied in a contract for their sale if the seller is a merchant with respect to goods of that kind. Under this section the serving for value of food or drink to be consumed either on the premises or elsewhere is a sale.

"(2) Goods to be merchantable must be at least such as: . . .

"(c) Are fit for the ordinary purposes for which such goods are used. . . .

"The issue also concerns the Alabama Extended Manufacturer's Liability Doctrine, which requires that 'a plaintiff must prove he suffered injury or damages to himself or his property by one who sold a product in a defective condition unreasonably dangerous to the plaintiff as the ultimate user or consumer. . . .' *Atkins v. American Motors Corp.*, 335 So.2d 134, 141 (Ala. 1976).

"The two standards go hand-in-hand, for it is apparent that a food product is defective or unreasonably dangerous if it is unmerchantable or unfit for human consumption. See *Matthews v. Campbell Soup Co.*, 380 F. Supp. 1061 (S.D. Tex. 1974).

"The Court of Civil Appeals rejected the adoption of the so-called 'foreign-natural' rule urged by Morrison's. This rule first appeared in *Mix v. Ingersoll Candy Co.*, 6 Cal. 2d 674, 59 P.2d 144 (1936), . . .

"The undesirability of the foreign substance test lies in the artificial application at the initial stage of processing the food without consideration of the expectations of the consumer in the final product served. Surely it is within the expectation of the consumer to find a bone in a T-bone steak; but just as certainly it is reasonable for a consumer not to expect to find a bone in a package of hamburger meat. It is entirely possible that a natural substance found in processed food may be more indigestible and cause more injury than many 'foreign' substances.

"The 'reasonable expectation' test as adopted by the Florida courts in *Zabner v. Howard Johnson's, Inc.*, 201 So.2d 824 (Fla. Dist. Ct. App. 1967), appears to us a more logical approach. Under that test, the pivotal issue is what is reasonably expected by the consumer in the food as served, not what might be natural to the ingredients of that food prior to preparation. *Id.* at 826 'Naturalness of the substance to any ingredients in the food served is important only in determining whether the consumer may reasonably expect to find such substance in the particular type of dish or style of food served.' *Id.*

"Adoption in this jurisdiction of the reasonable expectation test is compatible with the Alabama Extended Manufacturer's Liability Doctrine and the implied warranty of merchantability (§ 7–2–314). The terms 'defect,' 'unreasonably dangerous,' and 'merchantable' all focus upon the expectations of the ordinary consumer, possessed of the ordinary knowledge common to the community. *Casrell v. Altec Industries, Inc.*, 335 So.2d 128, 133 (Ala. 1976), quoting *Welch v. Outboard Marine Corp.*, 481 F.2d 252 (5th Cir. 1973).

"The Court of Civil Appeals held that what a consumer is reasonably justified in expecting is a question for the jury. *Morrison's Cafeteria of Montgomery, Inc. v. Haddox*, 431 So.2d 969 (Ala. Civ. App. 1982), citing *Hochberg v. O'Donnell's Restaurant, Inc.*, 272 A.2d 846 (D.C. App. 1971). We agree that in most instances this would be true. . . . As the court concluded in *Hochberg, supra,* after holding the question of reasonable expectation to normally be a jury question: 'It is a different matter if one is injured by a bone while eating a chicken leg or steak or a whole baked fish. There, it may well be held as a matter of law that the consumer should reasonably expect to find a bone.' 272 A.2d at 849.

"We agree with Judge Holmes in the instant case that, on the facts presented, the Court should find as a matter of law that a one-centimeter bone found in a fish fillet 'makes that fish neither unfit for human consumption nor unreasonably dangerous.' *Morrison's Cafeteria of Montgomery, Inc, v. Haddox*, 431 So.2d 969 (Ala. Civ. App. 1982), HOLMES, J., dissenting.

"Courts cannot and must not ignore the common experience of life and allow rules to develop that would make sellers of food or other consumer goods insurers of the products they sell. As has been pointed out, 'consumers do have rather high expectations as to the safety of the products which are offered for sale to them . . . [and] they have a rather low threshold for the frustration of these expectations.' Rheingold, *What Are the Consumer's 'Reasonable Expectations?'*, 22 Bus. Law. 589 (1967).

"On the facts presented here, we find as a matter of law that the presence of a one-centimeter bone did not render the piece of fish unreasonably dangerous. As Judge Holmes stated:

"I base this conclusion on several factors that are present in this case. First of all, it is common knowledge that fish have many bones. Furthermore, government regulations regarding fillets recognize this and allow for the presence of some bones in fillets. As one centimeter bone does not violate any of the government regulations regarding fillets. 50 C.F.R. § 263.101–.104 (1979). Finally, it was undisputed that, in light of the process used to mass produce fillets, it was commercially impractical to remove all bones.

"I stress that my opinion is based solely upon the facts of this case. For instance, if there had been a representation that the fish was boneless or if the bone had been larger or if there had been many bones, my conclusion might well be different. Under these facts, however, I would hold as a matter of law that the implied warranty of merchantability was not breached and that the AEMLD was not violated.

". . . For these reasons, the judgment of the Court of Civil Appeals is due to be reversed and the cause remanded.

"REVERSED AND REMANDED."

The Supreme Court of Oregon has made the reasonable expectations test a jury question, *Gardyjan v. Tatone*, 528 P.2d 1332 (1974). To the same effect, see *Williams v. Braum Ice Cream Stores, Inc.*, 534 P.2d 700 (Okla. App. 1974); *Thompson v. Lawson Milk Co.*, 48 Ohio App. 2d 143, 356 N.E.2d 309 (1976); *Stark v. Chock Full O'Nuts*, 77 Misc. 2d 553, 356 N.Y.S.2d 403 (App. Term. 1st Dep't 1974).

15:5 *Proof of Proximate Cause*

Insert at end of section, p. 411:

In *Jiles v. Church's Fried Chicken, Inc.*, 441 So.2d 393 (La. App. 1983), the Louisiana Court of Appeals found no liability, as a matter of law, for the salmonella poisoning of a child patron upon consuming defendant's chicken, absent proof that the presence of the salmonella bacteria was caused by defendant rather than by other sources of contamination.

15:7 *Defenses of Action for Breach of Implied Warranty of Fitness*

Insert at end of section, p. 412:

The following case illustrates the application of the reasonable expectations test to the consumption of fish poisonous in its natural condition.

HOCH v. VENTURE ENTERPRISES, INC.
473 F. Supp. 541 (D.V.I. 1979)

YOUNG, D.J.:

Factual Background

"This lawsuit stems out of an alleged case of fish poisoning suffered by plaintiff after consuming native hind fish at defendant's restaurant, Venture Enterprises, Inc., d/b/a Daddy's Restaurant (hereafter 'Daddy's'). Plaintiffs, their wives and two other couples went to Daddy's for dinner on the evening of March 4, 1976. Stephen Hoch and Joseph Gubernick ordered tha native hind fish, all the other members of the group ordered non-fish dinners. The dinners were served at approximately 10:00 P.M. and another member of the group, Alice Fioto, tasted a small amount of the native hind fish served to Gubernick. Around

1:00 A.M. the following morning, Gubernick and Hoch became ill, suffering stomach cramps, nausea, diarrhea malaise and a severe sensitivity to temperature changes. When the symptoms persisted, plaintiffs went to the emergency room at Knud Hansen Hospital where they were diagnosed and treated by Dr. Harold Hanno. Dr. Hanno diagnosed the plaintiffs as demonstrating symptoms of 'typical ciguatera poisoning.' Later, Alice Fioto reported that she felt slightly nauseous and suffered diarrhea the morning of March 5, 1976. Plaintiffs subsequently brought this suit against the Daddy's on the theory that Daddy's breached its express and implied warranty that the fish was wholesome and fit for human consumption. . . .

Motion for Partial Summary Judgment

"Plaintiffs move for entry of partial summary judgment in their favor on the issue of liability and assert three theories of liability in support, to wit: breach of defendant's express and implied warranty that the fish was fit for human consumption, and negligence *per se* relying on a safety regulation which prohibits the sale of contaminated food to the public. [Footnote omitted.] Defendant opposes said motion, arguing that material issues of fact are in dispute as to the issue of proximate causation; whether the cooked fish was unfit within the meaning of § 2-314 of the Uniform Commercial Code (hereafter U.C.C.) and whether the assumption of risk defense is applicable under the facts in the instant case.

"After carefully reviewing the memoranda of the parties and their supporting affidavits and documents, I conclude that there are material issues of fact which will be necessary for the jury to decide. First of all, on the record before me, I cannot find that plaintiffs have conclusively established the element of proximate causation. Rather, under the case authority [footnote omitted] cited by plaintiff, plaintiff has merely demonstrated that there is sufficient evidence in the matter *sub judice* to submit the issue of proximate cause to the jury. . . .

"Judge Christian's recent decision in *Battiste v. St. Thomas Diving Club*, 1979 St. Thomas Supp. 164 (D.C.V.I. 1979) provides as alternate basis for denying plaintiff's motion. *Battiste* involved a fish poisoning action for damages brought against Villa Olga Restaurant, wherein the parties filed cross motions for summary judgment. The defendant restaurant had argued that the implied warranty statute was inapplicable to fish poisoning because ciguatera fish poisoning is a latent natural condition in fish. The Court framing the issue as 'what legal standard governed the applicability of the implied warranty provisions of § 2-314 and § 2-315 to ciguatera fish poisoning' (1979 St. Thomas Supp. at 164) adopted a 'reasonable expectations test', which holds it is a question of fact whether a buyer could reasonably expect to find the substance in the food consumed. Only if the plaintiff did not reasonably expect to find such a substance, could it prevail on an implied warranty theory. Thus, under the *Battiste* rationale, there remains a factual question as to whether plaintiffs in the matter *sub judice* might have reasonably expected that their dinner would be contaminated by fish poisoning.

"There is yet a third basis on which to promise denial of plaintiff's motion. In *Bronson v. Club Comanche, Inc.*, 286 F. Supp. 21, 6 V.I.R. 683 (D.C.V.I. 1968), an action was brought against Club Comanche for alleged fish poisoning suffered after plaintiffs consumed a fish dinner in the restaurant. There, as here, plaintiffs sued on an implied warranty theory, relying on § 2-314 of the U.C.C. The Court held that the assumption of risk defense should be available to the defendant, noting:

> "[t]he form of contributory negligence which consists in voluntarily and unreasonably proceeding to encounter a known danger may be a defense in a case of strict liability, such as this. If the consumer is fully aware of the danger and nevertheless proceeds voluntarily to make use of the product and is injured by it, he is barred from recovery. This has sometimes, perhaps more accurately been described as ceasing to place any reliance on the implied warranty rather than as assuming the risk. [Footnote omitted.] 286 F. Supp. at 23, 6 V.I.R. at 687-688.

"Thus, in the matter *sub judice*, there remains a factual issue of whether in the instant case, the assumption of risk defense should be available to defendant. [Footnote omitted.] This will require a full factual development of the pertinent considerations, which the record presently lacks and, accordingly, Rule 56 [summary judgment] relief is not appropriate."

15:7a   *(New Section) Damages*

Insert immediately before 15:8, p. 412:

As a rule, upon a determination of tort liability, the wrongdoer is subject only to those direct and consequential compensatory damages proven by the victim. However, punitive damages to punish the wrongdoer and to deter others from misconduct are available in appropriate situations. In the following case, punitive damages against both the hotelkeeper and the hotel's franchisor were awarded to a food-service patron. The case arose out of food poisoning suffered from the on-premises consumption of food at the hotel.

AVERITT V. SOUTHLAND MOTOR INN OF OKLAHOMA
720 F.2d 1178 (10th Cir. 1983)

LOGAN, C.J.: "Defendants Sheraton Inns, Inc. and Southland Motor Inn Corporation of Oklahoma d/b/a Sheraton Inn-Skyline East Hotel (Southland) appeal from a judgment awarding punitive damages to plaintiff William Michael Averitt. Averitt brought this diversity suit against the defendants after he contracted shigella from eating at the Sheraton-Inn Skyline East Hotel in Tulsa, Oklahoma.

"On March 28, 1978, Averitt stayed at the Southland and dined at the hotel restaurant. Averitt became ill the next day. After he returned home to Dallas, his condition worsened. On April 5, after suffering from diarrhea for several days, he was admitted to a hospital. He was diagnosed as having ulcerative colitis, a chronic disease of the colon. On April 4, 1978, the manager of Southland was notified of an outbreak of food poisoning among guests of the hotel. That day the Tulsa City-County Health Department secured stool cultures from the hotel's employees. These cultures indicated that a hotel employee involved in food preparation had shigella. Although there was local publicity about the shigella outbreak, the hotel made no attempt to notify Averitt or other hotel guests that they had been exposed to shigella. Averitt did not learn of his exposure until a return trip to Tulsa some time later.

"Averitt brought suit against Southland on theories of negligence, strict liability, and breach of warranty, alleging that Southland sold Averitt food contaminated with shigella. Averitt also sued Sheraton Inns, Inc. on the theory that Southland was Sheraton's agent and that Sheraton was therefore responsible for Southland's torts. During trial, the plaintiff introduced into evidence health department inspection reports covering the period from January 8, 1974, to May 19, 1978. The reports indicated that Southland had committed numerous health and sanitary violations. The jury found against Sheraton and Southland and awarded the plaintiff $375,000 compensatory damages and $500,000 punitives damages. The defendants moved for a new trial challenging both the compensatory and punitive damages but then agreed with the plaintiff to pay compensatory damages and to 'forego their argument on their Motion for New Trial as to compensatory damages only, and their right to appeal as to only the amount of compensatory damages.'. . .

"Both defendants contend that the district court erred in admitting into evidence the health department inspection reports, that the evidence did not support an award of punitive damages, and that insufficient evidence of negligence existed to support any award. Sheraton asserts that the trial court erred in submitting the issue of agency or apparent agency to the jury and that Sheraton was thus wrongly held vicariously liable for the torts of Southland. . . .

"The jury verdict on the issue of compensatory damages represents a determination that the defendants breached a duty of care they owed to the plaintiff, that the breach caused the plaintiff's injury, and that Sheraton was liable for the torts of Southland because of an agency relationship. *See generally Chavez v. Sears, Roebuck & Co.*, 525 F.2d 827, 831 (10th Cir. 1975). In failing to appeal the award of compensatory damages, the defendants have left these determinations unchallenged.[1] We therefore address only whether the district court properly ad-

---

[1]"Even if these issues are properly before us, we conclude that the record provides sufficient evidence to support the jury's conclusions. The law is settled in Oklahoma that a principal can be held liable for punitive damages based on the conduct of its agent. *See Taxicab Driver's Local Union No. 889 v. Pittman*, 322 P.2d 159, 168 (Okl. 1957); *Kurn v. Radencie*, 193 Okl. 126, 141 P.2d 580, 581 (1943); *Schuman v. Chatman*, 184 Okl. 224, 86 P.2d 615, 618 (1938). We are satisfied that sufficient evidence supports the jury's verdict against Sheraton under the general agency principles set out in the trial court's order denying a new trial. *See Restatement (2d) of Agency* § 267 (1958). We are also satisfied that the record sufficiently supports the jury's verdict on the issues of negligence and causation.

[The circuit court's reivew of the district court's admission of the health reports is omitted.]

mitted into evidence the health department inspection reports on the issue of punitive damages and whether Southland's actions or omissions justify an award of punitive damages under Oklahoma law.

"Punitive damages are recoverable under Oklahoma law '[i]n any action for the breach of an obligation not arising from contract, where the defendant has been guilty of oppression, fraud or malice, actual or presumed.' Okla. Stat. tit. 23, § 9. Punitive damages are also recoverable when a defendant has been guilty of gross negligence that indicates a reckless disregard for the rights of others. [Citations omitted.] Whether punitive damages should be awarded is a question for the jury. 'Only where there is no evidence whatsoever that would give rise to an inference of actual malice or conduct deemed equivalent to actual malice may a trial court refuse to submit an exemplary damage instruction to the jury.' *Sopkin v. Premier Pontiac, Inc.*, 539 P.2d 1393, 1397 (Okl. App. 1975); *accord. Chavez v. Sears, Roebuck & Co.*, 525 F.2d 827, 829-30 (10th Cir. 1975); *Amoco Pipeline Co. v. Montgomery*, 487 F. Supp. 1268, 1272 (W.D. Okl. 1980).

"The defendants contend that the plaintiff introduced insufficient evidence that Southland was grossly negligent to justify submitting the question of punitive damages to the jury. We disagree. The plaintiff introduced evidence that Southland had repeatedly violated health department regulations by permitting unsanitary conditions to exist in the restaurant. The plaintiff also introduced evidence that Southland took no steps to notify guests of the hotel that they had been exposed to shigella, apparently because Southland feared that the publicity would hurt its business. We believe that this evidence justifies submitting the issue to the jury and that the jury could have found that Southland acted in reckless and conscious disregard for the rights of the plaintiff.

"AFFIRMED."

15:8   *Civil Liability for Injury Caused by Illegal Sale of Intoxicating Liquor—Dram Shop Acts*

Insert at end of third paragraph of section, p. 412:

In *McClennan v. Tottenhoff*, 666 P.2d 408 (1983), the Wyoming Supreme Court overruled its prior common-law doctrine immunizing a liquor vendor from liability to a third party arising out of the illegal sale of alcohol to a patron.

Insert at end of California Business and Professions Code, section 25602.3, p. 418:

In the following case, a California court of appeals has broadly construed the 1978 amendments to the California Civil and Business and Professions Codes, to protect the alcohol server. The amendments reaffirm the traditional common law rule that the consumption of alcohol, not its service, is the proximate cause of injuries arising therefrom.

CALENDRINO V. SHAKEY'S PIZZA PARLOR COMPANY, INC.
151 Cal. App. 3d 370, 198 Cal. Rptr. 697 (1984)

EVANS, A.J.: "Plaintiff appeals from a summary judgment entered upon defendant's [footnote omitted] motion. We affirm.

"On June 14, 1979, plaintiff, a minor, was served a number of mugs of beer over a two-hour span by defendant, a licensed purveyor. Thereafter, at approximately midnight, plaintiff went to a private party where he consumed large amounts of beer and hard liquor for six to six and one-half hours. Plaintiff remained at the party until 6:45 the following morning; at the time he was intoxicated. He accepted a ride home from Anthony Triggs, who was also intoxicated. [Footnote omitted.] Plaintiff was injured when Triggs' car was engaged in a single car accident.

"Triggs' intoxication was the direct cause of plaintiff's injuries. Plaintiff's theory of liability as against defendant, however, is that defendant served alcoholic beverages to plaintiff who was allegedly intoxicated. As a result of intoxication, plaintiff was alleged to be unable to care for and supervise his own conduct, and accepted a ride from an obviously intoxicated person to his physical detriment.

"Defendant's motion for summary judgment is based on the laws affecting liability for furnishing alcoholic beverages.

"The current law in California precludes plaintiff from establishing proximate cause which is the predicate to liability.

"It is now the law of this state that the consumption of alcoholic beverages rather than the furnishing of them is the proximate cause of injuries arising after the consumption of alcohol. The 1978 amendments to Civil Code section 1714 and Business and Professions Code section 25602 operate to bar a suit against providers of alcoholic beverages, social and licensed, brought by the intoxicated consumer as well as third persons injured by that consumer (see *Cory v. Shierloh* 29 Cal. 3d 430, 439 174 Cal. Rptr. 500, 629 P.2d 8). . . . .

"As the Supreme Court stated in *Cory v. Shierloh, supra*, 29 Cal. 3d in page 437, 174 Cal. Rptr. 500, 629 P.2d 8, '[t]he 1978 amendments are hardly models of draftsmanship.' However, in order to dispel any doubts harbored about the intent of the sections, the court expressly restated the result of the amendments was to preclude any actions by the consumer of alcoholic beverages or third persons from stating a cause of action for injuries against either the licensed purveyor or the social host providing the alcohol for consumption. (P. 437, 174 Cal. Rptr. 500, 629 P.2d 8.) The decision makes clear the amendments to Business and Professions Code section 25602 and Civil Code section 1714 reinstated the common law theory which precluded liability against a purveyor of alcoholic beverages prior to the *Vesely*, et al., decision.

"Defendant's motion for summary judgment successfully relied upon the provisions of Business and Professions Code section 25602 and Civil Code section

1714. Plaintiff relies on Business and Professions Code section 25602.1, which was added by the Statutes of 1978 (Stats. 1978, ch. 930, p. 2905, § 1). That section provides: 'Notwithstanding subdivision (b) of Section 25602, a cause of action may be brought by or on behalf of any person who has suffered injury or death against any person licensed pursuant to Section 23300 who sells, furnishes, gives or causes to be sold, furnished or given away any alcoholic beverage to any obviously intoxicated minor where the furnishing, sale or giving of such beverage to the minor is the proximate cause of the personal injury or death sustained by such person.'

"Plaintiff asserts that he has stated a good cause of action because he was a minor at the time his injuries were incurred and that the injuries were proximately caused by defendant serving him alcoholic beverages which impaired his judgment, causing him to ride with an intoxicated driver.

"However, we read section 25602.1 as providing a cause of action only for other persons injured by the intoxicated minor, and not for the intoxicated minor himself. The section '[e]xpresses a single exception to the . . . sweeping immunity' provided by section 25602 (*Cory v. Shierloh, supra*, 29 Cal. 3d at 436, 174 Cal. Rptr. 500, 629 P.2d 8), and, as an exception to the general rule, section 25602.1 must be narrowly construed (see *Goins v. Board of Pension Commissioners* (1979) 96 Cal. App. 3d 1005, 1009, 158 Cal. Rptr. 470, citing *Marrujo v. Hunt* (1977) 71 Cal. App. 3d 972, 977, 138 Cal. Rptr. 220). Section 25602.1 provides a cause of action for '*any person* who has suffered injury or death . . . where the furnishing, sale or giving of [an alcoholic] beverage to [an obviously intoxicated] minor is the proximate cause of the personal injury or death sustained by *such person*' (Emphasis added.) Interpreting the statute narrowly, we cannot construe the terms 'any person' and 'such person' to include the intoxicated minor himself. The purpose of the legislation amending Business and Professions Code section 25602 and Civil Code section 1714 was to abrogate the liability of the commercial purveyor of alcoholic beverages for injuries inflicted by the consumer of such beverages. If the narrow exception of Business and Professions Code section 25602.1 was intended to provide a cause of action not only for those injured by intoxicated minors, but also for the minors themselves, the Legislature would have specifically expressed such intention. . . .

"The judgement is affirmed.

"BLEASE, A.J., dissenting. . . .

"I dissent from the majority opinion because I do not see how 'person' can be read to exclude minors.

"Section 25602.1 excepts from the provisions of section 25602 '*any person* who has suffered injury or death . . . where the furnishing, sale or giving of [an alcoholic] beverage to [an obviously intoxicated] minor is the proximate cause of the . . . injury or death sustained by *such person*. (Emphasis added.) The majority opinion reads 'any person' to exclude the intoxicated minor, notwithstanding there are no words or context on which to hinge the claim. '[A]ny person who has suffered injury or death' plainly does not distinguish between a minor and other persons. Nor does 'such person,' referring to 'any person,' do the job.

"Moreover, I cannot see any reason for reading 'any person who has suffered injury' in section 25602.1 differently from 'any injured person' in section 25602 (which encompasses the consumer of alcohol; *Cory v. Shierloh, supra*, 29 Cal. 3d at p. 437, 174 Cal. Rptr. 500, 629 P.2d 8), the section to which 25602.1 is an exception.

"Nor does a rule of construction come to the aid of a statute plain on its face. There is no ambiguity in the statute. It should be applied as it reads."
Insert immediately before Matalavage v. Sadler, p. 424:

The case to follow interprets the New York Dram Shop Act not to apply to service of alcohol by a social host in a noncommercial setting. The court recognized a landowner's common law duty to supervise his or her premises, to include the conduct of social guests, but held that no notice of violent propensities of the guest was established, a necessary predicate to liability.

KOHLER v. WRAY
114 Misc. 2d 856, 452 N.Y.S.2d 831 (N.Y. Sup. Ct. 1982)

BOEHM, J.: "This is a motion to dismiss the complaint of plaintiff, Donald Kohler, Jr., or, in the alternative, for summary judgment. Plaintiff's claim against defendants Jack and Vicki Wray is grounded upon common law negligence and violation of the Dram Shop Act (General Obligations Law § 11–101).

"It appears that on February 21, 1981, the defendants invited several friends to their home for a housewarming party which featured a band and several kegs of beer. After the party had been in progress for some time the plaintiff arrived and was told by Jack Wray to help himself to the beer that was downstairs in the cellar. Plaintiff claims that at this time he was also encouraged by Wray to contribute some money so that more beer could be purchased.

"Not long after his arrival at the party, plaintiff approached Kelly Piersons who, unbeknown to plaintiff, was married and in the company of her husband, and asked her to dance. There is some dispute as to the intervening details, but within a short time plaintiff and Mr. Pierson exchanged blows, with the result that plaintiff's jaw was broken.

"Thereafter, the plaintiff commenced these lawsuits against the Wrays, alleging that they negligently caused or permitted Mr. Piersons to become intoxicated and that, knowing he was intoxicated, they negligently permitted him to assault and injure the plaintiff. In his bill of particulars, plaintiff also raises a violation of the General Obligations Law (GOL), presumably referring to § 11–101, New York's 'Dram Shop Act.' . . .

"GOL § 11–101 authorizes recovery for injuries caused by an intoxicated person from 'any person' who unlawfully contributes to his intoxication. It is settled, however, that liability under the statute does not flow from the mere service of alcohol to an intoxicated person, but instead requires a 'prohibited sale' as that term is defined by Alcoholic Beverage Control Law (ABCL) § 65 (*Gabrielle v. Craft,*, 75 A.D.2d 939, 428 N.Y.S.2d 84; *Huyler v. Rose*, 88 A.D.2d 755, 451 N.Y.S.2d 478; *Paul v. Hogan*, 56 A.D.2d 723, 392 N.Y.S.2d 766). No such sale has been alleged or shown to have occurred here.

"Although ABCL § 65 provides that 'no person shall sell, deliver or give away' alcohol to certain persons, the courts of this state have uniformly held that the law has no application to a social host in a non-commercial setting (see, *Huyler v. Rose, supra; Gabrielle v. Craft, supra; Paul v. Hogan, supra; Edgar v. Kajet*, 84 Misc. 2d 100, 375 N.Y.S.2d 548, aff'd, 55 A.D.2d 597, 389 N.Y.S.2d 631, mot. for lv. to app. dsmd. 41 N.Y.2d 802, 393 N.Y.S.2d 1026, 362 N.E.2d 626). Although the words 'give away' are included, the plain purpose of this statutory language was to include within the ambit of the sanctions 'those instances where the proprietor of a licensed establishment . . . provides the customer with the traditional "drink on the house.' The statute's title [Prohibited Sales] and its terms manifest the obvious intent to exclude from its coverage the social host who gratuitously provides his guest with an alcoholic beverage.' (*Gabrielle v. Craft, supra*, at 940, 428 N.Y.S.2d 84).

"Plaintiff's suggestion that defendant forsook the protection of the 'social host' exception to ABCL § 65 when they asked their guests to 'chip in' for the beer served is unpersuasive. In the circumstances of this case such conduct alone, unaccompanied by any exception of pecuniary gain, falls far short of the type of commercial activity that ABCL § 65 was intended to prohibit [citations omitted]. Accordingly, plaintiff's actions based upon a violation of GOL § 11-101 are dismissed.

"Nor does the common law recognize a right of action against a host based upon his serving alcohol to one who later injures another (*Paul v. Hogan, supra.*), and, insofar as plaintiff's second cause of action asserts such a claim, it, too, is dismissed.

"The common law recognizes a landowner's duty to take reasonable precautions to supervise a guest to prevent him from harming others, provided that the host 'knows that he can and has the opportunity to control the third party's conduct and is reasonably aware of the necessity of such control' (*id*, 724, 392 N.Y.S.2d 766; *Huyler v. Rose, supra; Mangione v. Dimino*, A.D.2d 128, 332 N.Y.S.2d 683). In addition, a landowner is under a duty to act in a reasonable manner to prevent harm to those on his property, and the standard of care must be determined in view of all the circumstances of the case (*Basso v. Miller*, 40 N.Y.2d 233, 241, 386 N.Y.S.2d 564, 352 N.E.2d 868; *Scurti v. City of New York*, 40 N.Y.2d 433, 437 387 N.Y.S.2d 55, 354 N.E.2d 794; unreported decision, *Treat v. Ponderosa Systems*, Index No. 81-2682, Special Term of Supreme Court, Sixth Judicial District, Broome County, April 27, 1982). Sympathetically read, the complaint adequately states a claim against defendants based upon breach of this duty (see *Huyler v. Rose, supra*).

"However, defendants also seek summary judgment. Although they have submitted nothing to relieve defendants, Vicki Wray, of liability, they have offered proof that Jack Wray had neither reason to anticipate nor opportunity to prevent Piersons from assaulting plaintiff. . . .

"In short, plaintiff has offered nothing to rebut defendant's proof that Jack Wray had neither notice of, nor an opportunity to prevent, the assault alleged by Kohler [footnote omitted] (see, *Burgess v. Garfield*, 1 Misc. 2d 60, 149 N.Y.S.2d 55).

"Plaintiff cites several cases which in his opinion foreclose a grant of summary judgment here. They are, however, distinguishable. Two of plaintiff's cases, *Huyler v. Rose (supra)* and *Molloy v. Coletti*, 114 Misc. 177, 186 N.Y.S. 730 dealt only with the sufficiency of the complaint, an issue which in this case has already been resolved in plaintiff's favor. The others, to the extent that they dealt with a host's liability for the torts of his guests, involved circumstances in which the defendant had been given advance notice of his guest's violent propensities and had an opportunity to guard against them (see, e.g., *Betancourt v. 141 East 57th St. Corp.*, 56 A.D.2d 823, 393 N.Y.S.2d 35 [assailant permitted to re-enter premises within minutes of his involvement in a violent fight]; *Treat v. Ponderosa Systems*, Sup. Ct. Broome County, 4/27/82 [unreported] [assailant had become 'high' on alcohol which he had unlawfully introduced and consumed in defendant restaurant with approval of defendant's employees]). In fact, in *Nallan v. Helmsley-Spear Inc.*, 50 N.Y.2d 507, 429 N.Y.S.2d 606, 407 N.E.2d 451 the Court of Appeals was careful to point out:

> "Of course, a possessor of land, whether he be a landowner or a lease-holder, is not an insurer of the visitor's safety. Thus, even where there is an extensive history of criminal conduct on the premises, the possessor cannot be held to a duty to take protective measures unless it is shown that he either knows or has reason to know from past experiences 'that there is a likelihood of conduct on the part of third persons . . . which is likely to endanger the safety of the visitor' (Restatement, Torts 2d, § 344, Comment *f*). Only if such conditions are met may the possessor of land be obliged to 'take precautions . . . and to provide a reasonably sufficient number of servants to afford a reasonable protection' (*id.*). (*Id.* at 519, 429 N.Y.S.2d 606, 407 N.E.2d 451.)

"Plaintiff here has shown nothing in either Pierson's conduct on the night of the party or his prior history which could have put defendants on notice that he was likely to be a danger to anyone at their party. In the absence of such proof, and considering defendant Jack Wray's showing of non-liability, plaintiff's claim against him must fall. . . ."

Insert immediately after Matalavage v. Sadler, p. 427:

An appellate court has interpreted New York's Dram Shop Act as prohibiting a tavern owner from avoiding or reducing liability, where an action is brought by a dependent of the intoxicated person (vendee), on the basis of the patron's contributory negligence. *Weinheimer v. Hoffman*, 470 N.Y.S.2d 804 (3d Dep't. 1983).

The objective test governing a commercial vendor's duty not to serve a patron alcohol, that the vendor knew or reasonably should have known that the patron was intoxicated, was reaffirmed by the Supreme Judicial Court of Massachusetts. Violation of a statute governing illegal sale of liquor was held to be some evidence of negligence. The prior requirement that the injured party prove scienter (guilty knowledge) was overruled. A parent was authorized to recover for emotional distress suffered as an on-the-scene bystander who witnessed his son's wrongful death. *Cimino v. Milford Keg, Inc.*, 385 Mass. 323, 431 N.E.2d 920 (1982).

The Washington Supreme Court has created a common-law cause of action in favor of the estate of an obviously intoxicated minor in a case arising out of an illegal commercial sale of liquor that caused the minor's death. The court stated that the illegal sale of alcohol to such a patron constitutes negligence *per se*. *Young v. Caravan Corp.*, 99 Wash. 2d 655, 663 P.2d 834, *opinion amended*, 672 P.2d 1267 (1983). Also see *Yost v. State*, 640 P.2d 1044 (Utah 1981). The Nevada Supreme Court has ruled otherwise in *Yoscovitch v. Wasson*, 645 P.2d 975 (1982).

15:9 *A Defense to Dram Shop or Common-Law Liability: Voluntary Intoxication of Patron*

Insert immediately before Williams v. Klemsrud, *p. 436:*

In this landmark case, the Supreme Court of Arizona overruled its prior common-law rule of tavernowner nonliability for alcohol-related injuries either to the intoxicated drinker or to third persons caused by the intoxicated drinker.

BRANNIGAN V. RAYBUCK
136 Ariz. 513, 667 P.2d. 213 (1983)

FELDMAN, J.: "Plaintiffs are the surviving parents of three boys, Michael William Brannigan, Michael J. Roberts and Danny Jordan, who were killed in a motor vehicle accident which occurred on October 8, 1978. The parents of all three filed wrongful death actions against the Raybucks (defendants), who operated a business under the style of 'Good Time Inn.' The parents alleged that the defendants had breached a duty of care by furnishing liquor to the boys and that this had been the cause of the accident in which all three were killed.

"Defendants moved for summary judgment in each of the cases, claiming that under the common law of Arizona a tavern owner was not liable for negligence in furnishing intoxicants to patrons who were underage or already intoxicated. The two trial judges who considered the cases in the superior court quite properly agreed that this was the law of Arizona and granted the motions for summary judgment. The cases were consolidated on appeal and in a memorandum decision [citations omitted] the court of appeals held that prior case law required it to apply the common law rule that a tavern owner is not liable for negligence in furnishing intoxicants to an underage or intoxicated patron who, as a result, subsequently injures either himself or some third person. The court of appeals therefore affirmed the summary judgments granted the defendants.

"All three plaintiff's joined in a petition for review to this court. We accepted review of this case and the transfer of the companion case of *Ontiveros v. Borak*, 136 Ariz. 500, 667 P.2d 200 (1983) in order to reconsider the common law rule of tavern owner's nonliability and to determine whether that rule should be retained as the common law of this state. . . .

"The facts are set out in the opinion of the court of appeals; we borrow their language: Roberts and Brannigan were passengers in a pickup truck driven by Jordan when the truck was involved in a one-car accident in which all three young men died. Roberts and Brannigan were both sixteen years of age and Jordan was seventeen years of age at the time of the accident. Viewing the evidence in a light most favorable to the plaintiffs, it is established that Jordan went to the Good Time Inn with his girlfriend on the evening of October 7, 1978, where he consumed several drinks of intoxicating liquor. He took his girlfriend home around midnight and returned to the bar, where he started drinking with Brannigan, Roberts and other friends. Several pitchers of beer and numerous drinks of tequilla were consumed by the boys. By the time they all left the bar at 1:00 a.m. on Sunday they were all intoxicated. The Maricopa County Medical Examiner's Report indicates that Jordan, the driver of the pickup, had a blood-alcohol level of .23. Within minutes of leaving the parking lot, Jordan crashed the pickup into a wall. There is testimony that the employees of the bar did not check for age cards and that the Good Time Inn, owned by Mr. and Mrs. Raybuck, was patronized by Jordan and other teenagers because they were not checked for proof of their ages.

"The grant of summary judgment by the trial court and affirmance by the court of appeals was predicated upon the principle that it is not the act of selling, but, rather, the act of consuming liquor that is the proximate cause of the injury sustained by either the intoxicated customer or some third person, so that the tavern owner is therefore not liable for negligence in selling the liquor. This is the common law rule which has obtained in Arizona. *Ontiveros, supra.* We have today abolished that rule, holding that it is unsuitable to present society and is based on reasoning repugnant to modern tort theory. We held that causation in dram shop cases 'should ordinarily be a question of fact for the jury under usual principles of Arizona tort law.'

Duty

"In *Ontiveros, supra*, we held today that the tavern owner was under a duty, imposed both by common law principles and statute, to exercise care in serving intoxicants to a patron who later injured a third party. The facts of the case at bench present a different question, since here one of the persons served, Jordan, inflicted the harm on himself as well as third persons. The third persons involved were not completely innocent participants, as in *Ontiveros*, but had participated with Jordan at the same 'party.'

"Thus, these cases present the question of whether the tavern owner has a duty to the patron to withhold intoxicants in order to prevent the patron from injuring himself. While this question is of particular significance in the Jordan case, it also exists in the other cases since one might well argue that Brannigan and Roberts contributed to their own demise by drinking with Jordan and getting in the truck with him. There was evidence that Jordan's state of intoxication was easily recognizable by both the barkeep and the passengers. In fact, the evidence indicates that Jordan 'staggered' from the saloon to the parking lot and a witness testified on deposition that as Jordan drove away, Mrs. Raybuck mentioned that 'those boys will be lucky if they make it home alive tonight.' While we have indicated above and in *Ontiveros, supra*, that we consider the act of furnishing liquor to be part of the chain of cause and effect leading to the accident, it is certainly to be acknowledged that the voluntary consumption is also part of that cause and effect. Therefore, we examine the question of duty in the context that the act of consumption by all three boys contributed to the occurrence of the accident.

"There are cases holding that the seller of liquor is not liable for the mere sale of liquor to an intoxicated person who subsequently causes injury to himself as the result of intoxication. *Noonan v. Galick*, 19 Conn. Supp. 308, 310, 112 A.2d 892, 894 (1955); see 48A C.J.S. *Intoxicating Liquors* § 428 at 134 (1981). A growing number of cases, however, have recognized that one of the very hazards that makes it negligent to furnish liquor to a minor or intoxicated patron is the foreseeable prospect that the patron will become drunk and injure himself or others. *See Vesely v. Sager*, 5 Cal. 3d 153, 164, 486 P.2d 151, 159, 95 Cal. Rptr. 623, 631 (1971). Accordingly, modern authority has increasingly recognized that one who furnishes liquor to a minor or intoxicated patron breaches a common law duty owed both to innocent third parties who may be injured and to the patron himself. *See Nazareno v. Urie*, Alaska, 638 P.2d 671 (1981); *Rappaport v. Nichols*, 31 N.J. 188, 156 A.2d 1 (1959); *Jardine v. Upper Darby Lodge No. 1973, Inc.*, 413 Pa. 626, 198 A.2d 550 (1964). These cases are but an example of the general rule that one who furnishes a dangerous instrumentality to a person not competent to use it is liable when that person misuses the item furnished and injures himself or another. *See Bernethy v. Walt Failor's, Inc.*, 97 Wash. 2d 929, 653 P.2d 280 (1982) (firearm given to intoxicated person who killed his wife). Restatement (Second) of Torts § 390 (1965) states:

"One who supplies . . . a chattel for the use of another whom the supplier knows or has reason to know to be likely because of his youth, inexperience or otherwise to use it in a manner involving unreasonable risk of physical harm to *himself* and others . . . is subject to liability for physical harm resulting to *them*.

"(Emphasis supplied.)

"We believe, therefore, that a supplier of liquor is under a common law duty of reasonable care in furnishing liquor to those who, by reason of immaturity or previous over-indulgence, may lack full capacity of self-control and may therefore injure themselves, as well as others.

"Most courts have, however, relied on statutes to find the existence of duty upon which to base a cause of action. *See Davis v. Shiappacossee*, 155 So.2d 365 (Fla. 1963); *Elder v. Fisher*, 247 Ind. 598, 217 N.E.2d 847 (1966); *Soronen v. Olde Milford Inn, Inc.*, 46 N.J. 582, 218 A.2d 630 (1966); *Smith v. Evans*, 421 Pa. 247, 219 A.2d 310 (1966); *Majors v. Brodhead Hotel*, 416 Pa. 265, 205 A.2d 873 (1965). . . .

"We believe that A.R.S. § 4-244(9), which prohibits furnishing 'spirituous liquor' to those under 19 years of age, and § 4–241(A), which requires a licensee to demand certain types of identification from those requesting service, constitute legislative recognition of the foreseeable danger to both the patron and third parties, and an effort to meet that danger by enactment of laws designed to regulate the industry, to protect third persons, and to protect those who are underage from themselves. Accordingly we find here, as in *Ontiveros, supra*, that the licensee and his employees have a duty recognized both by common law and statute to refrain from selling intoxicants to those whose subnormal capacity for self-control is or should be known or who are prohibited by statute from using alcoholic beverages. We hold, therefore, that defendants were under a duty to all three of the decedents.

<h3 style="text-align:center">Standard of Care</h3>

"Defendants argue with some persuasive force that in many cases unjust results will be reached by recognizing that the statute is, in part at least, a safety measure designed for protection of patrons and third parties. They contend that the statute will thus be considered to set the standard of care so that its violation will always result in a finding of negligence per se. It is the prevailing rule, recognized in Arizona, that a breach of a statute intended as a safety regulation is not merely evidence of negligence but is negligence per se. *Orlando v. Northcutt*, 103 Arix. 298, 300, 441 P.2d 58, 60 (1968); W. Prosser, *Handbook of the Law of Torts* § 36 at 197-200 (4th ed. 1971). It is true that *if* the statutory standard of conduct were applied rigidly, one who furnished liquor to a minor might be held to have breached his duty even though the minor produced false identification to satisfy the requirements of § 4-241, and one who furnished further intoxicants to an already intoxicated patron might be held liable even though the supplier had no way of knowing the patron had reached the point of intoxication.

"As in most things, however, the common law is not so rigid as to demand injustice. The actual rule on the negligence per se doctrine is that unless the statute is construed to impose an absolute duty, its violation may be excused when, for example, the defendant was 'unable after reasonable dilligence to comply.' Restatement of Torts, *supra*, § 288 A. . . .

"[Citations omitted.]

"We think this concept is applicable to the situation presented here. The legislature has not enacted a civil damage statute eliminating all excuse for the violation of the statute; thus, we are free to recognize that rule which we consider most likely to achieve just results. Prosser, *supra*, § 36, at 198. The statutes in question do not impose strict criminal liability. *Spitz v. Municipal Court*, 127 Ariz. 405, 407-08, 621 P.2d 911, 913-14 (1980). Even if they did, this would not prevent us from recognizing excusable violations when the statute is used to define a standard of care in civil cases. *See* Restatement of Torts, *supra*, § 288 A, comment b; Prosser, *supra*. We therefore hold that where a violation of the statutes pertaining to furnishing liquor to those who are underage or already intoxicated is shown, negligence exists as a matter of law, but under proper facts the jury may be allowed to find that the violation was excusable. [Footnote omitted.] *O'Donnell v. Maves*, 108 Ariz. 98, 100, 492 P.2d 1205, 1207 (1972); *Platt v. Gould*, 26 Ariz. App. 315, 316-17, 548 P.2d 28, 29-30 (1976).

"In dram shop cases, then, a licensee who has violated the statute may be able to show such violation excusable if he can establish, for instance, that the minor appeared to be of age and had what appeared to be proper identification as required by A.R.S. § 4-241 or that the demeanor or conduct of the person served was such that there was no reason to believe that he or she was intoxicated. The situations cited are intended as examples, and not as an exhaustive list.

Contributory Negligence—Assumption of the Risk

"We acknowledge that the boys in question were apparently of an age to understand and to control their conduct. The present record does not indicate that they were addicted to alcohol and therefore not responsible for their conduct. *Cf. Pratt v. Daly*, 55 Ariz. 535, 104 P.2d 147 (1940). The evidence establishes that they voluntarily obtained and consumed large amounts of intoxicating liquor and knew or should have known the danger involved in driving in that condition or riding with someone who was in that condition. No doubt their voluntary consumption was a cause of the accident. However, even assuming that the defenses of contributory negligence and assumption of the risk are available, [footnote omitted] under our constitution these defenses 'shall, in all cases whatsoever, be a question of fact and shall, at all times, be left to the jury.' Ariz. Const. art. 18, § 5. In Arizona, therefore, the court cannot find as a matter of law that the legal defenses of contributory negligence or assumption of risk exist; the jury is free to find in favor of the plaintiff even though the court ordinarily would find as a matter of law that the plaintiff has been contributorily negligent, or has assumed the risk. *Layton v. Rocha*, 90 Ariz. 369, 370, 368 P.2d 444, 445 (1962). We therefore do not reach the question of contributory negligence.

Other Arguments

"Here, as in *Ontiveros*, defendants raise various examples which they claim militate in favor of nonrecognition of liability. For instance, defendants argue that there will be difficulty in administering a rule of liability in hypothetical situations where: (1) a patron has one drink in the first saloon and 19 drinks in a second saloon; (2) the patron has 19 drinks in the first saloon and one drink in the second; (3) the patron has 10 drinks in each saloon. We find these hypothetical situations no more vexatious than in other cases. In the first example, for instance, one could argue that the acts of the first licensee were a contributing cause of the ultimate accident, but it is obvious that in the usual case there is no negligence in serving a sober, adult patron one drink. In the second example, the act of serving the last drink may well have been negligent, but, again, causation would have to be proved. In the third situation, each of the licensees may have negligently contributed to the result and both may probably be held liable. These and similar situations present the same problems of causation which exist in other tort actions. They are not beyond the ability of our system to handle. *Lewis v. Wolf,* 122 Ariz. 567, 572, 596 P.2d 705, 710 (App. 1979). We acknowledge that the system will not handle each case perfectly, but we think it better to adopt a rule which will permit courts to attempt to achieve justice in all cases than to continue to rely on one which guarantees injustice in many cases.

"Defendants argue that by changing the common law rule we will impose upon the liquor business a special duty of care not imposed on sellers of most other products. To an extent that is true, but alcohol is more dangerous than most products. We do no more than place upon those who furnish alcohol the burden of responding in damages for failure to use due care in furnishing a dangerous product. However, we do not place upon them any greater burden in conducting themselves than that which had already been imposed by the requirements of statute which make it unlawful to sell liquor to minors or intoxicated patrons. We agree with the New Jersey Supreme Court:

"Liquor licensees, who operate their businesses by way of privilege rather than as of right, have long been under strict obligation not to serve minors and intoxicated persons and if, as is likely, the result we have reached in the conscientious exercise of our traditional judicial function substantially increases their diligence in honoring that obligation then the public interest will indeed be very well served.

Rappaport v. Nichols, 31 N.J. at 205–06, 156 A.2d at 10.

"Defendants next argue, as did those in *Ontiveros,* that this court should await legislative action and should not abandon the common law rule in the absence of such action. As we indicated in *Ontiveros, supra,* we do not think lack of legislative intent with regard to the existence of a civil remedy is determinative. We believe there is a legislative objective to keep drunk drivers off the roads. The magnitude of the problem is documented in the statistics quoted in *Ontiveros.* The problem in Arizona seems, if anything, to be greater than in other parts of the country. According to the statistics cited in the amicus brief filed in this cause by Mothers Against Drunk Drivers, between one-third and one-half of all fatal automobile accidents in Arizona involve alcohol and Arizona ranks fourth highest in the country in alcohol-related deaths and injuries. *See, also, State ex. rel. Ek-*

strom v. Justice Court, 136 Ariz. 1, 4, 663 P.2d 992, 996 (1983) (concurring opinion). Adoption of a rule which will make those who furnish alcohol to those who are forbidden to use it civilly responsible to pay damages for the injuries caused by their violation of law is a step designed to meet a problem which has become acute. This is not judicial legislation, but merely the response of the common law to changed social conditions. If the legislature considers it to be unwise, it has the means of so informing us. . . .

"[The court's reasoning as to retroactive application of its decision is omitted.]

"We hold, therefore, that the former rule of nonliability based on causation is abolished, and the duty of a licensee to refrain from selling alcohol to minors and intoxicated patrons who may, as a result, injure themselves or others is recognized for this case, for all other pending cases, for those not yet filed which are not barred by the statute of limitations, and for all causes of action which may arise in the future.

"The decision of the court of appeals is vacated. The judgments below are reversed. The cases are remanded for further proceedings not inconsistent with this opinion."

CONGINI BY CONGINI V. PORTERSVILLE VALVE CO.
504 Pa. 157, 470 A.2d 515 (1983)

McDERMOTT, J.: "This appeal arises from an action in trespass for personal injuries sustained by Mark Congini in an automobile accident which occurred on December 22, 1978. His parents instituted suit on his behalf, and on their own behalf, in the Court of Common Pleas of Lawrence County against the Portersville Valve Company (Portersville). The defendant filed preliminary objections in the nature of demurrer. The trial judge, the Honorable William R. Balph, sustained the preliminary objections and the Conginis' complaint was dismissed on August 18, 1980.

"On appeal the Superior Court affirmed, relying in part on our decision in *Manning v. Andy*, 454 Pa. 237, 310 A.2d 75 (1973). [Footnote omitted.] Appellants petitioned this Court for allowance of appeal and we granted allocatur. . . .

"At the time of the accident in question Mark Congini was eighteen (18) years of age and an employee of Portersville. On December 22, 1978 Portersville held a Christmas party for its employees at which alcoholic beverages were served. Mark attended the party and, as a result of consuming an undisclosed amount of alcohol, became intoxicated.

"Mark's car was parked at Portersville plant, which was the scene of the party, and appellee, through one if its agents, had possession and custody of the car keys. Although Portersville's agent was aware of Mark's intoxicated condition, the keys were given to Mark upon his request so that he could drive from the plant to his home.

"While Mark was operating the car on the highway, he drove it into the rear of another vehicle which was proceeding in the same direction. As a result of this accident Mark suffered multiple fractures and brain damage which have left him totally and permanently disabled.

"In their appeal appellants have alleged several grounds of liability: first, that defendant was negligent in providing Mark with alcoholic beverages to the point that he became intoxicated; second, that defendant was negligent in surrendering the car keys to Mark, knowing that Mark was intoxicated and that he would drive; and third, that appellee, as a landowner, was negligent in breaching a duty owed to Mark as an invitee. Appellants have not alleged that appellee was a licensee of the Pennsylvania Liquor Control Board.

"The first issue before us is similar to that raised in *Klein v. Raysinger*, decided this day at ——Pa.——, 470 A.2d 507 (1983), i.e., the extent to which a social host can be held liable for injuries sustained by his guest to whom he has served intoxicating liquors. This case, however, differs in two respects: that the guest here was a minor; and that the plaintiff here is the guest to whom the intoxicants were served, rather than a third person injured by a person who was served alcoholic beverages. *See Klein, id.*

"As we note in *Klein*, our sister state jurisdictions are virtually unanimous in refusing to extend common law liability to an adult social host serving intoxicants to his adult guests. *Id.* at 510 (collected cases). However, there is no such unanimity in cases where an adult host has knowingly served intoxicants to a minor. [Citations omitted.]

"In *Klein v. Raysinger, supra*, we held that there exists no common law liability on the part of a social host for the service of intoxicants to this adult guests. In arriving at this decision we relied upon the common law rule that in the case of an ordinary able bodied man, it is the consumption of alcohol rather than the furnishing thereof, that is the proximate cause of any subsequent damage.

"However, our legislature has made a legislative judgment that persons under twenty-one years of age are incompetent to handle alcohol. Under Section 6308 of the Crimes Code [footnote omitted.] 18 Pa. C.S. § 6308, a person 'less than 21 years of age' commits a summary offense if he 'attempts to purchase, purchases, consumes, possesses or transports any alcohol, liquor or malt or brewed beverages.' Furthermore, under Section 306 of the Crimes Code, 18 Pa. C.S.A. § 306, an adult who furnishes liquor to a minor would be liable as an accomplice to the same extent as the offending minor.

"This legislative judgment compels a different result than *Klein*, for here we are not dealing with ordinary able bodied men. Rather, we are confronted with persons who are, at least in the eyes of the law, incompetent to handle the effects of alcohol. *Accord, Burke v. Superior Court, supra*, 129 Cal. App. 3d at 575, 18 Cal. Rptr. at 151; *Thaut v. Finely, supra* (1974); *Lover v. Sampson*, 44 Mich. App. 173, 205 N.W.2d 69 (1972). *See Davis v. Shiappacossee*, 155 So.2d 365 (Fla. 1963); *Chausse v. Southland Corp.*, La. App. 400 So.2d 1199 (1981) *cert. denied*, La., 404 So.2d 497 (1981); *Munford, Inc. v. Peterson*, Miss., 368 So.2d

213 (1979); *Wiener v. Gamma Phi Chapter of Alpha Tau Omega Fraternity*, 258 Or. 632, 485 P.2d 18 (1971). *See also, Cantor v. Anderson*, 126 Cal. App. 3d 124, 178 Cal. Rptr. 540 (1981).

"Section 286 of the Restatement of Torts Second provides:

"§ 286. When Standard of Conduct Defined by Legislation or Regulation Will Be Adopted

"The court may adopt as the standard of conduct of a reasonable man the requirements of a legislative enactment or an administrative regulation whose purpose is found to be exclusively or in part

"(a) to protect a class of persons which includes the one whose interest is invaded, and

"(b) to protect the particular interest which is invaded, and

"(c) to protect that interest against the kind of harm which has resulted, and

"(d) to protect that interest against the particular hazard from which the harm results.

"We have previously relied upon this Section and accepted it as an accurate statement of the law. *See Majors v. Brodhead Hotel*, 416 Pa. 265, 268, 205 A.2d 875 (1965); *Jardine v. Upper Darby Lodge, No. 1973*, 413 Pa. 626, 198 A.2d 550 (1964). *See also, Frederick L. v. Thomas*, 578 F.2d 513 (3d Cir. 1978).

"Section 6308 of the Crimes Code represents an obvious legislative decision to protect both minors and the public at large from the perceived deleterious effects of serving alcohol to persons under twenty-one years of age. Thus, we find that defendants were negligent per se in serving alcohol to the point of intoxication to a person less than twenty-one years of age, [footnote omitted] and that they can be held liable for injuries proximately resulting from the minor's intoxication. [Footnote omitted.]

"Our inquiry, however, cannot stop here. As noted above the plaintiff here was not an unwitting third party to the actor's negligence, but the person to whom the intoxicants were allegedly served. Nevertheless, for the purpose of deciding whether a cause of action exists, we see no valid distinction which would warrant a limitation on the action to third parties alone. [Citation omitted.]

"Under our analysis, an actor's negligence exists in furnishing intoxicants to a class of persons legislatively determined to be incompetent to handle its effects. It is the person's service which forms the basis of the cause of action, not whether or not a putative plaintiff is entitled to recover. Resolution of this latter issue requires a fuller record than the one which we have on demurrer.

"We note, however, that under the scheme set up by this Court in *Kuhns v. Brugger*, 390 Pa. 331, 135 A.2d 395 (1957) an eighteen year old person is 'presumptively capable of negligence.' [Footnote omitted.] We further note that an eighteen year old is liable as an adult for the offenses which he commits, and that by knowingly consuming alcohol an eighteen year old is also guilty of a summary offense. See 18 Pa. C.S. § 6308.

"Thus, although we recognize that an eighteen year old minor may state a cause of action against an adult social host who has knowingly served him intoxicants, the social host in turn may assert as a defense the minor's 'contributory' negligence. Thereafter, under our Comparative Negligence Act [footnote and citation omitted] it will remain for the fact finder to resolve whether the defendant's negligence was such as to allow recovery. *Accord Munford v. Peterson, supra; Chausse v. Southland Corp., supra.*

"Appellants have also asserted two separate issues, neither of which do we find meritorious. The first involves the alleged negligent entrustment of an automobile to one who is intoxicated. However, this cause of action has been recognized only in those situations where the person sought to be held liable was 'the owner or other person responsible for its (automobile) use.' *See* Anno.: *Liability Based on Entrusting Automobile to One Who Is Intoxicated or Known to Be Excessive User of Intoxicants.* 19 A.L.R.3d 1175 (1968). Appellants have cited no cases which extend this liability to persons who were not the owner or otherwise responsible for the automobile in question. *See e.g., Mills v. Continental Parking Corp.*, 86 Nev. 724, 475 P.2d 673 (1970) (holding parking lot attendant not liable for surrendering car to owner who was intoxicated.) The appellee here had no right of control over Mark Congini's car, and we see no basis upon which to extend liability to the situation posited here.

"Finally, appellants have argued that the defendants breached a duty as a landowner to Mark Congini. The Superior Court refused to discuss this issue, as they found that it was not fairly raised by the pleadings.

"Since there was nowhere pleaded that Mark Congini was required by his employer to attend the party in question, it appears at most that he was a gratuitous licensee. To such a person Section 341 of the Restatement of Torts, Second provides:

"§ 341. Activities Dangerous to Licensees
"A possessor land is subject to liability to his licensees for physical harm caused to them by his failure to carry on his activities with reasonable care for their safety, if, but only if,
"(a) he should expect that they will not discover or realize the danger, and
"(b) they do not know or have reason to know of the possessor's activities and of the risk involved.

"Appellants did not plead that Mark Congini was without knowledge of the possessor's activities, or of the risks involved in consuming alcoholic beverages. Indeed, it would have been impossible to contend that Mark Congini was ignorant of the appellee's activities, since that was the reason for his presence.

"Furthermore, appellant's injuries at most would seem to have resulted from 'existent conditions upon the premises' (i.e., the availability of alcohol), as opposed to 'any affirmative or "active" negligence on [the defendant's] part.' *See Potter Title and Trust Co. v. Young*, 367 Pa. 239, 244, 80 A.2d 76, 79 (1951). In such a case a possessor of land is not liable to a licensee in the absence of willful and wanton injury. *Knapp v. R.S. Noonan, Inc.*, 385 Pa. 460, 123 A.2d 429 (1956); *Potter Title and Trust Co. v. Young, supra.* Such liability was not pleaded by the appellants. We therefore, agree with the Superior Court that a cause of action under this theory was not stated.

"In light of appellee's potential liability as a social host, we reverse the order of the Superior Court and remand this case to the court of common pleas for proceeding not inconsistent with our opinion. As to appellants' other contentions, we affirm the order of the Superior Court. . . .

"[Concurring opinion omitted.]

"ZAPPALA, J., dissenting.

"In *Klein v. Raysinger*, ——Pa.——, 470 A.2d 507 (1983), we held that no duty exists under the common law which would impose liability upon a social host who serves alcohol to an adult guest for conduct of the guest which results in injury to himself or to a third party. We recognized that it is the consumption of alcohol, rather than the furnishing of alcohol to an individual, which is the proximate cause of any subsequent occurrence.

"In the instant case, however, the majority opinion concludes that liability of a social host may arise from the act of furnishing alcohol to a minor and that such liability may extend to harm suffered by the minor. By adopting this legal premise, the majority today is effectively overruling *Klein* [footnote omitted]. The analysis employed by the majority is clearly inconsistent with that enunciated in *Klein*, and for that reason I must dissent.

"The majority attempts to reconcile the inconsistency based upon a perceived public policy to protect minors and the public from the potentially harmful effects of alcohol. [Footnote omitted.] This public policy is gleaned from § 6308 of the Crimes Code which imposes criminal liability on a person under 21 who attempts to purchase, purchases, consumes, possesses or transports alcohol. Although the legislature may have determined that persons under 21 are incompetent to handle alcohol, as the majority suggests, it is evident that the legislature has defined the offense so as to render the minor culpable for his own conduct which violates the statute. A minor could not defend his conduct by demonstrating that an adult had furnished him with the alcohol. Thus, the statute which the majority interprets as evincing a policy to protect minors does not shield them from their acts which contravene the statute.

"The majority attempts to distinguish underage drinkers from those over 21 years by stating that minors are deemed incompetent to handle the effects of alcohol. This distinction is irrelevant, however, to the issue of whether a social host who furnishes alcohol to a minor may be held liable for injuries sustained by the minor or a third party as the result of the minor's actions.

"It is not the knowledge of a social host of the ability or inability of a guest to handle the effects of alcohol, or knowledge of a person's condition, which would give rise to a duty not to furnish alcohol to the guest. We declined to impose liability on that basis in *Klein*, when we refused to recognize a cause of action, urged by the Appellants therein, against a social host who serves alcohol to a visibly intoxicated person who the host knows, or should know, intends to drive a motor vehicle. I cannot agree, therefore, that liability should be imposed on a social host serving alcohol to a person under 21 based upon the rationale that minors are incompetent to handle alcohol. If it is consumption by an adult guest, rather than the furnishing of alcohol by a host, which is the proximate cause of subsequent occurrences, then it is not less compelling to conclude that it is the minor's voluntary consumption of alcohol which is the proximate cause of harm which results.

"I find it inconceivable that a minor or an innocent third party who suffers harm under the factual circumstances alleged in the instant case may assert a cause of action against a social host who has dispensed the alcohol, yet an innocent third party who suffers harm under the factual circumstances set forth in *Klein* would be precluded from asserting a similar cause of action. These inapposite results arise solely from the fortuitous circumstance of the age of the tortfeasor, rather than the conduct of the social host. I would hold, consistent with *Klein*, that no cause of action exists against a social host for providing alcohol to a guest under the facts alleged in this action. This matter is better left to legislative action than to judicial gymnastics."

The Connecticut Supreme Court has extended the liability of vendors and social hosts for the wanton and reckless sale to or service of an intoxicated person that causes that person to injure or cause the death of a third party. *Kowal v. Hofher*, 181 Conn. 355, 436 A.2d 1 (1980).

The extent to which a social host can be made responsible for alcohol "otherwise supplied" to a minor, in violation of the Iowa Code, was held not to apply to a property owner who permitted a beer party to be held on his property when he knew or should have known that minors would be present and as a result of which a minor plaintiff was injured. *DeMore by DeMore v. Dieters*, 334 N.W.2d 734 (Iowa 1983).

In *Sager v. McClenden*, 296 Or. 33, 672 P.2d 697 (1983), the Oregon Supreme Court ruled that no cause of action exists for patrons injured off the premises by reason of their own intoxication. This decision reaffirms the traditional voluntary intoxication doctrine applicable to adults and patrons (see *Wright v. Mofitt*, 437 A.2d 554 [Del. 1981]), in contrast to the judicial solicitude extended to minor patrons. See *Congini by Congini, supra*.

In *Brookins v. The Round Table, Inc.*, 624 S.W.2d 547 (Tenn. 1981), the Tennessee Supreme Court made a jury question of the issue of whether a minor's own intoxication, arising out of an illegal sale of alcohol, actively contributed to his own injuries.

Chapter 16. Innkeeper's Responsibility for Property of Guests

16:6 *Loss of Property Delivered to Innkeeper by Third Person for Guest*

Insert after Needles v. Howard, *p. 450:*

In *Berlow*, to follow, the Texas Court of Civil Appeals ruled that acceptance of a package for a departing guest in violation of that guest's instructions does not fall within the innkeeper's statute limiting liability for its loss.

BERLOW v. SHERATON DALLAS CORP.
629 S.W.2d 818 (Tex. Civ. App. 1982)

WHITHAN, J.: "This is an appeal from a judgment, on an alternative motion by defendant Sheraton Dallas Corporation (the hotel) for judgment on the verdict or judgment notwithstanding the verdict, that plaintiff (Berlow) take nothing in her suit against the hotel for the loss of a package containing jewelry. We reverse and render judgment in favor of Berlow.

"Berlow, a designer and manufacturer of jewelry, frequently authorized her parents (the Soifers) to represent her in showing and selling jewelry to fashionable department stores. In January, 1978, Berlow authorized the Soifers to show ten pieces of jewelry in Dallas. Berlow arranged to have a package containing the jewelry delivered by United Parcel Service (UPS) to her parents at the hotel. The package was marked 'insured' on the outside and showed Berlow's return address. The package did not arrive at the hotel during the four-day stay of the Soifers. During their stay, each of the Soifers asked frequently about it at the front desk and, before checking out, the Soifers informed front desk personnel that this was a very important package, although they deliberately refrained from telling them the contents or value of the package. They asked that the hotel refuse delivery of it, and personnel at the front desk agreed to refuse its delivery. Agreeing to and subsequently refusing delivery of packages upon the oral instructions of guests to front desk attendants was standard procedure for the hotel. Contrary to its agreement, however, when the package arrived the hotel took delivery of it, stored it at the front desk for a month, and then turned it over to the United States Post Office (USPO) without postage, marked 'Return to Sender.' This, too, was standard procedure for the hotel in dealing with packages stored at the front desk. No attempt was made to determine if the Soifers had been recent guests at the hotel, nor to contact Berlow. The package was lost. At trial, Berlow testifed that the fair market value of the jewelry was $10,231.00. . . .

"Berlow moved for judgment on the verdict and the hotel moved alternatively for judgment on the verdict or judgment notwithstanding the verdict. The trial court granted the hotel's motion and rendered judgment for it, without specifying on which ground judgment was being rendered. On appeal, if the judgment is proper in either respect, the trial court must be affirmed; thus a discussion of each ground on which judgment could have been entered is necessary.

I. The Hotel's Motion For Judgment on the Verdict

"The hotel contends that a judgment was proper on its motion for judgment on the verdict because, under Tex. Rev. Civ. Stat. Ann. art. 4593 (Vernon 1976), the risk of loss of the package was placed on Berlow as a matter of law. We do not agree. Article 4593 provides:

"Whenever any person shall allow his baggage or other property to remain in any hotel, apartment hotel or boarding house after the relation of innkeeper and guest has ceased without checking same, or shall leave his baggage or other property in the lobby of any hotel, apartment hotel or boarding house prior to checking it or becoming a guest, or shall forward any baggage to such hotel, apartment hotel or boarding house before becoming a guest, said hotel, apartment hotel or boarding house keeper may, at his option, hold such baggage or other property at the risk of the said owner.

"Under this statute, a hotel's liability is limited only under specifically enumerated circumstances, and, under the facts of this case, no such circumstances exist which would limit the hotel's liability. Berlow did not 'allow' the package to remain at the hotel, instead she, through the Soifers, elicited a promise from the hotel *not* to permit the package to enter the premises and was unaware that this promise was not carried out. Nor did Berlow forward the package to the hotel at her risk before the Soifers became guests. This section of the statute contemplates that the property reaches the hotel before the guest and awaits the guest's arrival at the owner's risk. In the present case, Berlow's package arrived only after the Soifers left. The hotel was not entitled to a judgment on the verdict under Article 4593.

"The hotel was likewise not entitled to a judgment on the verdict under the jury's finding that it was not grossly negligent. The hotel argues that the bailment of the package was merely gratuitous and, as a gratuitous bailee, it can be held liable only for gross negligence. See, *Citizen's National Bank v. Ratcliff & Lanier*, 253 S.W. 253 (Tex. Com. App. 1923, judgment adopted). Because we find for reasons explained below that the bailment of the package was a bailment for mutual benefit and not a gratuitous bailment, the hotel was liable for its ordinary negligence. *Citizens National Bank v. Ratcliff & Lanier*, 253 S.W. at 255; *Shamrock Hilton Hotel v. Caranas*, 488 S.W.2d 151 (Tex. Civ. App.—Houston [14th Dist.] 1972, writ ref'd n.r.e.). The hotel was not entitled to a judgment on the verdict on this ground.

II. The Hotel's Motion for Judgment Notwithstanding the Verdict

"Because judgment for the hotel was not proper on the verdict, the trial court may be affirmed only if it properly rendered judgment notwithstanding the verdict. Before a judgment notwithstanding the verdict is proper, there must be no evidence of probative force upon which the jury could have made the findings relied upon. *Harbin v. Seale*, 461 S.W.2d 591, 592 (Tex. 1970); Tex. R. Civ. P. 301. On appeal, all evidence must be considered in the light most favorable to the jury's findings, disregarding all contrary evidence. *Elliott v. Elliott*, 597 S.W.2d 795, 800 (Tex. Civ. App.—Corpus Christi 1980, no writ). *See also Rogers v. Searle*, 544 S.W.2d 114, 115 (Tex. 1976). We find that a bailment was established as a matter of law, that the bailment was one of mutual benefit as a matter of law, and that there was some evidence to support the jury's findings on negligence, proximate cause, and damages. Because the form or omission of special issues on some of the elements of bailment for mutual benefit are complained of in crosspoints by the hotel, each element will be discussed.

"In order to constitute a bailment there must be a contract, express or implied, delivery of the property to the bailee, and acceptance of the property by the bailee. *Sanroc Co. International v. Roadrunner Transportation, Inc.*, 596 S.W.2d 320, 322 (Tex. Civ. App.—Houston [1st Dist.] 1980, no writ). Uncontroverted evidence showed that the hotel, rather than refusing delivery, took possession of Berlow's package and stored it on the premises, under lock and key, for one month. Assuming custody of the package in this manner established an implied contract to bail the package. Delivery of the package and acceptance of it by the hotel were stipulated; thus bailment of the package was established as a matter of law. *See Sanroc Co. International v. Roadrunner Transportation, Inc.*, 596 S.W.2d at 322.

"That the bailment was one for mutual benefit and not merely gratuitous was also established as a matter of law. A bailment is for the mutual benefit of the parties, although nothing is paid directly by the bailor, where property of the bailor is delivered to and accepted by the bailee as an incident to a business in which the bailee makes a profit. *Wilson v. Hooser*, 573 S.W.2d 601, 602-603 (Tex. Civ. App.—Waco 1978, writ ref'd n.r.e.). The Soifers were paying guests at the hotel. It is not unusual for patrons to have packages delivered to them at a hotel, and, in this case, the evidence showed that the practice occurred frequently enough that the hotel developed standard procedures for dealing with packages. Although no direct charge was made, the price paid for the room also included the incidental services provided by the hotel. This provided consideration for the implied agreement to bail Berlow's package and established a bailment for mutual benefit as a matter of law.

"Having entered into a bailment for mutual benefit, the hotel became liable for its ordinary negligence. *Citizen's National Bank v. Ratcliff & Lanier*, 253 S.W. 253 (Tex. Com. App. 1923, judgmt. adopted); *Shamrock Hilton Hotel v. Caranas*, 488 S.W.2d at 155. The jury found that the hotel was negligent in its acceptance, care, and handling of the package, and there was some evidence to support this finding. The evidence showed that the hotel violated its own standard procedure, as well as its express agreement with the Soifers, to refuse delivery of packages when requested to do so. The evidence also showed that the package was stored for one month, during which the hotel made no attempt to contact the Soifers or Berlow, then delivered to USPO without postage. This raises some evidence upon which the jury could find the hotel negligent.

"By crosspoint, the hotel argues that, as a matter of law, it was not negligent. According to the hotel, because the package was delivered to USPO for return to Berlow, the liability for any loss rested with USPO as a subsequent bailee and not with the hotel. We do not agree. While the evidence showed that Berlow's package was lost while in the custody of USPO, it also showed that the hotel gave the package, which was insured when delivered to the hotel by UPS, to USPO without insurance or postage. This was evidence of negligence by the hotel sufficiently strong to require submission of the issue to the jury. The hotel, therefore, did not establish its non-negligence as a matter of law.

"There was also some evidence to support the jury's finding that the hotel's negligence was a proximate cause of Berlow's loss. In Texas, proximate cause is cause in fact plus foreseeability. *McClure v. Allied Stores of Texas, Inc.*, 608 S.W.2d 901, 903 (Tex. 1980). The evidence showed that instead of refusing delivery of the package, and thereby causing its immediate return to Berlow by UPS, the hotel took the package and attempted to return it, without insurance or postage, by a different method. This is some evidence that Berlow's loss was caused, in fact, by the hotel's negligent handling of the package. Moreover, because the package was given to USPO without postage, the jury could find that the hotel should have reasonably foreseen that the package would never reach Berlow.

"Likewise, there was some evidence to support the jury's finding that it was foreseeable that the package contained property of substantial dollar value. In *Shamrock Hilton Hotel v. Caranas*, 488 S.W.2d 151 (Tex. Civ. App. — Houston [14th Dist.] 1972, writ ref'd n.r.e.), the court upheld a hotel's liability for the loss of a woman's purse containing jewelry worth $13,000. The evidence showed that the woman left the purse in the hotel dining room where a bus boy found it and turned it over to the cashier. The cashier gave the purse to a man who claimed it, and the purse and jewelry were lost. Rejecting the hotel's argument that it was not foreseeable that the purse contained jewelry worth $13,000, the court, holding that foreseeability is a question for the jury to decide, stated 'it is known that people who are guests in hotels such as the Shamrock Hilton . . . not infrequently bring such expensive jewelry with them.' *Id.* at 155. In the present case, this 'known' practice of guests having valuables in hotels, together with evidence showing that the hotel provided a safe, used often, in which guests could store valuables and evidence showing that the package marked 'insured', was some evidence from which the jury could find it reasonable for the hotel to foresee that guests would bring or deliver items of value to the hotel. *See also Ampco Auto Parts, Inc. v. Williams*, 517 S.W.2d 401 (Tex. Civ. App. — Dallas 1974, writ ref'd n.r.e.). . . .

"Because there was some evidence on each element of recovery on Berlow's theory that she and the hotel entered into a bailment for mutual benefit, the trial court erred in granting the hotel's motion for judgment notwithstanding the verdict; thus judgment should be rendered for Berlow. The hotel, however, alternatively complains by crosspoint that the evidence was insufficient to support the jury's findings and requests reversal and remand rather than rendition. *See Muro v. Houston Fire and Casualty Insurance Co.*, 329 S.W.2d 326, 332, 333 (Tex. Civ. App.—San Antonio 1959, writ ref'd n.r.e.); Tex. R. Civ. P. 324; Calvert, 'No Evidence' and 'Insufficient Evidence' Points of Error, 38 Tex. L. Rev. 1 (1960). We have reviewed the evidence and find it sufficient to support the jury's findings. The hotel's crosspoints on this ground are overruled. . . .

"Reversed and judgment rendered in favor of Berlow for $10,231.00 damages and $10,500.00 attorney's fees."

16:14 *Scope of the* **infra Hospitium** *Requirement*

Insert at end of section, p. 467:

In *Vilella v. Sabine, Inc.*, 293 Okl, 636, 652 P.2d 759 (1982), reported at 16:16 *infra*, the Supreme Court of Oklahoma interpreted its innkeeper's liability statute as imposing liability for the loss of a guest's car and contents, absent proof of actual notice or delivery to an authorized employee. The statutory requirement "placed under his [the innkeeper's] care" was met by proof that the property was brought in to the inn in the usual and ordinary way and was not retained under the guest's exclusive control. A vehicle parked in an outside, unenclosed parking lot that was provided for the use of guests and was patrolled during the night was held within the ambit of innkeeper liability.

16:14a *(New Section) Liability as Bailee*

Insert immediately before 16:15, p. 467:

In the following case, the federal court of appeals for the District of Columbia reiterated the rule that the strict liability of an innkeeper for loss of guest property does not apply to public patrons of a hotel restaurant.

BLAKEMORE v. COLEMAN
701 F.2d 967 (D.C. Cir. 1983)

MIKVA, C.J.: ". . .

I. Background

"The decision in this case turns uniquely on the facts. The Blakemores were in Washington, D.C. to celebrate President Reagan's inauguration, staying as overnight guests at a hotel in Georgetown. Before returning home, they decided to have lunch at The Jockey Club, a restaurant with a reputation for elegance. Upon arriving at the restaurant, which was then part of The Fairfax hotel, the Blakemores checked their car and three large suitcases with the hotel doorman. At the same time, they carried two pieces of hand luggage—a briefcase and a small, carry-on bag—into the hotel themselves. It was the carry-on bag that contained the jewelry that eventually disappeared; specifically, the missing jewelry was in one of the two small jewelry pouches that the Blakemores had stored in the bag. The bag itself was made of leather, was two feet long by nine-and-one-half inches wide, and was closed only by means of a zipper. No other locks or safety devices secured the main compartment of the bag.

When the Blakemores entered the hotel, they checked their two bags with the hotel bellman, who proceeded to place the bags in a small holding room or checkroom adjacent to the lobby. That room had neither a door separating it from the lobby nor any posted sign that would limit the defendant's liability under D.C. Code Ann. § 34-101 (1981) (allowing hotels to limit liability if, *inter alia*, they conspicuously post such notice). The Blakemores did not inform the bellman of the valuable jewelry contained in their bags or ask about locked storage areas; neither did the bellman inquire whether such valuables existed or inform the Blakemores that safety deposit boxes or other locked storage compartments were available for their use.

"Following their lunch in the restaurant, the Blakemores returned to the hotel lobby to retrieve their belongings. Having done so, Mrs. Blakemore immediately opened the carry-on bag only to discover that one of the jewelry pouches was missing. It was at this point that the defendants actually were notified of the jewelry's existence and apparent disappearance. A search of the hotel by employees of The Fairfax and the police was unsuccessful in locating the missing pouch or any of the jewelry that it contained. . . .

II. Innkeeper's Liability

"Before discussing the issue of constructive knowledge that is central to this appeal, we must consider an alternative basis urged by the Blakemores for upholding the judgment of the district court. Specifically, the Blakemores argue that the trial judge should have found the defendants subject to innkeeper's liability, making them responsible for the contents of luggage belonging to their guests regardless of their knowledge about those contents. [Footnote omitted.] *See, e.g., Governor House v. Schmidt*, 284 A.2d 660 (D.C. 1971). It is true that application of the strict liability imposed on innkeepers would require affirmance of the district's court's judgment; but the Blakemores misconstrue the basis on which D.C. law premises an innkeeper-guest relationship. Indeed, in the latest case to define the scope of that relationship, *Wallace v. Shoreham Hotel Corp.*, 49 A.2d 81 (D.C. Mun. App. 1946), the D.C. Municipal Court of Appeals explicitly held that '[o]ne who is merely a customer at a bar, a restaurant, a barber shop or [a] newsstand operated by a hotel does not thereby establish the relationship of innkeeper and guest.' *Id.* at 82; *cf. Governor House*, 284 A.2d at 661-62 (applying innkeeper's liability in action brought by overnight guest of hotel); *Hotel Corp. of America v. Travelers Indemnity Co.*, 229 A.2d 158 (D.C. App. 1967) (same). Absent any indication that the D.C. courts have subsequently modified that definition, the federal courts are bound to follow that holding when applying D.C. law.

"Nor is there any sound justification for distinguishing between the Blakemores and other restaurant patrons simply because the restaurant they happened to visit is located within a hotel. *Cake v. District of Columbia*, 33 App. D.C. 272 (D.C. Cir. 1909), heavily relied on by the Blakemores, is not to the contrary. In that case, the court defined 'bona fide registered guests' to include customers partaking of a hotel's food or lodging. *Id.* at 277. That court, however, was interpreting language included in a criminal statute, and was not delineating the scope of the innkeeper-guest relationship created by the common law. Thus, the district court was correct to conclude that the Blakemores could not premise their action on the strict liability imposed on innkeepers.

III. Constructive Knowledge

"The Blakemores can sustain their damages award, therefore, only under a bailee-for-hire theory. The law of bailment for the District of Columbia, which the defendants admit is applicable to this case, requires that the subject matter of the bailment be delivered to, and accepted by, the bailee. It is not required, however, that the bailee have actual knowledge of the property in its custody in order to be liable for the property's eventual loss. Rather, when the property that is subject to the bailment is enclosed within a container, responsibility for its disappearance may rest with the bailee even though the bailee has only constructive or imputed knowledge of its existence. *See Dumlao v. Atlantic Garage, Inc.*, 259 A.2d 360 (D.C. App. 1969)(contents of an automobile); *Hallman v. Federal Parking Services*, 134 A.2d 382 (D.C. Mun. App. 1957) (same). Such constructive knowledge about the contents of a container has been defined to include those items that are in plain view, *see Dumlao*, 259 A.2d at 362, or that could be expected, given 'common knowledge and experience,' to be in a container under the specific facts and circumstances of a particular case, *see Hallman*, 134 A.2d at 385.

"The mere articulation of this legal standard inescapably leads to the conclusion that a finding of constructive knowledge is a mixed question of law and fact. As with a finding of negligence, the specific facts underlying a given situation must be determined by the trier of fact before the legal standard can be properly applied. In the usual trial setting, the trial judge will explain the legal standard in his or her instructions, but the jury, uniquely qualified to make factual determinations, will apply that standard to the particular facts at issue. *See generally W. Prosser, Handbook of the Law of Torts* § 37 (4th ed. 1971) (discussing respective functions of court and jury in finding of negligence). In the present case, therefore, whether the defendants had constructive knowledge that the Blake-mores' carry-on bag might contain valuable jewelry should have been left to the jury.

"The district court ruled first that '[t]he evidence mandated a finding of con-structive notice, leaving no question of fact for the jury in this regard,' RE 8, and then that '[a]rticles of jewelry are, as a matter of law, commonly and appropri-ately carried in hand luggage,' *id.* Both rulings, which had the effect of conclu-sively removing this issue from the jury's deliberations, were erroneous. [Foot-note omitted.]

"The first ruling quoted above—that the evidence 'mandated a finding' of constructive knowledge—effectively concluded that every reasonable juror nec-essarily would have found that the defendants had implied notice of the valuable jewelry contained in the Blakemores' carry-on bag. Although such a finding would not be clearly erroneous if the trial judge were serving as the trier of fact, the trial court committed reversible error when it removed the issue from the jury. The only fact that was conclusively established at trial was that the bag had some tangible contents. Whether those contents were valuable jewelry or just dirty laundry, however, could not be considered a foreclosed issue. Indeed, facts clearly existed from which conflicting inferences could be drawn. For example, it is conceded that the Blakemores arrived at the hotel only to have lunch, that they neither mentioned the valuables stored inside the bag or complained when the bag was placed in an unlocked holding room, and that the bag itself was un-locked. By themselves, these facts would seem to require submission of the case to the jury. *Cf. Dumlao,* A.2d at 362 (upholding a directed verdict in a bailment case when there was 'no evidence to show knowledge') (emphasis added). *Com-pare Wilkerson v. McCarthy,* 366 U.S. 53, 57, 69 S.Ct. 413, 415, 93 L.Ed. 497 (1949) ('It is the established rule that in passing upon whether there is sufficient evidence to submit an issue to the jury we need look only to the evidence and rea-sonable inferences which tend to support the case of a litigant against whom a pe-remptory instruction has been given.') with *Drapaniotis v. Franklin,* 504 F.2d 236, 237 (D.C. Cir. 1974) (per curiam) ('[i]n resolving [whether the trial court erred in directing a verdict for appellee] we must, of course, view the evidence, and the permissible inference therefrom, in the light most favorable to appel-lant') (citing *Brady v. Southern Railway,* 320 U.S. 476, 479, 64 S.Ct. 232, 234, 88 L.Ed. 239 (1943) and *Muldrow v. Daly,* 329 F.2d 886, 888 (D.C. Cir. 1964). *See generally Vander Zee v. Karabatsos,* 589 F.2d 723, 726-28 (D.C. Cir. 1978) (discussing standard for entering a directed verdict of j.n.o.v.), *cert. denied,* 441 U.S. 962, 99 S.Ct. 2407, 60 L.Ed.2d 1066 (1979). This is especially true when, as in this case, the trial judge takes an issue from the jury by ruling in favor of the party that bears tha burden of persuasion. *Cf. Lucas v. Auto City Parking,* 62 A.2d 557, 559 (D.C. Mun. App. 1941) (burden on plaintiff to prove bailment).

"Nor can we approve of the district court's ruling that valuable jewelry is, 'as a matter of law, commonly and appropriately carried in hand luggage.' To support that ruling, the trial judge relied on *Hasbrouck v. New York Cent. & H.R.R.*, 202 N.Y. 363, 95 N.E. 808 (N.Y. 1911), and the Blakemores cite *Sherman v. Pullman Co.*, 79 Misc. 52, 139 N.Y.S. 51 (App. Div. 1913). Even if these New York cases are somehow controlling in a diversity case applying D.C. law, they do not stand for the proposition stated. In *Hasbrouck*, for example, the specific paragraph relied on, 95 N.E. at 813, was an appellate court conclusion that there was sufficient evidence to support the trial judge's findings of fact; no conclusion of law about jewelry was made at the trial level. Similarly, in *Sherman*, the appellate court simply held that the lower court's conclusion that the term 'baggage' included jewelry found inside was not 'against the weight of the evidence.' 139 N.Y.S. at 52. Thus, in both cases the courts were affirming findings of fact made by trial judges serving as triers of fact; neither opinion is appropriate precedent for the lower court's action in the present case.

"In sum, a straightforward application of the law of bailment for the District of Columbia requires that the jury determine whether the defendants in this case had constructive knowledge of the existence of valuable jewelry in the Blakemores' carry-on bag. To this extent, the district court's judgment must be reversed, and the case remanded for a new trial.

IV. Proceedings on Remand

"Our holding requires that a retrial on all issues be held. Any decision concerning the defendant's constructive knowledge of valuable jewelry is too enmeshed with the other issues presented to allow for separate consideration.

"Even assuming the jury concludes that the defendants had constructive knowledge that valuable jewelry was contained in the Blakemores' carry-on bag, it does not follow that the defendants would be liable for an unlimited amount or value of jewelry. The defendants had a right to assume that patrons of the restaurant would not check articles having an unreasonably high value without informing the bellman. Thus, the trial judge should further instruct the jury to limit its potential damage award to the maximum value of goods which the defendants reasonably could expect to be left in baggage checked under the particular circumstances of the present case. Only in this way can the necessary and appropriate limits be set on the liability that might be imposed on the defendants.

"*It is so ordered.*"

16:15 *Liability as Bailee: Parking Lot Transactions*

Insert immediately after Garlock v. Multiple Parking Services, Inc., p. 478:

Other courts have adopted "foreseeability" as a measure of liability in parking lot cases. *Danielenko v. Kinney Rent A Car, Inc.*, 57 N.Y. 2d 198, 455 N.Y.S. 2d 555 (1982); *McGlynn v. Parking Authority of City of Newark*, 86 N.J. 551, 432 A.2d 99 (1981).

In *Danielenko*, the car that the plaintiff rented from the defendant [defendant both rented cars and owned the garage in New York City where he stored the cars] exploded when a bomb detonated under the front passenger seat while the plaintiff was driving. The plaintiff survived with serious injuries, and the blast destroyed some of the payroll that he was transporting.

The court held the defendant not liable, stating that sabotage of the type that occurred was not foreseeable. The court held that the "most foreseeable event that [could be] gleaned from the record is that defendant's automobiles could be stolen or parts taken from them." (Id. at 558.) The defendant met the duty to protect against such vandalism by renting the plaintiff a car that was in sound operating condition.

In *McGlynn*, while the court abandoned . . . "bailment" theory of responsibility and adopted the foreseeability standard, it did *not* abandon the presumption of negligence that attaches to the garage owner under the bailment theory. The court cited the garage owner's superior ability to control access to his garage as the reason for retaining the presumption.

In accord with *Garlock* are *Gauther v. Allbright New Orleans, Inc.*, 417 So.2d 376 (La. App. 1982), and *Glynn v. Newark Parking Authority*, 86 N.J. 551, 432 A.2d 99 (1981).

16:16 *Liability for Loss of Articles Left in Automobiles*

Insert after excerpt from Swarth v. Barney's Clothes, Inc., *p. 479:*
On the other hand, it has been held that, for the purpose of imposing liability on a parking lot owner under a "foreseeability" theory, cassettes and a tape deck are items reasonably found in cars today. *McGlynn v. Parking Authority of City of Newark*, 86 N.J. 551, 432 A.2d 99 (1981).
Insert at end of section, p. 479:

In most states, an innkeeper must be shown to have accepted complete and exclusive control over a guest vehicle and contents in order for a bailment to exist. In the case to follow, the Supreme Court of Oklahoma interpreted its innkeeper's statute to apply to a vehicle and contents under the care of the innkeeper.

VILELLA V. SABINE, INC.
293 Okl. 636, 652 P.2d 759 (1982)

SIMMS, J.: ". . . The cause of action arose under the following facts: On February 8, 1979, plaintiff's sons registered as paying guests at a motel in Oklahoma City operated by the predecessor corporation to defendant Sabine. Acting as his agents, plaintiff's sons were transporting his personal property to Pennsylvania in a truck and trailer. They inquired about a patrolled area where they could park the truck and trailer and were advised that the motel had an open parking lot, patrolled by a security guard during the night areas. During the evening hours of February 3 or the early morning hours of February 4, 1979, the vehicle and its contents were stolen from said parking lot. The defendant as owner and operator of the motel fully complied with the provisions of 15 O.S. 1981, § 503 [footnote omitted] and 503(a) in maintaining safety features for the motel doors, a safety deposit box for valuables, etc. [Footnote omitted.]

"The United States District Court certifies the following questions of law which may be determinative of the issues involved:

"1. Is a motel guest's vehicle and its contents parked in an outside, unenclosed, patrolled (at night) parking lot, provided for the use of the motel's guest, placed under the care of the motel within the meaning of 15 O.S. § 501?

"2. If yes, do the limitations of liability in § 503b apply to such vehicle and its contents stolen from such a parking lot described above when the motel complies with § 503?

I

"We answer question one in the affirmative on the basis of prior case law. In *Park-O-Tell Co. v. Roskamp*, 203 Okl. 493, 223 P.2d 375 (1950) the court found that property under 15 O.S. 1941, § 501, included an auto and its contents. [Footnote omitted.] § 501 is a codification of the common law which made the innkeeper a virtual insurer of the safety of property entrusted to his care by a guest. *Busby Hotel & Theatre Co. v. Thom*, 125 Okl. 239, 257 P. 314 (1927). Innkeepers were made strictly liable not only because of the traveler's vulnerability and the necessity of reliance on the innkeeper's good faith, but the innkeeper was considered in a better position to protect himself from loss by regulating charges to indemnify himself. [Footnote omitted.] Exceptions to this high standard of duty were the intervention of an Act of God, the public enemy, or negligence of the guest.

"For property to be 'under the care of the motel' it need not be exclusively within the control of the innkeeper. *Park-O-Tell, supra*, quoting an earlier case, [footnote omitted] clarified the meaning of the phrase under 15 O.S. 1981, § 501:

"The provision of this statute that the inkeeper is liable for goods of his guests, 'placed under his care', is declaratory of the common law, not restrictive thereof. Under such provisions it is not necessary, in order to render the innkeeper liable for their loss, that the goods be placed under his special care, or that notice be given of their arrival. It is sufficient if they are brought into the inn in the usual and ordinary way and are not retained under the exclusive control of the guest, but are under the general and implied control of the innkeeper.

"Some jurisdictions require the automobile to be in the custody and control of the innkeeper in a literal sense (e.g., the owner retains the keys, the innkeeper does not control the locking of the car or does not charge an extra fee for parking.) [Footnote omitted.] Neither *Park-O-Tell, supra*, nor our statute requires a showing of custody and control, only that the property be under the care of the innkeeper. [Footnote omitted.] Moreover, our legislature has not limited the liability of an innkeeper for the loss of an automobile by changing the common law rule and making the innkeeper liable as a bailee for hire. [Footnote omitted.]

II

"We answer the second question in the negative. The limitations of liability in 15 O.S. 1981, § 503b [footnote omitted] do not apply to a vehicle and contents, unless the items would fall under the provisions of § 503b.

"While we agree with defendant that the purpose of § 503a and b was to limit the liability of innkeepers in derogation of the common law, the limitation applies to only certain types of property as enunciated in § 503a, 'valuable property of small compass', and § 503b, providing for types of property that cannot be placed in a safety deposit box: 'trunks', 'valise', 'box or bundle', 'miscellaneous effects and property'. An early decision of our Court, *Busby Hotel & Theater Co. v. Thom, supra*, agreed with the contention that the intent of § 501 was to make innkeepers insurers of all losses to personal property placed under their care, except where *specifically exempted*.

"The 10th Circuit in *Solomon v. Downtowner of Tulsa*, 357 F.2d 449 (1966) recognized that § 503b was an exception to the strict liability rule of § 501 for certain kinds of property brought within the inn's care. *Solomon* involved an action against a motel owner for loss of jewelry (merchandise samples) from an automobile left in a motel parking lot while the plaintiff was checking out. Both car and jewelry were stolen, though the car was retrieved. The court upheld the award of damages to the car but denied recovery for the merchandise samples because the plaintiff had not followed the provisions of § 503b. The 10th Circuit, then, limited liability because of the nature of the property involved which fell specifically under § 503b; the court in no way intimated that liability would be so limited if a car and its contents [excluding items listed in § 503a and b] were stolen from the motel's parking lot.

"With no Oklahoma or 10th Circuit opinion directly on point, we look to another jurisdiction which has construed its statute limiting innkeeper's liability. In *Kushner v. President of Atlantic City, Inc.*, 105 N.J. Super. 203, 251 A.2d 480 (1969) plaintiff filed suit against an innkeeper for recovery of the value of his automobile which was allegedly lost or stolen while parked in the motel's lot. The defendant contended that the 'chattel' in the following statute included all kinds of property, including an automobile, and therefore defendant motel was liable only for a sum not to exceed $100.00:

". . . nor shall any such proprietor be liable for in any sum for the loss of any article or articles of wearing apparel, cane, umbrella, satchel, valise, bag, box, bundle or other chattel belonging to such guest, the same not being in a room or rooms assigned to such guest, unless the same shall be specially intrusted to the care and custody of such proprietor or his duly authorized agent, and if such property shall be so specially intrusted, the proprietor shall not be liable for the loss of the same in any sum exceeding one hundred dollars.

"The court held that such a construction would not be within the intention of the legislature which only sought abrogation of absolute liability for loss of a guest's personal property, *infra hospitium causa hospitandi*. [Footnote omitted.] Furthermore, the court said:

". . .the rule of *ejusdem generis* would mitigate against the asserted interpretation made by defendant. The list of articles in the second clause of R.S. 29; 2–3, N.J.S.A. other than the term 'chattel', is specific in scope, i.e., 'articles of wearing apparel, cane, umbrella, satchel, valise, bag, box, bundle, or other chattel belonging to such guest, the same not being in a room or rooms assigned to such guests . . .' *Ejusdem generis* may be applied to general words in conjunction with words of specific meaning, to limit them to the class expressly mentioned.

"We agree with the reasoning of the New Jersey Court and believe it expresses the intent of our legislature to limit liability [footnote deleted] under § 503b only to those items listed—such items of personal use, convenience, instruction or amusement which the ordinary innkeeper and traveler would regard as baggage or luggage and which it is customary or reasonable to expect a guest to consign or keep with the room assigned to him by the innkeeper—rather than to *all* personal property. . . ."

16:19 *Contractural Disclaimers of Liability for Automobiles*

Insert at end of section, p. 483:

In *Horowitz v. Ambassador Associates, Inc.*, 437 N.Y.S.2d 608 (N.Y. City Civ. Ct. 1981), an exculpatory clause in an agreement governing storage of a tenant's vehicle in landlord's residential garage was held void as violative of N.Y. Gen. Obligations Law, section 5–325, discussed in footnote 67, p. 483.

16:20 *Statutory Limitations of Liability for Automobiles*

Addendum to footnote 68, p. 483:

In *Vilella v. Sabine Inc.*, 652 P.2d 759 (Okla. Super. Ct. 1982) (reported at 16:16, *supra*), however, the court held that a vehicle and its contents are *not* "property" within the meaning of statutes limiting an innkeeper's liability for the lost property of guests.

Chapter 17. Exceptions and Limitations to Liability for Guest's Property

17:11 *Limited Liability for Money and Valuables*

Insert after first paragraph of section, p. 503:

No section of New York's General Business Law limits the liability of a discotheque owner for the loss of patrons' property. *Conboy v. Studio 54, Inc.*, 113 Misc. 2d 403, 449 N.Y.S.2d 391 (N.Y. Civ. Ct. 1982).

17:12   *Constitutionality of Statutory Limitations of Innkeeper Liability*

Insert at end of section, p. 508:
A Nevada innkeeper statute limiting the recovery on guests' property loss to $750 was upheld against an equal protection challenge in *Morris v. Hotel Riviera, Inc.*, 704 F.2d 1113 (9th Cir. 1983), because the statute was reasonably designed to foster a legitimate state interest in enhancing the tourist trade. The court noted that the statute reduced the possibility of fraudulent claims and properly considered the difficulties of preventing crimes related to personal property.

17:15   *Provision of Safes for Valuables*

Insert immediately after Zaldin v. Concord Hotel, *p. 513:*
The defendant in *Durandy v. Fairmont Roosevelt Hotel, Inc.*, 523 F. Supp. 1382 (E.D. La. 1981), was denied the protections of the Louisiana statute limiting innkeepers' liability because no employee was on duty at 5:30 A.M. to deposit plaintiff's jewelry in plaintiff's safe deposit box.

In the following case, the New York Court of Appeals indicated that it would inquire into the *adequacy* of an inn's safe before it would allow the innkeeper to avail himself of the protections afforded by New York statutes, which condition a limitation of innkeepers' liability on the provision of a safe.

GONCALVES V. REGENT INTERNATIONAL HOTELS, LTD.
58 N.Y.2d 206, 447 N.E.2d 693
reh'g denied, 59 N.Y.2d 761, 450 N.E.2d 254 (1983)

COOKE, C.J.: "A hotel will not be availed of limited liability provided by section 200 of the General Business Law for the loss of destruction of a guest's property delivered to it for safekeeping unless the hotel establishes that it provided a 'safe' within the meaning of that section. The hotel may be charged with its failure to provide an adequate facility.

"Plaintiffs in these two consolidated cases were guests in late November, 1979, at the Mayfair Regent, a Manhattan luxury hotel owned and operated by defendants. Each plaintiff was traveling with an extensive jewelry collection allegedly worth $1,000,000. As required by law, notices were posted in the hotel that a safe was available in the office for the secure storage of money, jewels, and other valuable items. Plaintiffs each delivered their jewelry over to the management for deposit. In doing so, they signed a 'Safe Deposit Box Receipt' which set forth certain terms and conditions. [Footnote omitted.]

"The security device provided by defendants consisted primarily of rows of safe-deposit boxes that required two keys—one held by the guest—to open. The safe-deposit boxes were housed in a room built of plasterboard with access controlled only by two hollow-core wood doors, one of which had an ordinary residential tumbler lock and the second of which had no lock at all. Plaintiffs claim that this room was unlocked, unattended, and open to the general public. Also, it is alleged that the card file, showing which guest was using each box and when property had been deposited and removed, was exposed to public scrutiny.

"On November 25, 1979, thieves entered the hotel and broke into a limited number of safe-deposit boxes, including those used by plaintiffs. The boxes were emptied of their valuables.

"Plaintiffs independently commenced these actions to recover for the theft of their jewelry. Plaintiff Goncalves stated four theories for relief in her third amended complaint: (1) gross negligence in providing security; (2) breach of contract by defendants' failure to fulfill an earlier promise to install a secure area for their safe-deposit boxes; (3) breach of duty as a bailee; and (4) breach of section 200 of the General Business Law by defendants' failure to provide a safe as required by that statute. Plaintiff Cecconi relied on two theories: (1) breach of duty as a bailee; and (2) negligence in providing security. Each plaintiff prayed for damages in the amount of $1,000,000.

"Defendants denied plaintiffs' allegations and raised three affirmative defenses in their answers. First, they relied on section 200 of the General Business Law as limiting plaintiffs' recovery to $500. Defendants also claimed breaches of the safe-deposit agreements occasioned by plaintiffs' deposit of goods worth more than $500. Last, defendants relied on the agreement to limit their liability to $500.

"The two actions were consolidated and defendants moved to dismiss the complaints or, in the alternative, have judgment entered against them in the amount of $500. Plaintiffs cross-moved to strike defendants' affirmative defenses and for summary judgment. Special Term directed entry of judgment of $500 against defendants in favor of each plaintiff. The cross motions to strike and for summary judgment were denied. The Appellate Division unanimously affirmed. This court granted leave to appeal, 57 N.Y.2d 601, 454 N.Y.S.2d ——, 439 N.E.2d 1245. The order below is now modified, 87 A.D.2d 1010, 450 N.Y.S.2d 644.

"The centerpiece of this appeal is section 200 of the General Business Law, which places a limitation on the absolute liability for the loss or destruction of a guest's property to which a hotelkeeper was subject at common law. That statute provides:

"§ 200. Safes; limited liability

"Whenever the proprietor or manager of any hotel, motel, inn or steamboat shall provide a safe in the office of such hotel, motel or steamboat, or other convenient place for the safe keeping of any money, jewels, ornaments, bank notes, bonds, negotiable securities or precious stones, belonging to the guests of or travelers in such hotel, motel, inn or steamboat, and shall notify the guests or travelers thereof by posting a notice stating the fact that such safe is provided, in which such property may be deposited, in a public and conspicuous place and manner in the office and public rooms, and in the public parlors of such hotel, motel, or inn, or saloon of such steamboat; and if such guest or traveler shall neglect to deliver such property, to the person in charge of such office for deposit in such safe, the proprietor or manager of such hotel, motel, or steamboat shall not be liable for any loss of such property, sustained by such guest or traveler by theft or otherwise; but no hotel, motel or steamboat proprietor, manager or lessee shall be obliged to receive property on deposit for safe keeping, exceeding five hundred dollars in value; and if such guest or traveler shall deliver such property, to the person in charge of such office for deposit in such safe, said proprietor, manager or lessee shall not be liable for any loss thereof, sustained by such guest or traveler by theft or otherwise, in any sum exceeding the sum of five hundred dollars unless by special agreement in writing with such proprietor, manager or lessee.

"Several issues requiring the explication of section 200 are raised. Plaintiffs argue that the statute limits absolute liability only, but does not exonerate a hotelkeeper whose negligence is the proximate cause of the loss of the goods delivered for safekeeping. Alternatively, plaintiffs propose that a hotelkeeper who does not provide a 'safe' within the meaning of the statute may not claim the benefits of section 200. Defendants argue that section 200 limits their liability no matter what the cause of loss and that they provided a 'safe' as required. Defendants further posit that the statute does not require a safe, but that '[an]other convenient place' will satisfy the conditions for invoking the section.

"At common law, an innkeeper was an insurer of goods delivered into his or her custody by a guest, and so was absolutely liable for the loss or destruction of such goods 'unless caused by the negligence or fraud of the guest, or by the act of God or the public enemy.' (See *Hulett v. Swift,* 33 N.Y. 571, 572.) The practical root of this rule lay in the days when travel was perilous, highway robbers abounded, and the only safe sanctuary at night usually was an inn (see *Hulett v. Swift, supra,* at pp. 572–573; Browne, *Bailments* [1896], pp. 81–83; Edwards, *Bailments* [2d ed. 1878], § 462, pp. 335–336; Schoulder, *Bailments* [3d ed. 1897], § 274, pp. 276–278; 43A C.I.S., *Inns, Hotels, and Eating Places,* § 36, p. 880; 9 A.L.R.2d 818). The obligation encompassed not only goods actually delivered into the innkeeper's possession, but also property in the guest's room (see *Ramaley v. Leland,* 43 N.Y. 539; cf. *Bendetson v. French,* 46 N.Y. 266). 'Undoubtedly an innkeeper, by the common law, is held responsible, in this capacity of exercising a public vocation, for whatever personal property of the guest the latter may have brought *infra hospitium.* Not only the guest's animals and private equipage may thus claim protection, his wearing apparel and personal jewelry, his baggage and travelling necessaries, but, indeed, money and valuables to an unlimited amount.' (Schouler, *Bailments* [3d ed. 1897], § 283, p. 288.)

"The common-law rule placed a heavy burden on the hotelkeeper, who could be held liable for a guest's loss although not having any culpability for the property's theft or destruction (see Edwards, *Bailments* [2d ed. 1978], § 463, pp. 336–337; see, also, Browne, *Bailments* [1896], pp. 83–84; 2B *Warren's Negligence* [3d ed.], *Hotelkeepers*, § 5.01). The New York Legislature early acted to restrict the innkeeper's exposure by providing a statutory exception to the common-law rule. In 1855, the predecessor statute to section 200 of the General Business Law was enacted (L.1855, ch. 421, § 1). Another law limiting the innkeeper's liability for loss by fire came into being 11 years later (L.1866, ch. 658; see, also, General Business Law, § 202). And the Legislature also limited the innkeeper's financial responsibility for guests' property such as clothing and other items that could not be expected to be placed in a safe (L.1883, ch. 227, § 2; see, also, General Business Law, § 201).

"Being in derogation of the common law, section 200 is to be strictly construed (see *Ramaley v. Leland,* 43 N.Y. 539, 541, *supra).* Moreover, to obtain its protection, the hotelkeeper must strictly adhere to its provisions (see *Millhiser v. Beau Site Co.,* 251 N.Y. 290, 295–296, 167 N.E. 447 [limitation not available when innkeeper's posted notices do not include information about limitation on liability]; see, also, *Zaldin v. Concord Hotel,* 48 N.Y.2d 107, 113–114, 421 N.Y.S.2d 858, 297 N.E.2d 370).

"Given this statutory framework, negligence by the hotelkeeper may arise in two ways. First, the hotelkeeper may be negligent in such a way that he or she fails to satisfy the conditions of the statute. Second, the hotelkeeper may fulfill the statute's conditions, but by some other negligent act cause the loss of property. The former may be charged against the hotelkeeper and the benefits of section 200 denied, but the latter does not remove the protection of the limited liability accorded to the hotelkeeper by the statute.

"Assuming that the proprietor meets the requirements of section 200, the statutory scheme limits his or her liability for general negligence. The terms of section 200 make no exception for loss caused by the negligence of the hotelkeeper. In contrast, sections 201 and 202 of the General Business Law each limit liability unless the loss occurs through the fault or negligence of the hotelkeeper. The Legislature has maintained these distinctions for at least 100 years (compare L.1855, ch. 421, § 1, with L.1866, ch. 658, and with L.1883, ch. 227). They should not be disturbed now.

"A sound basis for the statutory distinctions can be divined. Section 200 is concerned with property—'money, jewels, ornaments, bank notes, bonds, negotiable securities or precious stones'—which items tend to have a value disproportionate to their size and are easily stored in facilities to protect them against theft or destruction. The statute's message to hotelkeepers is clear: If you provide a facility that will protect such property against theft or destruction, then your absolute liability will be limited (unless you expressly agree to assume greater financial responsibility). This is economically sensible as well, as it encourages a hotel to initially invest in the construction of a secure receptacle, but permits long-term savings through lower insurance premiums and lower payments if losses do occur.

"The premise underlying this discussion is that an adequate facility is available to the guest. Section 200 requires that the proprietor 'provide a safe' as one of the conditions for receiving the protection of the statute. As recently noted in *Zaldin v. Concord Hotel*, 48 N.Y.2d 107, 113, 421 N.Y.S.2d 858, 397 N.E.2d 370, *supra,* the hotel is free to determine the extent to which it 'provides' a safe, but there must be strict conformity with the terms of section 200 in order to obtain the benefit of the statute. In *Zaldin,* it was held that a hotel could not deny access to its safe during certain hours and then claim the circumscribed liability of section 200 at all times. Analogously, a hotel that effectively fails to provide any safe at all, whether intentionally or because the receptacle is negligently constructed, also cannot claim the protection.

""What, then, is a 'safe' within the meaning of section 200 of the General Business Law? The Legislature has provided no definition. And while other sources provide guidance (see, e.g., Black's Law Dictionary [5th ed.], p. 1199 ['(a) metal receptacle for the preservation of valuables']; Webster's Third New International Dictionary [unabridged], p. 1998 ['a metal box or chest sometimes built into a wall or vault to protect money or other valuables against fire or burglary']), their terms lack the perspective necessary to determining whether any particular receptacle is adequate.[2] Nor is the question one that may be answered by prescribing uniform technical specifications and measurements. A large, luxury hotel has far different security needs than a small, low-priced motel catering to a different clientele. It would be inappropriate for this court, with its lack of expertise, to specify a single safe that must be used by all hotels and motels, not only because of their varying needs but also because of the flexibility that is left to the proprietor (see *Zaldin v. Concord Hotel,* 48 N.Y.2d 107, 113–114, 421 N.Y.S.2d 858, 397 N.E.2d 370, *supra;* see, also, *Akins v. Glens Falls City School Dist.,* 53 N.Y.2d 325, 331, 441 N.Y.S.2d 644, 424 N.E.2d 531).

"In determining an appropriate definition of a 'safe', there must be taken into account the risks that commonly threaten the type of property covered by section 200. Fire and theft, of course, come immediately to mind. Other dangers may also exist. To come within the contemplation of section 200 of the General Business Law, therefore, a 'safe' should be a receptacle that, under the circumstances, provides adequate protection against fire, theft, and other reasonably fore-

---

[2]It is worth noting, however, that the term "safe" has long enjoyed a similar definition. Thus, the 1940 edition of Bouvier's Law Dictionary defines the word as follows: "A place for keeping things in safety. Specifically, a strong and fireproof receptacle (as a movable chest of steel, etc., or a closet or vault of brickwork) for containing money, valuable papers, or the like." A similar definition is employed in the 1900 edition of Webster's Dictionary of the American Language.

seeable risks. In deciding this question, all aspects of a hotel's security system may be considered.

"Section 200 is an affirmative defense (see *Zaldin v. Concord Hotel, supra*, 48 N.Y.2d at p. 115, 421 N.Y.S.2d 858, 397 N.E.2d 370; *Faucett v. Nichols*, 64 N.Y. 377, 380; *Ramaley v. Leland*, 43 N.Y. 539, *supra*), and so the burden of proof lies on the defendant (see *Faucett v. Nichols, supra*). Whether a 'safe' was provided is a question of fact (cf. *Friedman v. Schindler's Prairie House*, 224 App. Div. 232, 236–237, 230 N.Y.S. 44, aff'd no opn. 250 N.Y. 574, 166 N.E. 329 [whether establishment was 'hotel' within scope of General Business Law a question of fact for jury]; *Peters v. Knott Corp.*, 191 Misc. 898, 82 N.Y.S.2d 650 [adequacy of posting of notices required by General Business Law a question of fact for jury]). This, of course, does not mean that the issue must always be submitted to the jury. As with any factual issue, a judge will make a determination on the evidence as a matter of law if there is no real controversy as to the facts (see *Basso v. Miller*, 40 N.Y.2d 233, 241–242, 386 N.Y.S.2d 564, 352 N.E.2d 868; see, also, *Licari v. Elliott*, 57 N.Y.2d 230, 237–238, 455 N.Y.S.2d 570, 441 N.E.2d 1088; *Akins v. Glens Falls City School Dist.* 53 N.Y.2d 325, 332, 441 N.Y. S.2d 644, 424 N.E.2d 531, *supra*). . . .

"In the present case, it was improper to award summary judgment. Plaintiffs submitted an affidavit by an expert having 29 years' experience in the design, installation, and sale of safes and vaults. This witness expressed his opinion that defendants' facilities were inadequate, stating that safe-deposit boxes can be invaded in less than 30 seconds and that they should be housed in a vault, not a room of plasterboard and wooden doors. Defendants relied on the existence and operation of the safe-deposit boxes. Under the circumstances, there exists a material issue of fact as to whether defendants' safe-deposit boxes constituted a 'safe' within the meaning of section 200.

"Defendants, relying on the language in the first clause requiring 'the proprietor . . . [to] provide a safe in the office . . . or other convenient place' (General Business Law, § 200), argue that a safe per se is not required by the statute. Defendants propose that this authorizes the hotel to provide a safe or another convenient place for storing valuables. This is not persuasive. Such an interpretation would allow a box or a bag kept behind the counter or a common coat closet to be interchangeable with a state-of-the-art steel vault. Clearly, this would defeat the policy underlying the statute, as discussed above. In addition, it is contrary to the long-standing comprehension that 'other convenient place' refers only to the *location* of the safe, and not to the nature of the receptacle itself (see Edwards, *Bailments* [2d ed. 1878], § 467, p. 341). To put it another way, the words 'other convenient place' relate to 'the office', not to the 'safe'; both the 'office' and the 'convenient place' specify the area in which the 'safe' is to be located. Finally, it is noted that the statute itself is entitled 'Safes; limited liability'; it does not refer to 'safes or other convenient places'. This may be taken as some indication that the Legislature intended that a safe, and nothing else, would suffice as a security device (see *McKinney's Cons. Laws of N.Y.*, Book 1, Statutes, § 123, subd. a, p. 246).

"As the matter must be returned for further proceedings, the court shall address the contention that defendants should not be allowed to take advantage of the agreements that were signed by the plaintiffs when they obtained the use of the safe-deposit boxes. Defendants assert that plaintiffs breached these contracts or, alternatively, that the agreements establish a maximum value of $500 for the property left in the boxes.

"The enforceability of the agreements can be decided without first determining whether defendants met the requirements of section 200. [Footnote omitted.] Assuming first that defendants did provide a 'safe' within the contemplation of the statute and met the other prerequisites for obtaining the benefits of that law, there is no need to present the agreements as they are merely cumulative to the protection afforded by the statute. More important, however, is the contracts' unenforceability under traditional precepts of contract law. The agreement recites: 'In consideration of the privilege herewith granted me by Mayfair House whereby I am allowed the sole use of an individual safe deposit box'. The contract is manifestly void for failure of consideration. To obtain the $500 limitation, the proprietor is required by statute to provide a safe to the guest. This statutory obligation cannot be transformed into a contractual performance, nor may the guest's statutory right be transformed into a contractual privilege. A promise to perform an existing legal obligation is not valid consideration to provide a basis for a contract (see *Ripley v. International Rys. of Cent. Amer.*, 8 N.Y.2d 430, 441, 209 N.Y.S.2d 289, 171 N.E.2d 443).

"Assuming that defendants did not provide the security required by section 200, then the agreements are unenforceable as against public policy. Allowing such agreements to be enforced would encourage hotels to provide lesser protection that is required by the statute. In addition, the present agreements result in a guest's waiver of rights without warning. Certainly, when the guest is justified in believing that the facilities are constructed to provide adequate protection against fire or theft or other reasonably foreseeable risk, the hotel should not be allowed to obtain a waiver of rights without revealing that it is actually proffering a lesser security (cf. *Gross v. Sweet*, 49 N.Y.2d 102, 108–110, 424 N.Y. S.2d 365, 400 N.E.2d 305).

"In summary, defendants may not invoke the protection of section 200 of the General Business Law without proving that [they] provided a 'safe' within the meaning of that law. There exists a material question of fact as to whether defendants supplied a receptacle that, under the circumstances, provided adequate protection against fire, theft, and other reasonably foreseeable risks. The safe-deposit box receipts, signed by each plaintiff, are unenforceable agreements and so may not be relied on by defendants in their defense.

"The parties' other contentions have been considered and are found to be without merit.

"Accordingly, the order of the Appellate Division should be modified, with costs to plaintiffs, by denying defendants' motion for summary judgment and by granting plaintiffs' cross motions to dismiss defendants' affirmative defenses to the extent of dismissing the second and third affirmative defenses, and, as so modified, affirmed.

"JASEN, J. (dissenting): . . .

"Certainly, in a common-law negligence action, the question of whether a person is crippled or whether there was physical contact between two vehicles or whether a hotel provided a safe could present factual questions calling for resolution by a jury. (See *Akins v. Glens Falls City School Dist.*, 53 N.Y.2d 325, 441 N.Y.S.2d 644, 424 N.E.2d 531.) A critical distinction, which the majority fails to perceive, must be drawn, however, where the Legislature has used such terms in a statute, in which case a purely legal question is presented, requiring the court, rather than a jury, to construe their meaning. Adopting a rule, as the majority does today, whereby a jury of lay persons is charged with the responsibility of giving content to statutory language, overrules well-established law without any justification for the change. Moreover, the new rule will destroy the confidence which lawmakers heretofore have had that the terms of their statutes will be construed and applied by the court in a uniform manner in accordance with the purposes sought to be achieved. Indeed, the wholly unacceptable result of the majority's holding will be that, as a practical matter, in every case where the plaintiff alleges that no 'safe' was provided within the meaning of the statute, the question will have to be submitted to a jury.

"The highest courts of three other States have addressed the same issue presented here and have unequivocally held that the question as to what constitutes a 'safe', as that term was used in various statutes, is a question of law. In *State v. Stoner* (473 S.W.2d 363 [Mo.]), the Supreme Court of Missouri held that a coin receptacle in a pay phone is a 'safe' within the meaning of a statute prohibiting possession of tools commonly used to break into safes. The court recognized that the content given such a term depended upon the intent of the Legislature in enacting the statute. Similarly, in *Smith v. Mine & Smelter Supply Co.*, 32 Utah 21, 25–26, 88 P. 683, the Utah Supreme Court held that whether or not a facility constituted a 'vault or safe' within the meaning of a statute regulating the storage of explosives is a question of law. Finally, in a case on point with the instant case, the Ohio Supreme Court held that the trial court properly charged the jury that a bank of metal safe-deposit boxes constituted a 'metal safe' as a matter of law. (*Chase Rand Corp. v. Pick Hotels Corp. of Youngstown,* 167 Ohio St. 299, 147 N.E.2d 849.)

"It is abundantly clear, therefore, based on the afore-mentioned cases and long-established principles of statutory construction, that the question whether or not the facility provided by defendant for the storage of its guests' valuables is a 'safe', as that term is used in section 200 of the General Business Law, is a pure question of law to be decided by this court.

"Turning to the case before us, I would hold that the subject facility is a 'safe' within the meaning of the statute. In arriving at this conclusion, it is necessary to first consider 'the context of the statute, the purpose and spirit of it, the surrounding circumstances, and—above all—the intention of the lawmakers.' (*McKinney's Cons. Laws of N.Y.*, Book 1, Statutes, § 235, citing *Mangam v. City of Brooklyn*, 98 N.Y. 585; *People ex rel. Lichtenstein v. Langan*, 196 N.Y. 260, 89 N.E. 921; and *People v. City of Buffalo*, 57 Hun. 577.)

"As previously stated, the principal purpose underlying the enactment of the statute before us was to protect hotels from undisclosed excessive liability by requiring guests who wished to have hotels safeguard property worth in excess of $500 to disclose the value of such property so that the hotel could take whatever steps necessary, based upon the value of the property, to assure its protection. (*Millhiser v. Beau Site Co.*, 251 N.Y. 290, 167 N.E. 447, *supra*.) The majority, however, appears to be of the view that the statute is primarily concerned with insuring the protection of guests' valuables. This misperception is apparent in the majority's assertion that (at p. 217, 460 N.Y.S.2d at p. 755, 447 N.E.2d at p. 698) [a] large, luxury hotel has far different security needs than a small, low-priced motel catering to a different clientele. It would be inappropriate for this court, with its lack of expertise, to specify a single safe that must be used by all hotels and motels, not only because of their varying needs but also because of the flexibility that is left to the proprietor'.

"The Legislature, in sharp contrast to the majority's position, made it clear that the differences between various types of hotels catering to different clienteles were no longer relevant with respect to an innkeeper's liability. This was done by requiring all hotels desiring to avail themselves of the statutory limitation of liability to provide a safe. By limiting a hotel's liability to $500 per guest, it should be abundantly clear that the Legislature envisioned that hotels would provide a safe of a type that would be adequate to safeguard $500 worth of property. It would be manifestly illogical to state, as one of the plaintiff's affiants did, that the Legislature intended to require a hotel, as a prerequisite to reliance on section 200, to install the same type of safes and vaults used by banks and other institutions that are responsible for safeguarding valuables worth millions of dollars merely to safeguard $500 worth of property. Indeed, the statute is designed to require guests to reveal the value of property they want the hotel to store so that the hotel can, if it chooses to by agreeing in writing, make arrangements elsewhere to provide the type of protection which may be unavailable at the hotel, but which is necessary to safeguard property worth significantly more than $500. Furthermore, the fact that some patrons frequenting a 'large, luxury hotel' have different security needs than those patronizing 'a small, low-priced motel' was precisely the reason why the Legislature enacted section 200. The type of safe provided is of secondary importance to the need of the hotel to be made aware of the value of such property. If value is undisclosed, the hotel is justified, under the express language of the statute, in assuming that the property so entrusted is worth $500 or less.[3] Consequently, if a 'safe' which is adequate to protect $500 worth of valuables is provided, the limitation of liability provided by section 200 is available. As the Supreme Judicial Court of Maine cogently observed in construing a similar statute: 'The hotelkeeper is not a banker; and he is not in the business of operating a safe deposit vault except as an incident to operating a hotel. It is not, therefore, unreasonable to restrict his liability for such incidental services rendered to his guests within such limits as will meet their ordinary needs. Those who carry with them large amounts of money or jewelry must take other measures for their protection. The added cost to the hotelkeeper of providing for such protection even as against the willful act or negligence of an employee, is in the last analysis one of his costs of operation reflected in the rates charged to all. Why should those guests who do not need such protection pay for the cost of those who do?' (*Levesque v. Columbia Hotel,* 141 Me. 393, 398, 44 A.2d 728.)

"While it would go too far to say that the Legislature cared nothing for the security of property belonging to the guests of a hotel, especially since the Legislature required that a safe be provided, it is imperative that the statute be construed in light of the fact that the *primary* concern of the lawmakers in enacting section 200 was to 'protect the hotel from an undisclosed excessive liability'. *(Millhiser v. Beau Site Co.,* 251 N.Y. 290, 294, 167 N.E. 447, *supra; Zaldin v. Concord Hotel,* 48 N.Y.2d 107, 112, 421 N.Y.S.2d 858, 397 N.E.2d 370, *supra.)*

"In light of the conceded purpose of the statute, I believe that the facility provided by the defendant here clearly falls within the meaning of the term 'safe' as it is used in section 200,[4] since it was more than sufficient to safeguard $500 worth of property per guest. This conclusion finds support in both the plain meaning of the term and the decisions in other jurisdictions that have addressed the issue.

"To assist a court in properly construing a term contained in a statute, resort may be had to definitions provided by lexicographers. (*Quotron Systems v. Gallman,* 39 N.Y.2d 428, 384 N.Y.S.2d 147, 348 N.E.2d 604; *McKinney's Cons. Laws of N.Y.,* Book 1, Statutes, § 234.) *Black's Law Dictionary* defines a safe as '[a] metal receptacle for the preservation of valuables.' (*Black's Law Dictionary* [5th ed.], p. 1199.) The identical definition is given in *Bouvier's Law Dictionary* and in *Words and Phrases* (38 *Words & Phrases,* 'Safe', 1982 Cum. Ann. Pocket Part, citing *Buntin v. State,* 117 Ga. App. 813, 162 S.E.2d 234). *Webster's Dictionary* defines a safe as 'a place or receptacle to keep articles (as pro-

---

[3]This is all the more so in a case such as this where both plaintiffs signed an agreement that they would not deposit more than $500 worth of property in their safety-deposit boxes and that they would not hold the defendant liable for more than $500 in the event their property was lost or stolen.

[4]The record reveals that defendant provided individually locked metal safety-deposit boxes for the use of its guests. The guest and the hotel each held a key to the guest's box. The safety-deposit boxes were housed in a separate room with sheetrock walls. Access to the room could be had only by passing through two-inch thick wooden doors, at least one of which was secured by an iron tumbler-type lock.

visions or valuables) safe.' (*Webster's Seventh New Collegiate Dictionary*, p. 757.) Finally, the term 'safe' is defined once again in *Words and Phrases* as, *inter alia,* 'a receptacle in which valuables are placed to complete their safety.' (38 *Words & Phrases,* 'Safe', p. 9, citing *Columbia Cas. Co., v. Rogers Co.,* 157 Ga. 158, 160– 161, 121 S.E. 224.) The individually locked metal safety-deposit boxes, enclosed in a sheetrock room, which were provided by defendant, fall within all of these commonly accepted definitions of the term 'safe'.

"In addition to the afore-mentioned definitions and the intent of the Legislature to protect hotels from excessive undisclosed liability, our holding finds further support in the decisions of at least two other States that have addressed the issue. A Federal District Court in Michigan held that a defendant hotel provided a 'metal safe or a suitable vault' within the meaning of a Michigan statute similar to New York's where it had made available safety-deposit boxes which contained a locking apparatus that could be released only upon the simultaneous application of two keys, one of which was held by the guest while the other was in the possession of the hotel. (*Oppenheimer v. Morton Hotel Corp.,* 210 F. Supp. 609, aff'd/324 F.2d 766.) The court reasoned that since these boxes were similar to the kind employed in banks, they constituted a 'safe' within the contemplation of the statute. The defendant in this case provided an identical facility.

"In a similar case, *Chase Rand Corp. v. Pick Hotels Corp. of Youngstown,* 167 Ohio St. 299, 305, 147 N.E.2d 849, *supra,* which the *Oppenheimer* court relied on, the Ohio Supreme Court held that 'as a matter of law the bank of metal safe deposit boxes constituted "a metal safe," and that such boxes complied with [the Ohio statute].'

"There can be little doubt that the defendant's safe-deposit box facility was a 'safe' as that term is commonly defined, as it has been construed by other courts and, most especially, as the New York Legislature intended it to be construed. Nor is it insignificant that in the century and a quarter that this statute has been on the books, there is nothing in the reported cases to suggest, until now, that the availability of the statutory protection might turn on the type of 'safe' provided by the innkeeper.

"Finally, some mention should be made as to the enforceability of the agreements signed by plaintiffs limiting the hotel's liability to $500. I agree that the agreements signed by the parties purporting to limit the hotel's liability to $500 do not operate to achieve any such limitation of liability in the cases before us, but I reach this conclusion for quite different reasons than does the majority. I cannot agree that the agreements were unenforceable for lack of consideration. The promise of the hotels to provide safe-keeping facilities would support their guests' promises to limit the liability of the hotels. (See 1 Corbin, *Contracts,* § 136, p. 579; *Restatement, Contracts* 2d, § 74.) To suggest that the promise of the hotels could not serve as consideration because it merely restated their statutory obligation is incorrect. Section 200 imposes no obligation on a hotel to provide a safe for storage of valuables; the statute merely conditions the limitation of the hotels' liability to $500 on the provision of such a safe.

"These agreements, however, would not serve to limit the liability of the hotels in the circumstances of these cases. As contracts of exoneration, rather than of indemnity, they would not serve to exculpate the hotels for liability for their own negligence in the absence of an explicit reference to exoneration for such liability. (*Gross v. Sweet,* 49 N.Y.2d 102, 424 N.Y.S.2d 365, 400 N.E.2d 306.)

"For the reasons stated, I would hold that defendant's liability is limited to $500 and affirm the order of the Appellate Division awarding both plaintiffs said sum."

17:15a   *(New Section) Provision of Security Box in Guest Room*

Insert immediately before 17:16, p. 513:

Recently, hotel operators have voluntarily installed in-room security boxes as an added means of protecting guest valuables. Their use has raised the issue of whether such devices nullify innkeeper statutes requiring guests to deposit valuables in a hotel safe or vault or in most instances forgo the right to hold the innkeeper liable for their loss.

In 1981, Hawaii amended its hotel statute (Hawaii Revised Statutes, chapter 486K) to add a new subdivision (5) to section 486K–1:

(5) "Security box" means any metal or alloy box, used in a hotel for the safekeeping of any valuables, which may be securely locked with a locking mechanism that meets or exceeds Underwriters Laboratories standards and which shall be secured in a manner which precludes its removal from the room.

Section 486K–4 was also amended to add a new subdivision (b):

(b) If the keeper of a hotel provides a security box in the room of any guest and prominently posts a notice stating that a security box is provided in which valuables may be deposited and explains the liability for losses therefrom, the keeper of the hotel shall not be liable in any sum for any loss sustained by the guest unless the loss is due to the negligence or fault of the keeper of the hotel.

Conference Committee Report No. 12, dated April 21, 1981, set forth the reasons for the amendments as follows:

The purpose of this bill is to limit the liability of hotels that provide security boxes for the safekeeping of guests' valuables.

Presently, hotels are not liable for any sum for any loss of valuables if: (1) a safe or vault is provided for the safekeeping of guests' valuables; (2) a notice stating that fact is posted in a conspicuous place in the room; and (3) the guest nevertheless fails to make use of the safe or vault. If a guest does deposit his valuables in the safe or vault, the hotel's liability is limited to $500.

Hotels find, however, that most patrons are not willing to take the time and effort of placing their valuables in the office safe. Consequently, burglaries in hotels have become a serious and growing problem for the tourist industry. In addition to the possibility of burglary, there is the growing threat of mugging and robbery for the visitor.

Your Committee finds that another means of security for hotel room guests should be made available. Though security devices have been available to hotels for several years, the question of liability has prevented their installation and use. This bill is intended to encourage hotels to provide their guests with this added measure of security.

In the absence of similar statutory changes by other states, innkeepers would be well advised to follow the Hawaii model so as to make it clear that the installation and use by the guest of such in-room security boxes is for the guest's convenience only and in no way affects the guest's continuing duty to deposit valuables in the hotel safe or vault.

17:16   *Notices Required to Be Posted*

Insert immediately after Depaemelaere v. Davis, *p. 517:*

The Appellate Term, First Department, affirmed *DePaemelaere* without opinion. See 79 Misc. 2d 800, 363 N.Y.S.2d 323 (1974).

17:19   *Deposit of Valuables of Daily Use—Jewels and Ornaments*

Addendum to first paragraph, p. 521:

Under South Carolina law, a guest must deposit in the innkeeper's safe jewels "not ordinarily carried upon the person" before the innkeeper will be held liable for their loss. In *Bischoff v. Days Inns of America, Inc.,* 568 F. Supp. 1065 (D. S.C. 1983), the court held that, though the diamond rings at issue could have been ordinarily "worn upon the person or clothing" (*id*. at 1067), the court would consider them "not ordinarily carried upon the person" for purposes of the law's application.

Insert at end of section, p. 521:

In the following case, the Supreme Judicial Court of Maine distinguished between a watch as ornament and as an object of utility in regard to the loss of a guest's diamond wristwatch from her hotel room arising out of an assault upon her person inflicted by an intruder. The court's discussion of the inn's nonliability for personal injuries is omitted.

BREWER v. ROOSEVELT MOTOR LODGE
295 A.2d 647 (Me. 1972)

DUFRESNE, C.J.: ". . . Absent statutory regulations limiting their liability, innkeepers and hotel keepers are by the common law insurers of the property of their guests committed to their care and are liable for its loss by theft or otherwise, or for injury to it, except when caused by the act of God, the public enemy, or the neglect or fault of the guest or his servants. And the liability extends to all types of personal property of the guest, including moneys and watches, which are placed within the inn or hotel, and is not limited to such as are reasonably necessary for the current use of the guest. *Wagner v. Congress Square Hotel Co.,* 115 Me. 190, at 191–192, 98 A. 660 (1916); *Levesque v. Columbia Hotel,* 141 Me. 393, 44 A.2d 728 (1945).

"The evidence disclosed that the defendant motel corporation was 'duly licensed' as an innkeeper within the City of Waterville. . . . Thus, were it not for our present statute regulating the nature and extent of liability for loss or injury to guests' property (30 M.R.S.A., §§ 2901, 2902, 2903 and 2904), the defendant's responsibility in the instant case for the loss of Mrs. Brewer's watch would be unquestionable. . . .

"Our present Act displaces the common law except where, within the statutory ceiling of liability, the common law remains operative. Section 2901, [footnote omitted] as interpreted by this Court in *Wagner, supra,* limits the innkeeper's liability to $300 for the loss of any of the articles or property of the kind specified therein and this, whether the conditions of the section respecting safe, vault, locking doors, windows and transoms, the posting of the law itself, have been complied with or not. The property covered by section 2901 includes the guest's money, bank notes, *jewelry,* articles of gold and silver manufacture, precious stones, *personal ornaments,* railroad mileage books or tickets, negotiable or valuable papers and bullion.

"Section 2902 [footnote omitted] permits the innkeeper to make special arrangements to receive for deposit in the safe or vault *any* property upon such terms as they may in writing agree. But, under this section, liability for loss of the articles or property accepted for deposit under section 2901, where all the conditions of section 2901 have been met, within the limit of $300 as provided by section 2901 (exclusive of the situation where by specific terms a different arrangement is made in writing between the innkeeper and his guest), is not that of absolute liability under the common law, but the innkeeper is liable for theft or negligence on his part or that of any of his servants.

"[Reference to section 2903 omitted as inapplicable.]

"Section 2904 [footnote omitted] determines the responsibility of any innkeeper for loss of or injury to his guest's personal property other than the property described in sections 2901, 2902 and 2903 and unequivocally states that liability within the limits therein provided shall be that of a depository for hire (excepting losses by fire not intentionally produced by the innkeeper or his servants). This section permits an innkeeper to assume greater liability by agreement in writing. It also covers property of the guest kept by the innkeeper after the relationship of innkeeper and guest has ceased or property received by him prior to the inception of the relationship, where the holding of the baggage or property may be, at the option of the innkeeper, at the risk of the owner. It is to be noted that section 2904 is general in scope and covers *all* innkeepers.

"The plaintiff contends that the defendant corporation never qualified for the statutory exemption from the common law rule of absolute liability, because, although licensed as an innkeeper, it never furnished the proper bond pursuant to 30 M.R.S.A., § 2753. . . . Assuming for the purposes of this decision that the bond was statutorily insufficient . . . , nevertheless, we conclude that the plaintiff's contention must fail. . . . Proper licensing pursuant to statute was not included as one of the required conditions under which the exemption from common-law absolute liability was granted to innkeepers in case of loss of or injury to their guest's property. The legislative language is clearly to the contrary.

"Thus, before she can recover the maximum amount of $300 under the terms of the statute for her diamond wrist watch regarding which she testified to a fair market value of approximately $400 at the time of loss on the theory of common-law absolute liability because the defendant innkeeper had not complied with the conditions of section 2901, the plaintiff must bring herself within the terms of that section. Otherwise, her recovery would be governed by the limitations of section 2904. The plaintiff's diamond wrist watch, to be covered under section 2901, must be either 'jewelry' or a 'personal ornament.' The evidence does not reveal of what metal manufacture the watch was; we cannot surmise or conjecture that it might be an article of gold or silver manufacture as described in the reference section.

"In *Ramaley v. Leland,* 43 N.Y. 539, 3 Am. Rep. 728 (1871), the New York Court said:

> "A watch is neither a jewel or ornament, as these words are used and understood, either in common parlance or by lexicographers. It is not used or carried as a jewel or ornament, but as a timepiece or chronometer, an article of ordinary wear by most travelers of every class, and of daily and hourly use by all. It is as useful and necessary to the guest in his room as out of it, in the night as the day-time. It is carried for use and convenience and not for ornament. But it is enough that it is neither a jewel or ornament in any sense in which these words have ever been used.

". . . The Nebraska Court in *Leon v. Kitchen Bros. Hotel Co.,* 1938, 134 Neb. 137, 277 N.W. 823, 115 A.L.R. 1078, after citing *Wagner v. Congress Square Hotel Co., supra,* with approval, reached the same result as did the New York Court in the case of a lady's platinum diamond wrist watch. It concluded that if the Legislature had intended to include in that part of the statute an article of such general and common use as a watch, it would have used the word 'watch' and not relied on the terms 'jewelry' and 'personal ornaments.' We fully agree. We are aware that the Tennessee Court has ruled to the contrary. *Rains v. Maxwell House Co.,* 1904, 112 Tenn. 219, 79 S.W. 114, 64 L.R.A. 470, 2 Ann. Cas. 488.

"By this conclusion we do not suggest that a given article is, ipso facto, precluded from qualifying as 'jewelry' or 'personal ornaments' solely because it includes a 'watch.' A time-piece might be designed and arranged as a part of an item such that it, and its practical function of telling time, are truly incidental to a manifestly predominant overall purpose of the article as an adornment—in which situation it might legitimately qualify as 'jewelry' or 'personal ornament' within the meaning of the present statute. On the other hand, that which in its objective nature is revealed as primarily and essentially aimed at the practical function of telling time and, is, therefore, basically a 'watch' does not become transformed into 'jewelry' or a 'personal ornament', for purposes of the present statute, solely because it might be rendered interesting or unusual by some accompanying decoration even in the form of precious stones.

"The criterion of judgment, therefore, is the predominant function of the article as disclosed objectively by its nature, construction and assemblage.

"Our conclusion in the instant situation is that the evidence is insufficient—insofar as it has shown the article here involved to be only a 'diamond wrist watch' of market value of approximately $400.00 at the time of the loss— to sustain the ultimate burden of proof reposing upon plaintiff to establish that the article was 'jewelry' or a 'personal ornament' because its predominant function was other than that normally conveyed by the basic designation that it was a 'watch'—a mechanism to serve the utilitarian function of providing its wearer with information as to the time of day.

"Since the plaintiff's wrist watch did not come within any of the types of property enumerated in sections 2901, 2902 or 2903 of the statute, it came within the terms of section 2904 which limits the responsibility of the innkeeper to that of a depository for hire, and in the case of miscellaneous effects including personal belongings to the limit of $50. As stated in *Wagner v. Congress Square Hotel Co., supra,* at page 195 of volume 115 of the Maine reports, at page 662 of volume 98 of the Atlantic Reporter, '[a] depository for hire is liable only for failure to exercise ordinary care, or, as it is sometimes expressed, such care as men of ordinary prudence usually exercise over their own property under like circumstances.' The Justice below ruled as a matter of law that there was no obligation on the part of the defendant innkeeper to anticipate the unforeseeable intrusion of the plaintiff's assailant into her chambers through the open bathroom window and thus there was no breach of due care for which the defendant was responsible in damages . . . for the theft of her property. In this, there was no error.

"The entry will be [:]

"Appeal denied.

"All Justices concurring."

17:20   *Extent of Liability for Property Deposited in Safe*

Insert at end of section, p. 525:

The following case reiterates the settled doctrine that in order for a hotel to avail itself of the innkeeper's statutory limitation of liability for losses of deposited guest valuables, it must strictly comply with the statutory requirements.

ZACHARIA V. HARBOR ISLAND SPA, INC.
684 F.2d 199 (2d Cir. 1982)

WINTER, C.J.: ". . . Florida provides hotels with a statutory method of limiting their liability for the loss of valuables which they accept for safekeeping from guests. The pertinent statutory language reads:

"liability . . . shall be limited to $1,000 for such loss, if the [hotel] gave a receipt for the property (stating the value) on a form which stated, in type large enough to be clearly noticeable, that the [hotel] was not liable for any loss exceeding $1,000 and was only liable for that amount if the loss was the proximate result of fault or negligence of the operator.

"Fla. Stat. § 509.111(1) (1979).

"On November 17, 1979, the plaintiff, Mrs. Sarah Zacharia, checked into defendant's Harbor Island Spa Hotel in Miami Beach. She signed a registration card which stated 'HOTEL'S LIABILITY IS LIMITED AS PROVIDED IN POSTED "IMPORTANT NOTICE TO GUESTS".' Soon thereafter, she sought the use of a Hotel safe deposit box to store her valuables. At the Hotel's request, she signed two cards. The first, Card (1), was entitled 'Harbor Island Spa, Inc. —Statement of Value.' The second, Card (2), was entitled 'Safe Deposit Box —Statement of Value.' . . . Both cards state that the Hotel's liability is limited to $1,000 for loss of valuables deposited in a safe deposit box. Each contains language certifying that the aggregate value of items on deposit will at no time exceed $1,000. The limitation provisions of Card (1), however, were crossed out and Zacharia was not asked to fill in the blanks on Card (2) for her name, the Hotel's name and the date of deposit. The parties dispute what she was told by Hotel employees, Zacharia claiming the desk clerk told her not to worry about the cards which were merely for the Hotel's record, the Hotel denying such statements were made.

"On some 36 occasions Zacharia sought access to the safe deposit box and signed the reverse side of Card (2) in order to verify her identity. Neither on the first nor on any later occasion was she given any document evidencing either a deposit of valuables or the potential limitation on the Hotel's liability.

"On December 7 or 8, 1979, many safe deposit boxes, including Zacharia's, were emptied by a thief, apparently a desk clerk who vanished at the same time as the contents of the boxes. Zacharia's claim of loss is in excess of $10,000. The Hotel, on the other hand, is prepared to present evidence that her original claim escalated sharply after a phone call to New York from the Hotel lobby.

". . . Section 509.111(1) provides that a hotel's liability may be limited only if the hotel 'gave a receipt for the property (stating the value).' Plaintiff was given no document of any kind in connection with use of the safe deposit box. All of the documentation was retained by the Hotel in accord with its established practices. Moreover, on Card (1), 'Harbor Spa, Inc. —Statement of Value,' the critical portion relating to limitation of liability was crossed out. Finally, the blanks within the text of Card (2) 'Safe Deposit Box—Statement of Value,' relating to plaintiff's name, the name of the Hotel, and date of deposit, were not filled in.

"We can only speculate as to the result a Florida court would reach on these facts. Relevant Florida decisions, however, emphasize that the burden of compliance is on the hotel rather than on the guest, since the hotel has 'superior position and knowledge . . . with regard to the mandates of the statute,' *Garner v. Margery Lane, Inc.,* 242 So.2d 776, 778 (Fla. 4th Dist. Ct. App. 1970), and that compliance by the hotel must be 'strict.' *Id.* at 779 (quoting *Fuchs v. Harbor Island Spa,* 420 F.2d 1100, 1103 (5th Cir. 1970)). In a case decided under an earlier but pertinent version of the statute, *Safety Harbor Spa, Inc. v. High,* 137 So.2d 248 (Fla. 2d Dist. Ct. App. 1962), limitation of liability was denied where the hotel failed to keep track of continuing deposits and withdrawals by a guest. The Court noted that such a step was for the hotel's own protection and held it liable for an amount in excess of $1,000 because it was not in 'strict compliance.' *Id.* at 249. The most recent Florida case, *Great American Insurance Co. v. Coppedge,* 405 So.2d 732 (Fla. 4th Dist. Ct. App. 1981) indicates in *dicta* that documentation must be given to the guest if liability is to be limited under the present statute. Id. at 735.

"We hold that the Hotel's casual attitude toward even the plainest requirement of the statute deprives it of the benefit of the limitation of liability. There is no ambiguity as to the statute's requiring that a document constituting a statutory receipt must be *given* to the guest depositing valuables. This receipt requirement is obviously designed to emphasize to the guest the statutory limitation since access to the valuables on each occasion is only by production of this document to Hotel officials. No document was given to Zacharia then or on any of the numerous occasions on which she entered the box. Although additional valuables might have been deposited at any time, the Hotel made no attempt to give direct notice to Zacharia of its purported limited liability except on the first deposit. While the Hotel asked plaintiff to sign two forms indicating future deposits would leave the aggregate value under $1,000, these forms were never completed, and on Card (1), the critical language was crossed out. Whether the desk clerk actually said not to worry about the cards since they were only for Hotel records is less significant than the conduct of the Hotel in keeping the cards, for that conduct expressed exactly the same idea.

"The non-compliance here was more than technical, yet defendant has not cited a single Florida case in support of its position. Florida decisions dealing with related issues directly hold that hotels seeking the shelter of the statute bear a 'burden' of 'strict compliance,' *Garner, supra,* and imply that compliance must be in connection with every use, *High, supra.* While no absolutely dispositive Florida decision has been rendered, existing case law clearly weighs in plaintiff's favor.

"We hold therefore, that the statutory limitation of liability is inapplicable.

Defendant may use documents signed by Zacharia at trial to attack her assertions as to the value of the items deposited.

"Reversed and remanded."

17:21 *Extent of Liability for Failure to Deposit Valuables Where Loss Is Caused by Negligence of Innkeeper*

Insert immediately before Levitt V. Desert Palace, Inc., *p. 526:*

The distinction between misfeasance and nonfeasance in regard to losses of valuables from the guest room, where the guest fails to deposit such valuables in the hotel safe, deserves fuller treatment. The following Arizona case, *Terry v. Linscott Hotel Corp.*, cited in footnote 44, p. 526, is a leading opinion favoring innkeeper nonliability.

TERRY V. LINSCOTT HOTEL CORP.
126 Ariz. 548, 617 P.2d 56 (1980)

O'CONNOR, J.: "Jewelry and other items belonging to appellants were stolen from their rooms while they were guests at the Scottsdale Hilton Inn. They brought suit for the loss against appellees, owners of the Inn. Appellees moved for partial summary judgment as to that portion of the loss which was jewelry based on A.R.S. § 33–302(A), which restricts the liability of innkeepers. The trial court granted appellees' motion for partial final summary judgment. We affirm.

"The loss occurred on December 28, 1977. Some unknown thieves stole the jewelry and other items while appellants were away from their rooms. The first count of appellants' complaint simply alleges the loss, appellees' status as innkeepers, and appellants' status as guests, and seeks recovery for the loss. Count two of the complaint alleges a cause of action for negligence, as follows:

"The theft of plaintiffs' personal property from their locked room is the direct and proximate result of the defendants' negligence, carelessness and recklessness in failing to provide adequate security, failing to provide plaintiffs with the degree of care and protection to which they were entitled as paying guests, and in failing to warn plaintiffs of the series of thefts and burglaries which had occurred at the Scottsdale Hilton prior to December 28, 1977.

"Appellees served interrogatories on appellants asking them to state each act or omission which appellants alleged constituted negligence on appellees' part. Appellants answered as follows:

"Failure to provide adequate security including the use of security guards, interior hall security personnel and adequate locking and securing devices on the doors.

"Failure to increase effective security measures with full knowledge of the high incident rate of theft in the Scottsdale Hilton.

"Failure to warn the plaintiffs of the number of thefts and burglaries committed in the Scottsdale Hilton prior to December 28, 1977.

"A.R.S. § 33–302 reads in part as follows:

"A. An innkeeper who maintains a fireproof safe and gives notice by posting in a conspicuous place in the office or in the room of each guest that money, jewelry, documents and other articles of small size and unusual value may be deposited in the safe, is not liable for loss of or injury to any such article not deposited in the safe, *which is not the result of his own act.*

"B. An innkeeper may refuse to receive for deposit from a guest articles exceeding a total value of five hundred dollars, and unless otherwise agreed to in writing shall not be liable in an amount in excess of five hundred dollars for loss of or damage to property deposited by a guest in such safe *unless the loss or damage is the result of the fault or negligence of the innkeeper.*

"C. The innkeeper shall not be liable for loss of or damage to merchandise samples or merchandise for sale displayed by a guest unless the guest gives prior written notice to the innkeeper of having and displaying the merchandise or merchandise samples, and the innkeeper acknowledges receipt of such notice, but in no event shall liability for such loss or damage exceed five hundred dollars *unless it results from the fault or negligence of the innkeeper.* [Emphasis added.]

"The notice placed in appellants' rooms reads as follows in large size print:

"PLEASE

"Safety Deposit Boxes for your valuables are available at the Reception Desk. We recommend that you deposit all valuables.

"We also suggest you double bolt your door when using the patio door to the swimming pool.

"Arizona Statutes do not hold hotels liable for missing valuables, nor do we have insurance coverage.

"So . . . ,

"please deposit your valuables.

"There is no dispute that the hotel maintained a fireproof safe as required by A.R.S. § 33–302(A).

"On appeal, appellants argue that partial summary judgment for appellees was improper for two reasons. First, they argue that A.R.S. § 33–302(A) was intended to relieve an innkeeper of his common law strict liability for the guest's property, but not from the effects of his own negligence. Second, appellants contend that the trial court erred in holding as a matter of law that the notice placed in appellants' rooms complied with the statute.

Innkeeper Liability

"The common law rule imposed a strict rule of liability upon an innkeeper and was founded upon the public policy of an earlier day. We quote from the case of

Minneapolis Fire & Marine Insurance Co. v. Matson Navigation Co., 44 Hawaii 59, 61, 352 P.2d 335, 337 (1960):

> "The imposition of strict liability on the innkeeper found its origin in the conditions existing in England in the fourteenth and fifteenth centuries. Inadequate means of travel, the sparsely settled country and the constant exposure to robbers left the traveler with the inn practically his only hope for protection. Innkeepers themselves, and their servants, were often as dishonest as the highwaymen roaming the countryside and were not beyond joining forces with the outlaws to relieve travelers and guests, by connivance or force, of their valuables and goods. Under such conditions it was purely a matter of necessity and policy for the law to require the innkeeper to exert his utmost efforts to protect his guests' property and to assure results by imposing legal liability for loss without regard to fault.

"Statutes such as A.R.S. § 33–302 were enacted as law enforcement improved and travel was less hazardous. The need to limit an innkeeper's potential liability became apparent. As it stated in an annotation at 37 A.L.R.3d 1276, 1279–80 (1971):

> "The statutes defining the limits of an innkeeper's liability for loss of or injury to his guest's property represent a legislative intent to soften what has been termed an unduly harsh common-law rule.

> "In former times, there were a number of sound reasons to justify the public policy of imposing a strict rule of liability on innkeepers. And so, at common law, the innkeeper was practically an insurer of property brought by a guest to his inn and he was relieved of liability for the loss of such property only where the loss occurred through an act of God, through an act of a public enemy, or through the fault of the guest himself.

> "Since the passing of years has erased much of the need for such absolute liability, the modern innkeeper is often permitted by statute to lessen his responsibility to certain limits, if he provides suitable locks on his guests' rooms, provides a safe for the protection of their valuables, and provides adequate notice of the presence of that safe and, in some cases, of his limited liability. [Footnotes omitted.]

"A.R.S. § 33–302(A) provides that an innkeeper who maintains a fireproof safe and posts the required notice is not liable for loss of jewelry or articles of unusual value 'which is not the result of his own act.' Subsection B provides that the innkeeper is not liable for more than $500.00 for the loss of jewelry or valuable items placed in the innkeeper's fireproof safe unless otherwise agreed to in writing, or unless the loss is 'the result of the fault or negligence of the innkeeper.' Subsection C has a separate provision limiting liability of the innkeeper for loss or damage to merchandise samples unless it 'results from the fault or negligence of the innkeeper.'

"Appellant argues that the phrase in subsection A, 'which is not the result of his own act,' preserves a cause of action against the innkeeper for his negligent inaction in failing to provide adequate security and in failing to warn appellant of the number of thefts within the hotel.

"There are cases from some jurisdictions holding that innkeeper's liability statutes were intended to relieve only the innkeeper's liability as an insurer, but not to preclude recovery for loss caused by the innkeeper's negligence. *See, e.g., Shiman Bros. & Co. v. Nebraska Nat. Hotel Co.,* 143 Neb. 404, 9 N.W.2d 807 (1943); *Hoffman v. Louis D. Miller & Co.* 83 R.I. 284, 115 A.2d 689 (1955); *Shifflette v. Lilly,* 130 W.Va. 297, 43 S.E.2d 289 (1947). Other jurisdictions have interpreted the provisions of particular statutes as limiting the amount of recovery for loss of a guest's property even when caused by the innkeeper's negligence. *See, e.g., Ricketts v. Morehead Co.,* 122 Cal. App. 2d 948, 265 P.2d 963 (1954); *Pfennig v. Roosevelt Hotel,* 31 So.2d 31 (La. 1947); *Levesque v. Columbia Hotel,* 141 Me. 393, 44 A.2d 728 (1945); *Goodwin v. Georgian Hotel Co.,* 197 Wash. 173, 84 P.2d 681 (1938).

"We are guided in our analysis of the statute in question by the customary principles of statutory construction. Statutes are not to be construed as effecting any change in the common law beyond that which is clearly indicated. [Citations omitted.] Where a statute is in derogation of the common law, and is also remedial in nature, the remedial application should be construed so as to give effect to its purpose. . . . *Albuquerque Hilton Inn v. Haley,* 90 N.M. 510, 512, 565 P.2d 1027, 1029 (1977). *See also* A.R.S. § 1–211; *State v. Allred,* 102 Ariz. 102, 425 P.2d 572 (1967).

"In interpreting a statute, full effect is to be given to the legislative intent, 'and each word, phrase, clause and sentence must be given meaning so that no part will be void, inert, redundant or trivial.' *Adams v. Bolin,* 74 Ariz. 269, 276, 247 P.2d 617, 621 (1952). [Citation omitted.]

"The term 'negligence' includes both action and inaction, commission and omission. A.R.S. § 1–215(20); *Salt River Valley Water Users' Associaton v. Compton,* 39 Ariz. 491, 8 P.2d 249, on rehearing 40 Ariz. 282, 11 P.2d 839 (1932). The word 'act,' however, 'denotes the affirmative. Omission denotes the negative. Act is the expression of will, purpose. Omission is inaction. Act carries the idea of performance. Omission carries the idea of refraining from action.' *Randle v. Birmingham Railway, Light & Power Co.,* 169 Ala. 314, 324, 53 So. 918, 921 (1910). W. Prosser, *Law of Torts* § 56, at 338–39 (4th ed. 1971) states:

"In the determination of the existence of a duty, there runs through much of the law a distinction between action and inaction. In the early common law one who injured another by a positive, affirmative act, was held liable without any great regard even for his fault. But the courts were far too much occupied with the more flagrant forms of misbehavior to be greatly concerned with one who merely did nothing, even though another might suffer harm because of his omission to act. Hence there arose very early a difference, still deeply rooted in the law of negligence, between 'misfeasance' and 'non-feasance'—that is to say, between active misconduct working positive injury to others and passive inaction or a failure to take steps to protect them from harm. The reason for the distinction may be said to lie in the fact that by 'misfeasance' the defendant has created a new risk of harm to the plaintiff, while by 'non-feasance' he has at least made his situation no worse, and has merely failed to benefit him by interfering in his affairs. [Footnotes omitted.]

"Applying these concepts to A.R.S. § 33–302, we hold that the legislature, by using the word 'act' in subsection A, intended to eliminate the common law liability of innkeepers and to encourage hotel guests to deposit their jewelry and valuable possessions in the innkeeper's fireproof safe, failing which the guest may not recover a loss from the innkeeper unless the loss results from some *active misfeasance* of the innkeeper, or unless adequate notice of the existence of the safe has not been provided to the guest. Concerning loss of items which are in fact deposited by the guest for keeping in the innkeeper's safe, the legislature, by using the words 'fault or negligence' in subsection B, intended to make the innkeeper liable to the guest for any loss occurring thereafter which is the result of the innkeeper's negligent action or inaction.

"Since appellants did not deposit their valuables in the safe, active misfeasance of the innkeeper must be shown. Appellants' only allegations of fault by appellees for the loss of their jewelry are allegations of failure of appellees to provide adequate security precautions and failure to warn appellants about the number of thefts in the hotel. These are allegations of non-feasance or acts of omission. Therefore, assuming adequate compliance by appellees with the statutory notice requirements, no cause of action exists in favor of appellants for the loss of their jewelry, which was not deposited in the safe while they were guests at appellees' hotel, based on appellees' failure to warn them of the number of thefts and to provide adequate security. . . .

"[The court's discussion of adequacy of notice to the guest of the statutory limitation is omitted.]

"For the foregoing reasons, the partial summary judgment of the trial court is affirmed."

Insert immediately before Hanover Insurance Co. v. Alamo Motel, *p. 530:*

In 1979, Nevada amended its statute by adding the following new paragraph:

> If an owner . . . of any hotel . . . provides a fireproof safe or vault in which guests may deposit property for safekeeping, and notice of this service is personally given to a guest or posted in the office and the guest's room, the owner . . . is not liable for the theft of any property which is not offered for deposit in the safe or vault by a guest unless the owner or keeper is grossly negligent. Nev. Rev. Stat., section 651.010(2) (1979).

To the same effect, construing Nevada law, see *Kabo v. Summa Corp.*, 523 F. Supp. 1326 (E.D. Pa. 1981), and *Levin by Levin v. Desert Palace Inc.*, 465 A.2d 1019 (Pa. Super. 1983).

Insert at end of section, p. 533:

In *Laubie v. Sonesta International Hotel Corp.*, 398 So.2d 1374 (La. 1981), the Supreme Court of Louisiana interpreted its innkeepers' civil code provisions to limit liability arising out of contracts of deposit of guest property for safekeeping but not to limit liability arising out of innkeeper negligence or other torts causing loss of guest property. This decision was cited and followed in a federal lawsuit where guest jewelry was lost through theft from the guest room by violence. There was no one present at the front desk to accept the guest's jewelry for safekeeping before she retired for the night. This omission was held to constitute negligence, to which the Louisiana civil code limiting liability for undeposited valuable property was held not to apply. *Durandy v. Fairmont Roosevelt Hotel, Inc.*, 523 F. Supp. 1382 (E.D. La. 1981). To the same effect, see *Kraaz v. La Quinta Motor Inns, Inc.*, 410 So.2d 1048 (La. App. 1982).

The Louisiana legislature thereupon amended the statute, La. Civ. Code Ann., article 2971 (West), to limit liability under either theory. (See 17:28, appendix B, p. 554, for state limitation of liability statutes.)

17:25a   *(New Section) Liability for Guests' Property after Guests' Departure*

Insert immediately before 17:26, p. 541:

In *Great American Insurance Co. v. Coppedge*, 405 So.2d 732 (Fla. App. 1981), *rev. denied*, 415 So.2d 1359 (1982) the plaintiff hid her jewelry in her nightstand while she was a guest at the Diplomat Hotel. After she checked out, a maid found her jewelry and turned it over to the director of hotel security, who claimed, at trial, that he misplaced it. For purposes of examining the hotel's liability, the Florida Appeals Court deemed plaintiff a "guest" at the time the jewels became missing. The court noted that to do otherwise would bring about the absurd result under Florida statutory law of limiting the hotel's liability while plaintiff was actually a guest and not limiting its liability when plaintiff had departed.

17:28   *Statutory Limitations of Liability for Property Other than Valuables*

Insert immediately before Appendix A, p. 551:

The following case illustrates the unwillingness of a federal district court to extend New York's innkeeper's liability statute governing losses of guest property from the room to luggage intentionally taken from the room by the innkeeper's employees, and intentionally transported to Saudi Arabia by mistake.

BHATTAL v. GRAND HYATT–NEW YORK
563 F. Supp. 277 (S.D.N.Y. 1983)

BRIEANT, D.J.: "Defendant, an innkeeper, seeks summary judgment in its favor in this alienage case, regulated by New York law. Plaintiffs, residents and citizens of India, registered as guests in defendant's Grand Hyatt Hotel in Midtown Manhattan on July 19, 1981 and were assigned Room 2946. [Footnote omitted].

"Following the customary practice in first class hotels in this City of the sort operated by defendant, plaintiffs turned over to the bell captain various pieces of personal luggage, which are now said to have contained valuables of great significance, and this luggage was duly transferred by defendant's employees to plaintiffs' assigned hotel room.

"Plaintiffs did not request that any of their valuables be placed in the safe depository provided by the hotel, nor did they enter into any 'special agreement' with the hotel concerning their valuables, as is contemplated by § 200 of the New York General Business Law.

"Shortly after arriving at their room with the luggage, plaintiffs left the hotel for luncheon with friends, locking their door with a key provided by defendant. On returning earlier the same evening, plaintiffs discovered that their luggage and the contents thereof were missing.

"All things in the modern world which go wrong for reasons other than the application of Murphy's Law, seem to go wrong because of a particular sort of mechanical malevolence known as 'computer error.' Apparently defendant's front desk relies heavily on computer support, and as a result of computer error, employees of defendant transported plaintiffs' luggage from plaintiffs' room to JFK International Airport, along with the luggage of aircraft crew members of Saudi Arabian nationality, who had previously occupied Room 2946. In other words, the computer omitted to notice that the room had been vacated and relet to plaintiffs, and hotel employees responding to computer direction, included plaintiffs' luggage along with the other luggage of the departing prior guests. This is not to suggest that the Grand Hyatt-New York is a hotbed house, but apparently it was operating at 100% occupancy with no lost time between the departure of the Saudi Arabian aircraft crew members who had previously occupied the room, and the arrival of plaintiffs.

"Needless to say, plaintiffs' luggage departed for Saudi Arabia and has not since been seen. A missing pearl is always a pearl of the finest water, and accordingly plaintiffs demand damages in the amount of $250,000.00, together with costs and attorneys' fees.

"There seems to be no disputed issue of fact as to what happened to the luggage.

Defendant's motion relies on § 200 of the New York General Business Law, which reads in relevant part as follows:

"§ 200. *Safes; limited liability*

"Whenever the proprietor or manager of any hotel, motel, inn or steamboat shall provide a safe in the office of such hotel, motel or steamboat, or other convenient place for the safe keeping of any money, jewels, ornaments, bank notes, bonds, negotiable securities or precious stones, belonging to the guests of or travelers in such hotel, motel, inn or steamboat, and shall notify the guests or travelers thereof by posting a notice stating the fact that such safe is provided, in which such property may be deposited, in a public and conspicuous place and manner in the office and public rooms, and in the public parlors of such hotel, motel, or inn, or saloon of such steamboat; and if such guest or traveler shall neglect to deliver such property, to the person in charge of such office for deposit in such safe, the proprietor or manager of such hotel, motel, or steamboat shall not be liable for any loss of such property, sustained by such guest or traveler by theft or otherwise; but no hotel, motel or steamboat proprietor, manager or lessee shall be obliged to receive property on deposit for safe keeping, exceeding five hundred dollars in value; and if such guest or traveler shall deliver such property, to the person in charge of such office for deposit in such safe, said proprietor, manager or lessee shall not be liable for any loss thereof, sustained by such guest or traveler by theft or otherwise, in any sum exceeding the sum of five hundred dollars unless by special agreement in writing with such proprietor, manager or lessee.

"Section 201 of the New York General Business Law, also of interest here, provides in relevant part that:

"§ 201. *Liability for loss of clothing and other personal property limited*

"1. No hotel or motel keeper except as provided in the foregoing section shall be liable for damage to or loss of wearing apparel or other personal property in the lobby, hallways or in the room or rooms assigned to a guest for any sum exceeding the sum of five hundred dollars, unless it shall appear that such loss occurred through the fault or negligence of such keeper. . . .

"The motion thereby presents the question of whether these statutes limit the liability of an innkeeper, in a case where the innkeeper, by his own agents, intentionally and without justification, took custody and control of plaintiffs' luggage and contents, without plaintiffs' authorization, and intentionally, although inadvertently, caused the luggage to be transported to Saudi Arabia. The Court concludes that the statutes do not extend so far as to protect the innkeeper under these facts.

"Essentially what has taken place here is a common law conversion of property by defendant's agents. A fair reading of the amended complaint as amplified by the papers submitted on this motion indicates that plaintiffs state a claim for unintentional conversion under New York law, although not specifically so labelled. See *Meese v. Miller*, 79 A.D.2d 237, 436 N.Y.S.2d 496 (4th Dept. 1981). Intentional use of property beyond the authority which an owner confers upon a user or in violation of instructions given is a conversion. *Quintal v. Kellner*, 264 N.Y. 32, 189 N.E. 770 (1934).

"Here, defendant's employees entered plaintiffs' locked room, without plaintiffs' permission or knowledge, and removed their luggage, commingled it with the luggage of the Saudi Arabian aircraft crew members and placed it on a bus headed for Kennedy Airport. The Court infers that if the luggage was not stolen at Kennedy Airport, it arrived in Saudi Arabia and was eventually stolen by a Saudi thief who still had the use of at least one good hand. In this instance, the intentional acts of the defendant clearly constituted conversion under New York law.

"Sections 200 and 201 of the New York General Business Law were adopted in the middle of the nineteenth century to relieve an innkeeper from his liability at common law as an insurer of property of a guest lost by theft, caused without negligence or fault of the guest. *Millhiser v. Beau Site Co.*, 251 N.Y. 290, 167 N.E. 447 (1929). These statutes and the cases cited thereunder by the defendant extend to the situation where there is a mysterious disappearance of valuable property, either as a result of a theft by an employee of the hotel—or a trespass or theft by an unrelated party, for whose acts the innkeeper is not responsible. The statutes are also intended to protect the innkeeper from the danger of fraud on the part of a guest in a situation where the property said to have disappeared never existed at all, or was taken or stolen by or with the privity of the guest. *Weinberg v. D-M Restaurant Corp.*, 53 N.Y.2d 499, 442 N.Y.S.2d 965, 426 N.E.2d 459 (1981); *Salisbury v. St. Regis Sheraton Hotel Corp.*, 490 F. Supp. 449 (S.D.N.Y. 1980); *Federal Insurance Co. v. Waldorf-Astoria*, 60 Misc. 2d 996, 303 N.Y.S.2d 297 (Sup. Ct. N.Y. Co. 1969); *Reichman v. Compagnie Generale Transatlantique*, 290 N.Y. 344, 49 N.E.2d 474 (1943); *Honig v. Riley*, 244 N.Y. 105, 155 N.E. 65 (1926); *Adler v. Savoy Plaza, Inc.*, 279 App. Div. 110, 108 N.Y.S.2d 80 (1st Dept. 1951); *DePaemelaere v. Davis*, 77 Misc. 2d 1, 351 N.Y.S.2d 808 (Civ. Ct. N.Y. Co. 1973).

"The reason for providing a hotel safe in compliance with § 200 and the reason for limiting a hotel's liability under § 201 is to protect against just such situations. When a hotel room is let to a guest, the innkeeper has lost a large measure of control and supervision over the hotel room and its contents. While housekeeping and security staff can enter the room at reasonable hours and on notice to any persons present therein, essentially, for most of the time at least, property of a guest which is present in a hotel room can be said to be under the exclusive dominion and control of the hotel guest, rather than the innkeeper.

"We have been cited to no case extending the limited immunity provided by statute against the common law liability of innkeepers, where the liability sought to be founded on the innkeeper was based on the exercise of unlawful dominion and control by the innkeeper himself, or his agents and employees acting in the course of their employment; as contrasted with mysterious disappearances due to causes unknown, or criminal acts of third parties or employees acting for themselves rather than for the employer. As noted above, it was only for the latter class of cases that the statutes granted immunity.

"Since §§ 200 and 201 of the New York General Business Law operate in derogation of the common law liability of an innkeeper as insurer, courts have traditionally construed their application strictly. *Millhiser v. Beau Site Co., supra; Ramaley v. Leland*, 43 N.Y. 539 (1971); *Jones v. Hotel Lanham Co.*, 62 Misc. 620, 115 N.Y.S. 1084 (Sup. Ct. N.Y. Co. 1909).

"In *Millhiser v. Beau Site Co.*, the plaintiff placed a package containing jewelry worth $369,800 in a safety deposit box maintained by the defendant hotel pursuant to § 200 of the New York General Business Law, without disclosing to the defendant's desk clerk the contents of the package or the value thereof. Upon retrieving the package, the plaintiff discovered that $50,000 worth of jewelry was missing. Subsequently, an employee of the defendant was arrested and convicted for the theft of the gems but the jewelry was never recovered.

"In construing § 200, the New York Court of Appeals held that this provision limited the liability of an innkeeper for thefts of guests' property committed by its employees. However, the Court also stated that § 200 did not operate to limit the liability of an innkeeper for thefts committed by the innkeeper itself:

". . . [S]uch a theft would be by the hotel keeper from the guest and not a theft from the hotel keeper. We read the statute to [limit the liability of the the hotel keeper for] . . . a theft of . . . articles from the hotel keeper and not a theft by the hotel keeper from the guest. The act of the defendant's employee in stealing the jewelry was a wrongful act, outside the scope of his employment and for his own enrichment. It was not in any sense the act of the defendant. [Citations omitted.] 251 N.Y. at 295, 167 N.E. 447.

"Applying this rationale to the case at bar, the Court is compelled to conclude that §§ 200 and 201 do not limit the liability of an innkeeper for its conversion of guests' property. In this case, the plaintiff's luggage was not converted or stolen from the hotel by means of an employee theft or a fraud perpetrated by a third party. See *Adler v. Savoy Plaza, Inc.*, 279 App. Div. 110, 108 N.Y.S.2d 80 (1st Dep't. 1951). Rather, employees of the defendant, acting *within* the scope of their employment and relying on the accuracy of their employer's computer, intentionally converted the luggage of the plaintiffs by removing it from plaintiff's room and delivering it to an aircraft bound for Saudi Arabia. The theft (by unknown parties) occurred after the conversion. . . .

"The Court finds no genuine issue as to any material fact concerning the liability of the defendant for the conversion of the property of the plaintiffs. Accordingly, on the Court's own motion and pursuant to Rule 56(d), F.R. Civ. P., partial summary judgment is granted in favor of the nonmoving plaintiffs against defendant Hyatt Corporation. *Doe v. United States Civil Service Commission*, 483 F. Supp. 539, 571 (S.D.N.Y. 1980).

". . . So ordered."

Appendix B.   *Limitation of Liability Statutes*

Addendum to Hawaii Rev. Stat. §§ 486K–1, 486K–4 pp. 551, 552. amended by L. 1981, c. 83, § 1. Only significant changes are noted.

Addendum to Ind. Code § 32–8–28–2, p. 554: amended by P.L. 187, § 97, 1982

Addendum to La. Civ. Code Ann. § 2971 (West), p. 554: amended by Acts 1982, No. 382 § 1

Addendum to Minn. Stat. §§ 327.01 to .04, p. 554: repealed by Laws 1982, c. 517, § 9. See now § 327.70 *et seq.*

Addendum to Wis. Stat. Ann. §§ 160.31 to .33, p. 555: renumbered 50.80 to 50.82 by L. 1975, c. 413, § 15

Chapter 18. Innkeeper's Duty to Nonguests

18:7   *Right of Nonguest Forfeited by Misconduct*

Insert at end of section, p. 561:

Whatever rights a nonguest may acquire upon lawful admission to business premises open to the public, such entry is not unrestricted. Lawful entry is lost when a person refuses to obey a lawful demand to leave by the owner, operator, or other person in charge.

In *Safeway Stores Inc. v. Kelly,* 448 A.2d 856, 863 (D.C. 1982), the District of Columbia Court of Appeals reviewed the authorities on the question of what constitutes unlawful entry upon commercial premises. The following excerpt restates the applicable law, including mention of hotel and restaurant cases:

> . . . Absent a constitutional or statutory right to remain, a person lawfully on the premises of a commercial establishment is guilty of unlawful entry if he refuses to leave the premises after a demand by the person lawfully in charge. *Grogan v. United States,* D.C. App., 435 A.2d 1069, 1071 (1981) (individuals protesting abortions declined to leave clinic after ordered to do so); *Kelly v. United States,* D.C. App., 348 A.2d 884, 886 (1975) (unregistered guest failed to leave after returning to hotel despite warning not to); *Feldt v. Marriott Corp.,* D.C. App., 322 A.2d 913, 915 (1974) (barefoot woman refused manager's request to leave restaurant); *Drew v. United States,* D.C. App., 292 A.2d 164, 166, *cert. denied,* 409 U.S. 1062, 93 S.Ct. 569, 34 L.Ed.2d 514 (1972) (man failed to leave restaurant after owner asked him to leave despite previous warning not to return); *United States v. Bean,* D.C. Sup. Ct. (Cr. No. 50426–70, May 12, 1971) (Greene, C.J.) (man with prior arrest for shoplifting failed to leave store after ordered to do so). See *O'Brien v. United States,* D.C. App., 444 A.2d 946, 948 (1982).

Chapter 19. Responsibility of Restaurant Keeper for Patron's Property

19.7   *Limitation of Liability for Articles Checked*

Correction: Unofficial citation for *Weinberg v. D-M Restaurant Corp.,* case title in the text p. 589, should read: 400 N.Y.S.2d 524.

Insert at end of Weinberg v. D-M Restaurant Corp., p. 590:

In the following landmark case, the New York Court of Appeals, among other rulings, reaffirmed its prior holding in *Honig v. Riley* (see p. 588 of original text, *supra*) limiting liability for the loss of articles checked in a restaurant checkroom to seventy-five dollars, absent any declaration of excess value, regardless of the fact that the loss was caused by the gross negligence of the restaurant.

WEINBERG V. D-M RESTAURANT CORP. [WEINBERG II]
53 N.Y.2d 499, 426 N.E.2d 459 (1981)

MEYER, J.: "Section 201 of the General Business Law has no bearing upon an action against a restaurant owner sued for the conversion of a coat checked by a patron. It does limit recovery by a patron who sues for negligence: to the value of the coat if negligence be shown, a fee or charge is exacted for checking the coat, and a value in excess of $75 is declared and a written receipt stating such value is issued when the coat is delivered to the checkroom attendant; to $100 if a value in excess of $75 is declared and the other conditions are met but negligence cannot be shown; to $75 in any event if no fee or charge is exacted or a value in excess of $75 is not declared and a written receipt obtained when the coat is delivered. . . .

I

"Plaintiff's complaint contained but one cause of action predicated upon the negligence of defendant restaurant owner. Defendant moved for summary judgment limiting plaintiff's recovery to $75. The affidavits presented by defendant established that neither defendant's president nor anyone else in his employ could explain the disappearance of the Russian sable fur coat which plaintiff checked with defendant's checkroom attendant, that no value had been declared by plaintiff nor had any writen receipt stating a value been given, acknowledged that no sign had been posted but stated that section 201 of the General Business Law did not require posting by a restaurant, and quoted a portion of plaintiff's deposition in which she acknowledged that no charge had been made for the checking of the coat. Plaintiff cross-moved for summary judgment. Her affidavit noted the admission of defendant's president that tipping was discretionary and characterized it as contrary to common knowledge. Attached to it also was the deposition of the coatroom attendant in which she conceded that on the night in question she received $20 to $30 in tips.

"Special Term denied both the motion and cross motion. On appeal the Appellate Division modified and remanded for trial as to damages, holding that plaintiff was entitled to judgment on liability but that on the issue of damages there existed questions of fact concerning whether defendant restaurant had 'exacted' a fee or charge and whether the loss was the result of theft by defendant, its agent, servants or employees (60 A.D.2d 550, 400 N.Y.S.2d 524). On remand the Trial Judge, after testimony by defendant's president that the checkroom attendant received an hourly rate of pay plus a percentage of the tips given her, the owner receiving the balance of the tips, ruled that notwithstanding that there was no sign concerning tips nor other open solicitation of them and that some people received their coats without leaving any tip, the gratuities paid the checkroom attendant constituted, as a matter of law, the exaction of a fee within the meaning of the section. He noted further that the issue of theft by defendant or its employees had become academic, that were that not so he would have directed a verdict for plaintiff on that ground also because defendant had presented no evidence on the question of theft. He submitted to the jury, therefore, only the question of the value of plaintiff's coat. The jury fixed that value at $7,500 and judgment was entered for that sum plus interest and costs.

"On appeal from the judgment entered on the jury's verdict, the Appellate Division affirmed, without opinion, but granted defendant leave to appeal to our court from the final judgment. . . . For the reasons stated below we hold that (1) the tip or gratuity customarily given a checkroom attendant is not a 'fee or charge . . . exacted' for the checking service within the meaning of section 201 of the General Business Law; (2) restaurants are not required to post the provisions of section 201 in order to be entitled to its limitation of liability; and (3) in granting summary judgment to plaintiff rather than defendant and in affirming the judgment entered February 7, 1979 the Appellate Division erred; its order of affirmance must, therefore, be modified and judgment directed to be entered for plaintiff in the amount of $75 with interest from March 3, 1975.

II

"Subdivision 1 of section 201 of the General Business Law provides in relevant part: '[A]s to property deposited by guests or patrons in the parcel or check room of any hotel, motel or restaurant, the delivery of which is evidenced by a check or receipt therefor and for which no fee or charge is exacted, the proprietor shall not be liable beyond seventy-five dollars, unless such value in excess of seventy-five dollars shall be stated upon delivery and a written receipt, stating such value, shall be issued, but he shall in no event be liable beyond one hundred dollars, unless such loss occurs through his fault or negligence.' In a case strikingly similar to the instant case, *Honig v. Riley,* 244 N.Y. 105, 155 N.E. 65, that language was construed by this court. Plaintiff Honig sought to recover the value of the fur coat she left at the checkroom of defendant's restaurant on New Year's Eve 1925. She received a check but was not questioned as to value and made no statement to the attendant concerning value. The Trial Judge charged that plaintiff was entitled to full value of the coat if they found defendant to have been negligent. On appeal by defendant from a judgment of $850 entered on the jury's verdict and affirmed by the Appellate Term and the Appellate Division, this court reversed and directed reduction of the judgment to $75. In an opinion by Judge CARDOZO, we said (244 N.Y., at pp. 108–109, 155 N.E. 65):

"The defendant maintains that where property is deposited in a parcel or check room without statement of value or delivery of the prescribed receipt, there is a limit of liability to $75 for loss from any cause. Disclosure of the value, if followed by a receipt, will extend liability for fault or negligence up to the limit of the value stated, though even then the liability, if any, as insurer will be $100 and no more. The plaintiff on her side maintains, and the courts below have held, that the exemption from liability in excess of $75 where the value is not disclosed, is not to be read as a limitation of liability for loss from any cause, but is confined to losses not due to the fault or negligence of the proprietor.

"We think the defendant's construction is the true one, however clumsy and inartificial may be the phrasing of the statute. A limitation of liability affecting merely the measure of recovery is applicable, if not otherwise restrained, to loss for any cause. . . . From the beginning of the section to the end, the exemption from liability in excess of the prescribed maximum is absolute where value is concealed. Only where value is stated and a receipt delivered is the exemption made dependent upon freedom from negligence or other fault.

"Under that reading of the statute plaintiff's recovery is limited to $75, no value having been declared or receipt obtained, unless it can be found that a 'fee or charge [was] exacted.' The ruling of the lower courts that the acceptance by the checkroom attendant of a gratuity in which the restaurant owner shares constitutes an 'exaction', made not as a finding of fact but as a matter of law was, however, erroneous. Though tips may constitute compensation to an employee for purposes of the Workers' Compensation Law [Citations omitted]; [(]see Ann., 75 A.L.R. 1223), of the income tax (Ann., 10 A.L.R.2d 191) and of unemployment compensation taxes (Ann., 83 A.L.R.2d 1024), it does not follow that a tip to an employee may be regarded for all purposes as compensation to the employee [citations omitted] or as a part of the employer's income (Ann., 73 A.L.R.3d 1226 [sales tax]). As to the employer the test generally is whether the payment is a 'service charge' exacted by the employer or a voluntary payment by the patron to the employee (*Beaman v. Westward Ho Hotel Co.*, 89 Ariz. 1, 357 P.2d 327; see Ann., 73 A.L.R.3d 1226, 1231). So in *Beaman* the Arizona Supreme Court held a service charge collected by the hotel, where direct tipping of employees was not permitted, to be subject to sales tax. In so doing, it distinguished the customary employee gratuity saying (89 Ariz. at pp. 4–5, 357 P.2d 327) 'A tip is in law, if not always in fact, a voluntary payment' (see, also, *Peoria Hotel Co. v Department of Revenue*, 87 Ill. App. 3d 176, 179, 408 N.E.2d 1182, 42 Ill. Dec. 473). The United States District Court for the Southern District of New York reached a result similar to *Beaman* in *Restaurants & Patisseries Longchamps v. Pedrick*, D.C. 52 F. Supp. 174, but noted (at pp. 174–175) that 'A patron in a restaurant is under no compulsion to leave a "tip"' (see, also, *United States v. Conforte*, 9th Cir. 624 F.2d 869, 874, cert. den. 449 U.S. 1012, 101 S.Ct. 568, 66 L.Ed.2d 470).

"The more clearly should such a distinction be made when, as here, we deal with a statute not at all concerned with the compensation of the *employee* or the

[208]   Supplement to "Laws of Innkeepers"

taxes payable to the State, but rather with whether the *employer* in permitting gratuities to be paid to the employee has exacted a fee or charge [citation omitted]. So a restaurant owner or hotel that imposes a fixed charge for the service of checking a coat and does not leave to the patron the decision whether to give and what amount to give may properly be said to have exacted a service charge or fee (semble *Aldrich v. Waldorf Astoria Hotel,* 74 Misc. 2d 413, 414, 343 N.Y.S.2d 830 [35 cents per garment paid; held a 'fee or charge']).

"When the service cannot be obtained without the payment of a fixed sum a fee has been exacted, but when, as the papers on the summary judgment motions showed, plaintiff acknowledges that no charge was made and presents no evidence that there was a sign indicating a fixed charge, or of solicitation of any kind, or that the giving and the amount were other than discretionary with the customer, there has, as a matter of law, been no exaction of a fee or charge.

III

"Plaintiff argued on the original motions, and the dissenter in this court agrees, that section 201 is not applicable because defendant failed to comply with subdivision 2 of the section. That subdivision requires that 'A printed copy of this section shall be posted in a conspicuous place and manner in the office or public room and in the public parlors of such hotel or motel.' While that provision was not added to the section until 1960 (L. 1960, ch. 840), section 206 has since 1909 required posting of a printed copy of section 201. Section 206 is by its terms limited, however, to a 'hotel or inn' just as subdivision 2 of section 201 is limited to a 'hotel or motel.' To read subdivision 2 to require posting by a restaurant because subdivision 1 groups 'hotel, motel or restaurant' together is to fly in the face of usual rules of statutory construction that a statute (in this instance, subdivision 2's posting requirement) is to be read and given effect as it was written, and that the courts under guise of interpretation may not enlarge or change the scope of a legislative enactment [citations omitted]. Nor is the dissent's reliance upon the language of *Honig v. Riley (supra)* a proper basis for concluding otherwise. No issue of posting was presented in that case. Moreover, since section 201 contained no posting requirement when *Honig* was decided and no mention was made in the opinion of section 206, the phrases from that opinion quoted by the dissent cannot be fairly read as having been written with respect to the point for which those phrases are now cited. If posting by restaurants is to be required as a condition of the limitation of liability granted them by subdivision 1 of section 201, it is the Legislature rather than this court that must impose the requirement.

IV

"Though neither the posting nor the fee exaction provisions of section 201 limit defendant's right to the benefits of its provisions, plaintiff, pointing to the statement in *Honig v. Riley supra,* 244 N.Y. at p. 110, 155 N.E. 65, that 'The statute is aimed at loss or misadventure. It has no application to theft by the defendant or his agents,' contends she is entitled to affirmance of the judgment because defendant failed to come forward with proof that the coat had not been stolen by its employees. The difficulty with plaintiff's position is that the complaint declares for negligence only and has never been amended either by motion addressed to Special Term or by a motion to conform pleadings to proof at the end of the trial. Quite simply, plaintiff cannot recover on a conversion theory which she has never pleaded.

"Accordingly, the Appellate Division's order of February 7, 1979 should be modified, with costs to defendant in all courts, by reducing the amount awarded to plaintiff to $75 with interest from March 3, 1975.

"FUCHSBERG, J. (dissenting):

"Invited, of course, to do so by its management , plaintiff, a restaurant patron, deposited her fur coat, now found to have been worth $7,500, at the defendant's cloakroom at the plush Rainbow Grill in Rockefeller Center. Without explanation, it was never to be returned. Yet, the majority would relegate her to a recovery of $75. Neither the history or public policy of the statutory scheme which governs such a case, nor the common sense or the elementary fairness that go with a living law will abide such a result. I therefore vote to uphold the Trial Term award to the plaintiff for the full amount of her loss as thereafter unanimously affirmed by the Appellate Division. Here follow my reasons, grounded, I would like to believe, on principle, practicality and, withal, sound law.

"I start with section 201 of the General Business Law, which as we have seen, so drastically and arbitrarily limits the amount which even the grievously damaged patron-bailor may recover for the loss of property entrusted without separate fee to restaurants, hotels or, since they arrived on the scene, motels. Indeed, its provisions, enacted, as the legislative history makes clear, at the instance of restaurant and hotel industry functionaries, are so harsh that, even when a restaurateur, hotelkeeper or motel owner to whom an article is committed is proved to have knowingly engaged a dishonest checkroom attendant, collectable damages may not exceed the more munificent sum of $100. This cap, I might add, has remained unaltered since it was fixed in the antedeluvian monetary times of 57 years ago.

"But, as one might have suspected, there had to be and, indeed, are compensating provisions designed to ameliorate the confiscatory nature of this scheme or at least to warn those who otherwise could be caught within its web. So, when a patron requests a receipt containing the declared value of the item he or she decides to check, the limitations are inoperative, and the restaurant, hotel or motel resumes its traditional liability for full value (General Business Law, § 201).

"Now, it goes without saying that, unless a restaurant proffers receipts and invites declarations, or unless patrons in some other manner are advised of the existence of this option (or, for that matter, of the limitations that prevail in the absence of its exercise), it would be but a secret, and, therefore, ineffective privilege. It was to avoid this paradoxical consequence that the Legislature, apparently recognizing that almost no one is likely to consult the Consolidated Laws before deciding to dine out, enacted section 206 as an auxiliary to the statutory scheme. In my view, this provision, a precondition to the enforcement of the limitation preferences granted restaurants by section 201, requires them to informatively post a printed copy of the statute in a conspicuous place and manner. This, concededly, the defendant here did not do. Yet, because the posting appendage, though part of what Judge CARDOZO called a 'connected plan' embracing both restaurants and hotels (*Honig v. Riley,* 244 N.Y. 105, 109, 155 N.E. 65), does not refer to restaurants by name, the majority, by choosing to deal with section 206 as though it stood in isolation rather than as a dependent part of a whole, would stultify the salutary purpose it was intended to achieve.

"It takes no missionary zeal to observe that, while canons of construction are helpful, they can never take the place of reasoned analysis [citations omitted]. Signposts at best, they are not to be followed blindly when they appear to point in the wrong direction. All the more is this so when we treat with a statute which Judge CARDOZO also deservedly characterized as 'clumsy and inartificial' (*Honig v. Riley, supra,* 244 N.Y. at 109, 155 N.E. 65). For, the notion that, because words are plain, their meaning is also plain is 'merely pernicious oversimplification' (*United States v. Monia,* 317 U.S. 424, 431, 63 S.Ct. 409, 87 L.Ed. 376 [FRANKFURTER, J., dissenting], quoted in *People v. Brooks,* 34 N.Y.2d 475, 478, 358 N.Y.S.2d 395, 315 N.E.2d 460). So, when words, read literally, lead to an unreasonable result plainly at variance with the policy of legislation as a whole, a court must look 'to the purposes of the act' [citation omitted]. Or, as we suggested, in *Brooks,* the goal of judicial inquiry is not always to be satisfied by a 'mechanical' reading of a statute, but rather by understanding that its phrases have ' "some purpose or object to accomplish, whose sympathetic and imaginative discovery is the surest guide to their meaning" ' (*People v. Brooks, supra,* 34 N.Y.2d at 478, 358 N.Y.S.2d 395, 315 N.E.2d 460, quoting *Cabell v. Markham,* 2d Cir. 148 F.2d 737, 739 [LEARNED HAND, J.]).

"Turning then to the purpose of the statute before us now, its genesis goes back to the days when, if food and drink were to be provided outside the home, it was primarily the business of the innkeeper to provide it. In this unitary concept, the same responsibility was borne toward the wayfarer who applied for lodging and the one who applied for a meal. One of these in the beginning was that of absolute liability, as an insurer, for the loss of a guest's property and, later, a combination of statutorily fixed limited liability matched by compulsory safeguards against loss (*Zaldin v. Concord Hotel,* 48 N.Y.2d 107, 111–112, 421 N.Y.S.2d 858, and authorities cited therein). However, with time, as a growing urban population developed an everincreasing habit of taking meals at restaurants, the obligation of its proprietors was reduced to that imposed by the general law of negligence (*Montgomery v. Ladjing,* 30 Misc. 92, 61 N.Y.S. 840; *Simpson v. Rourke,* 13 Misc. 230, 34 N.Y.S. 11).

"Then, the year 1924 saw the birth of the legislation which Judge CARDOZO so critically was to describe that same year and which we, as his successors, today confront. Its intended goal and format, as described in hotel terms by the counsel to the New York State Hotel Association and the Hotel Association of New York City, who did the drafting, is revealing: 'Heretofore the hotelkeeper has been practically at the mercy of the unscrupulous guest and has often been compelled to pay heavy claims for the loss of property from store-rooms and checking-rooms in cases where, when the property was originally deposited with the hotel-keeper, he had no knowledge of the real value thereof nor was such value called to his attention by the guest. The . . . bill relieves the situation and at the same time works no hardship on the guest, for all he is required to do is to notify the hotelkeeper of the value of the property at the time of depositing the same. Fur-thermore, when so notified, the hotelkeeper at all times continues to be liable for the full value of such property in case of negligence, *and copies of the law are required to be posted, pursuant to Section 206 of the General Business Law*' (emphasis added; legislative bill jacket, Document No. 3, L. 1924, ch. 506).

"As formally enacted, however, the bill, to be known as section 201, without further definition, put restaurants within the ambit of its general protection. Then, significantly, when it was construed by this court, Judge CARDOZO made clear that, however ineptly presented, its inclusion of restaurants made them part of an integrated whole. Specifically, he not only referred to them 'in conjunction with the provisions immediately preceding it as part of a connected plan,' but also declared that 'the statute is not aimed at the protection of proprietors of res-taurants exclusively'. Crucially, he went on to say that, '*[f]or the purpose of the new exemption, proprietors of inns and proprietors of restaurants are grouped as a single class*' (*Honig v. Riley*, 244 N.Y. 105, 110, 155 N.E. 65 *supra* [emphasis added]). [Footnote omitted.]

"That sensible crossover among the different sections of the General Business Law was intended is well illustrated by these observations. For 'the new exemp-tion' for 'proprietors of restaurants' to which *Honig* refers is also contained in ar-ticle 12 of the General Business Law under what ordinarily might be regarded as the misleading heading 'Hotels and Boarding Houses'. It follows from this most confusing arrangement that the posting requirements applicable to hotels, if they are to make any sense, must be deemed equally applicable to restaurants.

"It was in the same vein that, in 1960, section 201 was amended to include, as had been the case with restaurants, the newly emerging motel industry as well. On that occasion, in language again reflecting the recognized trade-off between the benefits and obligations of the statutory framework, the Department of Com-merce and the Association of the Bar of the City of New York advised the Gover-nor that those desiring the protection should be 'subjected to the posting provi-sions of the law' (legislative bill jacket, Document Nos. 14, 31, L. 1960, ch. 840).

"Sound policy too supports this conclusion. In the past, this court, dehors the present context, has repeatedly emphasized that it would be misleading and unfair to allow a hotel to assert a limited liability when it had not posted a copy of a statute so that a guest would be 'notified of the true situation and acts with knowledge' (*Millhiser v. Beau Site Co.*, 251 N.Y. 290, 296, 167 N.E. 447). It would be equally misleading and unfair for one who patronizes a restaurant to be confronted with a defense of limited liability without such notice. (See also, *Klar v. H. & M. Parcel Room*, 270 App. Div. 538, 542, 61 N.Y.S.2d 285, aff'd 296 N.Y. 1044, 73 N.E.2d 912 [claim check limiting damages recoverable for loss at parcel room in railroad terminal, though otherwise comporting with public policy, held inadequate in absence of 'conspicuous signs . . . calling attention to the limitation . . . or that there was any opportunity afforded to plaintiffs to assent to or dissent from the alleged contract']).

"In fine, history and policy lead to inexorable conclusions: The Legislature did not intend to extend the salutary benefits of section 201 of the General Business Law to the proprietors of either restaurants, hotels or motels without appropriate notice of the condition—exaction of a receipt containing a statement of value —without which the most extensive loss would bring but a pittance. When the bill was originally enacted, it would have served nothing but an impermissibly overprecious and overliteral reading to assume it intended to charge only hotels with its posting requirement, when, though its hotel sponsors had ignored restaurants, the Legislature affirmatively and expressly took the trouble to include them within the 'connected' statutory scheme [citation omitted].

"Therefore, while, no doubt, the statutory language could be clearer, it surely is remiss not to give effect to the clearcut underlying intent that, at least for checkroom posting purposes, restaurants are in the 'same class' with the other kinds of establishments to be found in the related subdivisions of the statute. . . ."

Since *Weinberg*, the New York State legislature has amended section 201 of the General Business Law to increase the liability limitations for checkrooms in hotels, motels, and restaurants. Chapter 182 of the Laws of 1983 relating to such increased limits reads (changes indicated with italics):

. . . as to property deposited by guests or patrons in the parcel or *checkroom* of any hotel, motel or restaurant, the delivery of which is evidenced by a check or receipt therefor and for which no fee or charge is exacted, the proprietor shall not be liable beyond *two hundred* dollars, unless such value in excess of *two hundred* shall be stated upon delivery and a written receipt, stating such value, shall be issued, but he shall in no event be liable beyond *three* hundred dollars, unless such loss occurs through his fault or negligence.

Subsection 2 of section 201 was also amended, adding the following language:

No hotel, motel or restaurant proprietor shall post a notice disclaiming or misrepresenting his liability under this section.

In a 1982 case, the court addressed a number of important issues, not the least of which was whether a discotheque may avail itself of the protection afforded under section 201(1) of the New York General Business Law. The reasoning of the court follows.

Conboy v. Studio 54, Inc.
113 Misc. 2d 403, 449 N.Y.S.2d 391 (N.Y. City Civ. Ct. 1982)

Saxe, J.: "The issue that I must decide is whether the statutory limitation on liability in subdivision 1 of section 201 of the General Business Law provides a monetary haven for a discotheque.

"The section states in part: '[A]s to property deposited by guests or patrons in the parcel or check room of any *hotel, motel* or *restaurant,* the delivery of which is evidenced by a check or receipt therefor *and for which no fee or charge is exacted,* the proprietor shall not be liable beyond seventy-five dollars, unless such value in excess of seventy-five dollars shall be stated upon delivery and a written receipt, stating such value, shall be issued, but he shall in no event be liable beyond one hundred dollars, unless such loss occurs through his fault or negligence." (Emphasis supplied.)

"On January 23, 1982, the claimant, his wife and a group of friends convened for a party at Studio 54 (Studio) in Manhattan. Studio, licensed by the New York City Department of Consumer Affairs as a cabaret, is a discotheque, where patrons dance to recorded music usually played continuously on high fidelity equipment. (*Random House Dictionary of the English Language* [unabridged ed. 1973].) Often a psychedelic light show accompanies the music and provides background and impetus for the free-spirited patrons who pay $18 per person to dance to the deafening and often overwhelming disco music played continuously on the sophisticated sound system. A cabaret is defined as 'Any room, place or space in the city in which any musical entertainment, singing, dancing or other form of amusement is permitted in connection with the restaurant business or the business of directly or indirectly selling to the public food or drink'. (Administrative Code of City of New York, § B32–296.0, subd. 3.)

"No food is sold or served here—not even a single peanut or pretzel to accompany the alcoholic and soft drinks available for purchase.

"The Conboy party checked their coats, 14 in all, with the coatroom attendant. They received seven check stubs after paying the 75 cent charge per coat. A bailment of the coats was created. (See, generally, 9 N.Y. Jur. 2d, *Bailments and Chattel Leases,* § 1.) Mr. Conboy did not issue a statement concerning the coat's value to the attendant.

"After their evening of revelry, they attempted to reclaim their coats. Mr. Conboy's one-month-old, $1,350 leather coat was missing. It has not been found and, accordingly, he has sued Studio for $1,350.

"Under traditional bailment law, once the goods were delivered, the failure of the bailee (Studio) to return them on demand, created a prima facie case of negligence. The burden of coming forward with evidence tending to show due care shifted to Studio. (*Claflin v. Meyer*, 75 N.Y. 260, 264; *Singer Co. v. Stott & Davis Motor Express*, 79 A.D.2d 227.) Studio did not come forward with any evidence to meet this burden. Mr. Conboy is entitled to a judgment.

"Studio, relying on subdivision 1 of section 201 of the General Business Law, contends that its liability is limited to $75 since no value was declared for the coat. Its argument is incorrect for two reasons.

"First, the statute applies to a hotel, motel or restaurant and then only to property deposited by a patron in a checkroom 'the delivery of which is evidenced by a check or receipt therefor and for which no fee . . . is exacted'. The statute offers innkeepers and restaurant proprietors who comply with it a reduction of the innkeeper's common-law insurer liability as to guests' property deposited with them. (See, generally, Navagh, A New Look at the Liability of Inn Keepers for Guest Property under New York Law, 25 Fordham L. Rev., 62; *Steiner v. O'Leary*, 186 Misc. 236, aff'd 186 Misc. 577.) Compliance with the terms of the statute relieves the innkeeper or restaurant owner of this common-law responsibility, where applicable. (*Weinberg v. D-M Rest. Corp.*, 53 N.Y.2d 499; *Zaldin v. Concord Hotel*, 65 A.D.2d 670, mod. on other grounds 48 N.Y.2d 107.) The statute is in derogation of the common law and is therefore strictly construed. (*Briggs v. Todd*, 28 Misc. 208 [App. Term, 1st Dept.].)

"That being said, it need only be noted that the statute offers its protection to restaurants, hotels and motels, *not* discotheques which appear to be modern-day versions of dance halls. (Cf. Administrative Code, § B32–296.0, subd. 1.)

"Simply put, a discotheque may qualify as a restaurant but there is no logic in giving it that classification unless one of its principal activities is the furnishing of meals. Certainly, Studio should not be classified as a restaurant, because it serves no food. A licensed cabaret, such as Studio, is permitted to engage in the restaurant business (Administrative Code, § B32–296.0, subd. 3) but is not required to.

"The term 'restaurant' was first used in America to refer to dining rooms found in the best hotels and to certain high-class *a la carte* restaurants. (*People v. Kupas*, 171 Misc. 480.) Today, a restaurant would be thought of as an establishment that sells food and drink or where meals may be purchased and eaten. (*People v. Gobeo*, 6 N.Y.S.2d 937; see, also, *Donahue v. Conant*, 102 Vt. 108.) The limitations on liability set forth in the statute are therefore not applicable here. (McKinney's Cons. Laws of N.Y., Book 1, Statutes, § 240.) It may be illogical to condition limitation of liability on the sale of meals, but that is what the statute says and it is for the Legislature to change, not this court.

"Even if I might have concluded that Studio could be treated as a restaurant, it still would not have benefited from the liability limitation provided by the statute because of the fact that a charge was exacted for each coat checked. (*Aldrich v. Waldorf Astoria Hotel*, 74 Misc. 2d 413.)

"Studio claims however that their liability may nevertheless be limited by the posting of a sign in the coatroom. The sign states: 'Liability for lost property in this coat/check room is limited to $100 per loss of misplaced article. This notice is posted pursuant to Section 201, General Business Law of New York State.'

"My holding to the effect that subdivision 1 of section 201 of the General Business Law is not applicable here, does not make the posting of the sign a useless act, for it may still function as a common-law disclaimer. To bind Conboy to this limitation, I must find however that he had notice of the terms of the disclaimer and agreed to it. (*Klar v. H. & M. Parcel Room*, 270 App. Div. 538, 541, aff'd 296 N.Y. 1044.) Studio did not establish that the sign was posted in a conspicuous manner. (*Klar v. H. & M. Parcel Room, supra*, at 542; *Aldrich v. Waldorf Astoria Hotel, supra.*)

"I hold that Conboy is not bound by the posted disclaimer of liability.

"As to damages, Conboy is entitled to the 'real value' of the coat. (*Alebrande v. New York City Housing Auth.*, 44 Misc. 2d 803, rev'd on other grounds 49 Misc. 2d 880 [App. Term, 1st Dep't].) Real value, especially with respect to used clothing or household furnishings that are lost or damaged is not necessarily its market value which presumably would reflect a deduction for depreciation. (*Supra*, at p. 808; *Teich v. Andersen & Co.*, 24 A.D.2d 749.) In fact, the real value may be measured by the price paid when new for the lost or damaged goods. (*Lobell v. Paleg*, 154 N.Y.S.2d 709, 713.)

"One commentator has offered a reason that the strict market value approach is not favored: 'No judge buys his clothing second hand and none would expect any owner to replace his clothing in a second hand store. Hence no judge expects to limit the cost of replacing clothing to a market no one should be expected to use.' (Dobbs, *Remedies*, § 5.12, p. 397.)

"I therefore hold that Conboy may be compensated on a basis that will permit him to replace the very same coat purchased new—$1,350.

"Judgment for claimant in the sum of $1,350."

Chapter 20. The Innkeeper's Lien

20:21 *Statutory Lien as Disposition of Property without Due Process of Law*

Insert immediately after Anastasia v. The Cosmopolitan National Bank of Chicago, *p. 612:*

In *Culbertson v. Leland*, 528 F.2d 426 (1975), the Ninth Circuit Court of Appeals held that, under the Arizona Innkeeper's Lien Statute, the hotel manager's seizure by self-help of lodgers property constituted state action requiring constitutional due process, which was not afforded the affected hotel lodgers.

Chapter 22. Crimes against Innkeepers

22:2 *Hotel Fraud Acts Are Not Collection Aids*

Insert at end of section, p. 628:

The following case illustrates the unwillingness of courts to convict for mere nonpayment in a nonhotel food-service context.

STATE v. WAGENIUS

99 Idaho 273, 581 P.2d 319 (1978)

BAKES, J.: ". . .

V

"In No. 12070, *State v. DeVoe*, we are also presented with substantive questions of law as well as procedural issues already discussed.

"The magistrate found DeVoe guilty of a violation of I.C. § 18-3107, which provides in pertinent part:

"18-3107. FRAUDULENT PROCUREMENT OF FOOD, . . . —It shall be unlawful for any person to obtain food . . . at any . . . restaurant . . . with intent to defraud the owner or keeper thereof by not paying for the same. . . .

" I.C. § 18-3108 establishes the following presumption for proof of fraudulent intent:

"18-3108. PROOF OF FRAUDULENT INTENT IN PROCURING FOOD . . .—Proof that . . . any person absconded without paying or offering to pay for such food . . . shall be prima facie proof of the fraudulent intent mentioned in the preceding section.

"At trial DeVoe admitted that he and a companion had left the restaurant without paying for the food and drinks they had ordered and consumed, but maintained that he had not intended to defraud the restaurant, but had merely forgotten to pay the bill, primarily because he had been intoxicated at the time. At the close of the testimony, the magistrate stated:

"I think what it really boils down to is the question as to whether there was an intent to defraud and as to whether intoxication is any excuse for that. I think the law is pretty clear on it that intoxication is no defense. It doesn't appear to me apart from what I've heard here today that either one of you were so intoxicated and so drunken that you could not have possibly formed the necessary intent to violate the law.

I would merely point out under 18-3108 of the Idaho Code it does say that if you abscond without paying or offering to pay for the food, lodging or other accommodations, that's prima facie evidence of a fraudulent intent. And it does appear to the Court that you did, even from your own admissions, leave without paying for it. Apparently, your basis of defense was that you merely forgot and didn't have the intent or that you were so intoxicated, you didn't know what you were doing. However, I have to draw the question of intent from the the circumstantial evidence and the facts as it appears to the Court. . . .

"And, again, I don't think intoxication under the law is any defense, and certainly it doesn't appear to me that either one of you was so drunk that you couldn't possibly form the necessary intent. You both knew what you were doing. . . .

"And, therefore I do feel beyond a reasonable doubt it has been shown that you did fraudulently procure the food and lodging and that you did abscond or leave without paying for it.

"It is clear from a reading of I.C. § 18-3107 that fraudulent intent is a necessary element of the crime with which the defendant is charged. I.C. § 18-3108 further provides that a *prima facie* case of fraudulent intent is made by 'proof that . . . any person *absconded* without paying or offering to pay for such food.' (Emphasis added.) Since the state's case was based upon the *prima facie* case resulting from the defendant's alleged absconding, the question which this appeal poses is whether or not there is any evidence in the record to support the trial court's finding that the defendant 'absconded.'

"All of the dictionary definitions of 'abscond' indicate that to abscond means to depart clandestinely, secretly, or surreptitiously. *See Black's Law Dictionary* (4th ed. 1968); *Webster's New International Dictionary* (3d ed.). It is not sufficient that the state prove merely that the defendant left the premises without paying. There must be some evidence, either direct or circumstantial, that the departure was secretive, clandestine, or surreptitious in order for it to constitute 'absconding.' The record suggests that the magistrate may not have recognized this distinction when he stated, 'I do feel beyond a reasonable doubt that it has been shown that you did fraudulently procure the food and lodging and that you did *abscond or leave* without paying for it.' (Emphasis added). The appellant alleges that there is no evidence in the record to show that he 'absconded,' i.e., that he left secretly, clandestinely or surreptitiously.

"The entire case of the prosecution consisted of the testimony of the security guard who observed the defendant and his companion enter the restaurant in an 'intoxicated condition' at approximately 11:00 P.M. and stay until roughly 1:45 A.M.

"His testimony is not clear as to whether or not he observed them leave. On direction examination he stated,

"I observed these two gentlemen get up and walk out of the coffee shop and then proceed to walk out of the building itself.

"When asked if he followed them immediately, he said:

"No, I did not. The waitress came over and told me that they had left their ticket on the table. I went over and picked it up and followed them and caught them outside as they were proceeding to leave.

"However, in response to a later question by the prosecuting attorney in his direct examination as to whether or not he picked up the meal ticket as soon as the defendant and his companion left the table, he answered:

"No, I was doing-I was in the other part of the building at the time checking the bar and everything. And I came back in and the waitress told me that these two gentlemen had walked out on their ticket. So I went over there and got the ticket off the table and proceeded to get these gentlemen back inside.

"On cross examination, by the defendant, who appeared *pro se*, the security guard testified:

"Q. You didn't see us actually leave walking out of the building—from like over by the restaurant area?

"A. No, I did not.

"Q. So you wouldn't be able to see that we were like running out of there or something like that?

"A. No, I didn't cause—at the time the waitress said you just walked out.

"Q. And when we were outside, we didn't try to run or take off, split up or divide. . . .

"A. No, no, I didn't.

"Q. And when you first called to us, it wasn't like 'You're under arrest'. You just called and said 'Come on back' and we went back just to see what was going on or what was happening.

"A. Right.

"The foregoing testimony is the only evidence relating to the manner in which the defendant and his companion left the restaurant. The question which we must decide is whether or not, based upon that evidence, the magistrate was justified in finding that the defendant 'absconded' as we have defined that term above. We think not. There is nothing in that testimony which would justify a finding that what the defendant did was secretive, clandestine or surreptitious. Without such evidence the defendant's conduct would not constitute 'absconding' within the meaning of I.C. § 18-3108, and therefore there was no 'prima facie case of fraudulent intent.' There is nothing else in the record from which the Court would be justified in finding the necessary element of fraudulent intent required by I.C. § 18-3107. The magistrate's finding that defendant DeVoe was guilty of violating I.C. § 18-3107 is not supported by the evidence and is therefore reversed. *See State v. Erwin*, 98 Idaho, 736, 572 P.2d 170 (1977). . . .

"DONALDSON, J.: ". . . dissenting.

"I dissent from Part V of the majority opinion. My brethren in the majority have departed from their normally rational temperament and here employ a limited and technical construction of I.C. § 18-3107 and § 18-3108.

"The majority reverses in Part V based on its interpretation of the requirements of I.C. § 18-3107 as defined by I.C. § 18-3108 [footnote omitted] and particularly the word 'abscond.' The obvious infirmity in the majority's reasoning is their construction that overlooks our role as appellate justices; that we are merely asked to judge the works and actions of normal human beings. 'The law is not a series of calculating machines where definitions and answers come tumbling out when the right levers are pushed.' William O. Douglas, *The Dissent: A Safeguard of Democracy*, 32 J. Am. Jud. Soc. 105 (1948).

"A plain reading of the two statutes involved would give fair notice to all that a person is subject to criminal liability should that person leave a restaurant with the intent of not paying for the food he just ate. Somehow the majority, by referring to a dictionary definition for one of the 86 words in I.C. § 18-3108, finds a hidden meaning in those statutes.

"It must be remembered: 'As in other sciences, so in politics, it is impossible that all things should be precisely set down in writing; for enactments must be universal, but actions are concerned with particulars.' Aristotle, 2 Politics at 8.

"A short analysis will show the fallacy inherent in the type of legal interpretation employed by the majority opinion. The majority requires the state to prove DeVoe 'absconded' [footnote omitted] from the premises. This is explained to mean DeVoe must be shown to have secretly, clandestinely, surreptitiously left the restaurant. The statute does not require such.

"What the statute does require is an intent to defraud. Idaho Code § 18-3107 sets out the crime of which DeVoe is accused. The word 'abscond' appears only in the next section, I.C. § 18-3108. The purpose of this second section is to give the state one way, but by no means the only way, to prove a violation of I.C. § 18-3107. [Footnote omitted.]

"The majority reverses the finding of the trial court because of the trial judge's use of the word 'abscond.' However, the trial judge understood very well the requirement of the statute. He stated, 'I think what it really boils down to is the question as to whether there was an intent to defraud and as to whether intoxication is any excuse for that. . . .'

"Proving fraudulent intent is not easy, considering the very personal nature of fraud. Again, in the words of the trial judge, 'I have to draw the question of intent from the circumstantial evidence and the facts as it appears to the Court.'

"These statements show the trial judge understood the requirements of I.C. § 18–3107 and applied them at trial. The testimony at trial consisted of the security guard at the restaurant, the defendant DeVoe and a co-defendant who ate with DeVoe. DeVoe's defense was that he was too intoxicated to form the intent to defraud and that he had must merely forgotten to pay the check. The judge heard this testimony and chose to disbelieve it. His finding of guilt was based on his opinion that DeVoe did possess the fraudulent intent, the finding was not based on an erroneous reading of the law. The trial judge held:

"It doesn't appear to me . . . that either one of you were so intoxicated and so drunken that you could not have possibly formed the necessary intent to violate the law.

"[C]ertainly it doesn't appear to me that either one of you was so drunk that you couldn't possibly form the necessary intent. You both knew what you were doing. . . .

" 'The determination of the credibility of witnesses and the weight to be given their testimony are exclusively within the province of the trier of facts.' *Comish v. Smith*, 97 Idaho 89, 91, 540 P.2d 274, 276 (1975).

"Recognition of the trial court's advantages has resulted in a rule regarding the scope of review. 'The special deference accorded the findings of fact of the court below is a recognition of the special opportunity of the lower court to assess the credibility of the witnesses in the proceeding there. I.R.C.P. 52(a)' *Prescott v. Prescott*, 97 Idaho 257, 261, 542 P.2d 1176, 1180 (1975).

"Intent to defraud is a question of fact within the province of the trial court. Because the evidence in this case consisted of the testimony of three persons, the trial judge is in a far better position than we to ascertain whether DeVoe possessed the requisite intent.

"[W]hether a fraudulent intent exists is said to be a question of fact for a trial court rather than of law for an appellant tribunal.' *Grant v. Segawa*, 44 Cal. App. 2d Supp. 945, 112 P.2d 784, 786 (1941).

"The trial judge could well have found this intent to defraud by the fact that DeVoe left without even taking the check from the table. In fact, the trial judge did find DeVoe possessing the requisite intent and he chose to disbelieve the intoxication defense. There is evidence to support this finding. This finding should not be disturbed, especially on the ground of a dictionary definition of one word that is not a part of the crime.

"SHEPARD, C.J., concurs."

22:4   *Hotel Accommodations Must Have Been Obtained by Fraud*

Insert at end of section, p. 632:

In the following case, a finding of statutory hotel fraud was affirmed over the guest's argument that the innkeeper had agreed to defer payment until the end of the guest's stay. Such an agreement was held other than an "express agreement for credit" found in the statute exempting the guest from criminal prosecution.

COMMONWEALTH V. WILSON

16 Mass. App. 369, 451 N.E.2d 727 (1983)

HALE, C.J.: "The defendant was charged with violating G.L. c. 140, § 12, under a complaint which alleged that the defendant 'did without an express agreement for credit, procure food, entertainment or accommodation from an innkeeper without paying therefor and with intent to cheat and defraud the owner, thereof.' A jury of six in a District Court returned a verdict of guilty, and the defendant was sentenced. He claims error in the denial of his motion for a required finding of not guilty.

"The case is before us on an appendix consisting of the docket entries, the face page of the complaint, an 'Agreed Statement,' the motion for a required finding and the claim of appeal. It is agreed that in May of 1981, the defendant arrived at the complainant's motel in Ipswich and said that he was in the process of moving and wanted a room at the motel for an indefinite period. The defendant was known to the owner. The defendant asked if he could pay for the charges upon leaving the motel, and the owner said that was fine with her. Thereafter the defendant stayed at the motel for a total of thirty-three days until June 24, 1981. A day or two prior to checking out, the defendant had informed the owner of his intention, and she had instructed her bookkeeper to prepare a bill. The owner was not present when the defendant checked out on June 24, but the motel manager gave the defendant a bill dated that day. The bill was not paid. When several attempts to obtain payment failed, the owner filed the complaint.

"General Laws c. 140, § 12, as amended through St. 1977, c. 284 § 1, provides in pertinent part:

"Whoever puts up in a hotel, motel . . . and, without having an express agreement for credit, procures food, entertainment or accommodation without paying therefor, and with intent to cheat or defraud the owner or keeper thereof . . . shall be punished. . . .

If there was not an express agreement for credit, that payment for such . . . accommodation . . . was refused upon demand, shall be presumptive evidence of the intent to cheat or defraud referred to herein.

"The only express agreement between the parties was that the defendant could pay his bill when he checked out.

"The defendant contends (1) that the agreement was an express agreement for credit as contemplated by the first paragraph of G.L. c. 140, § 12, and (2) that the Commonwealth cannot take advantage of the 'presumption' [footnote omitted] in the second paragraph of § 12 as it did not introduce evidence that would 'indicate that the defendant failed to make an agreement for credit.' We treat the two contentions together.

"There is nothing in the arrangement made at the time the defendant arrived at the motel that speaks to an extension of credit beyond the defendant's time of departure from the motel. The charges became due when the defendant checked out. A bill was presented to the defendant at check out, and it was not paid. We construe the agreements for credit referred to in § 12 as contemplating an agreement to delay payment until some time after a person terminates his relation as a guest at the place of accommodation. See *Cottonreeder v. State*, 389 So.2d 1169, 1171 (Ala. Cr. App. 1980). We regard such a credit agreement to be separate and distinct from the normal procedure of deferring payment until all requested services have been received.

"The jury were warranted in finding beyond reasonable doubt (*Commonwealth v. Latimore*, 378 Mass. 671, 677-678, 393 N.E.2d 370 [1979]), that the presentation of the bill was a demand for payment for the motel accommodations furnished to the defendant, which was refused. They could have inferred from the facts which are set out in the 'Agreed Statement' that there was no agreement for credit with respect to that bill and that the defendant had the intent to cheat the owner of the motel.

  "Judgment affirmed."

Law Review Articles

Table of Cases

Library of Congress Cataloging in Publication Data

Sherry, John Harold.
  The laws of innkeepers.

  Updated by: 1985 supplement / by John E. H. Sherry.
  Bibliography: p. 645–651.
  Includes index.
  1. Hotels, taverns, etc.—Law and legislation—United States.   I. Sherry, John E. H.
KF951.A7S5   1981   343.73′07864794   81-67174
ISBN 0-8014-1421-0   347.3037864794